DOMESTIC MANNERS
OF THE
AMERICANS
By
FRANCES TROLLOPE

Edited By
JOHN LAURITZ LARSON
Purdue University

Brandywine Press · **St. James, New York**

1st Printing 1993

Telephone Orders: 1-800-345-1776

Printed in the United States of America

ISBN: 1-881089-13-4

TABLE OF CONTENTS

iv

INTRODUCTION

to the Abridged Edition of
Frances Trollope's
Domestic Manners of the Americans
by John Lauritz Larson

In 1832 Frances Trollope published a two-volume narrative of life in the United States entitled *Domestic Manners of the Americans*. This work placed her among a host of scribbling European travelers who visited the new American republic, took in all that they could see, and tried to interpret for Old World audiences the peculiar character, conditions, and pretensions that gradually were shaping American culture. Neither the first, nor the most important, nor the best prepared tourist to witness the emergence of a distinctly American society, Mrs. Trollope stood out as one of the most sharp-eyed observers of domestic details, which she reported in frank and stinging anecdotes that instantly offended her American readers and thereby helped confirm her notoriety.

Dozens of travelers had published before Mrs. Trollope: French aristocrat F. J. Marquis de Chastellux (1786), naturalist F. A. Michaux (1806), frontier prairie developer Morris Birkbeck (1818), English political radical William Cobbett (1818), and many more—each pursuing a personal interest, connection, or promotion. Later in the century, as the genre grew more popular, established writers tried their hands at this lucrative field— Charles Dickens (1842), Frances Trollope's son Anthony (1862), and Rudyard Kipling (1891) to name just three. Mrs. Trollope's work appeared during an explosion of interest fueled by the narratives of Frances (Fanny) Wright, Basil Hall, Harriet Martineau, Frances (Fanny) Kemble, Richard Cobden, Francis Lieber, Robert D. Owen, and—most famous of all—Alexis de Tocqueville. By 1835, when the first volume of Tocqueville's magisterial *Democracy in America* appeared, the American character as a subject for speculation clearly had captured the interest and imagination of readers in the Old World and the New.[1]

What attracted most tourists to America and stimulated their literary efforts was America's experiment in liberty and equality. With their triumphant Revolution, Americans claimed to have established a "new order for the ages," and by the 1830s people everywhere wished to know if it was true. Through the miracle of political self-creation, the former British colonists had brought into being the modern world's first revolutionary republic. In the Declaration of Independence, their explanation of themselves to a "candid world," American founders had proclaimed the unalienable right of all people to tear down traditional regimes and raise up new ones legitimated by nothing more than the consent of the people to be governed. The radicalism of that notion is hard to recognize two hundred years later, now that much of the world has come to embrace the principles of civil liberty and political legitimacy first tested in the American Revolution. In 1776, however, and for two generations thereafter, the passion of the Americans for equality, self-government, and personal liberty was perceived in the United States and across Europe as a great experiment the outcome of which remained uncertain.[2]

By the time of Frances Trollope's arrival in 1828, white Americans had become more literally free and equal than any of the founders could have predicted. Rising economic prosperity, fueled by war in Europe and by America's rich stock of natural resources, created a fine field for personal success in the new United States. The opening of a vast frontier region west of the

[1]For samples of this literature see Henry Steel Commager, ed., *America In Perspective: The United States through Foreign Eyes* (New York, 1947); and Oscar Handlin, ed., *This Was America: True Accounts of People and Places, Manners and Customs, as Recorded by European Travelers to the Western Shore in the Eighteenth, Nineteenth, and Twentieth Centuries* (Cambridge, Mass., 1949).

[2]For the issue of radicalism see Gordon S. Wood, *The Radicalism of the American Revolution* (New York, 1992); an excellent introduction to the grand claims of the revolutionary generation is Michael Lienesch, *New Order for the Ages: Time, the Constitution, and the Making of Modern American Political Thought* (Princeton, 1988).

Appalachian Mountains brought millions of acres of cheap land to market and stimulated both internal migration and immigration from abroad. The promise of the Revolution's rhetoric, to establish equality, liberty, and self-government, fostered an ever-more democratic style of politics in which ordinary farmers and tradesmen—and eventually all adult white males—participated with increasing enthusiasm. The unfolding of these many kinds of opportunities under the banner of republican democracy also tore down habits of deference and structures of social class hierarchy and replaced them with a popular commitment to equality of opportunity if not of station. All this was taking shape at a frightening pace in the early decades of the nineteenth century. By the 1820s Americans themselves were beginning to feel a little confidence and pride in their emerging democratic culture, and Europeans were becoming more curious than ever about the fate of this experimental nation.[3]

What had driven these American to declare such extreme, untested ideas about liberty, equality, and human rights to be "self-evident truths"? And what was becoming of their country—of society, culture, and politics—when guided over time by such abstract and novel principles? These were the questions that drew foreign tourists to American shores. Some came predisposed to praise the experiment, having drunk from the same cup of Enlightenment radicalism in the salons of Europe. Some came equally determined to find chaos and anarchy, which traditional ideas about authority and government predicted must result from American liberation. Many Europeans were scandalized by the reckless individualism, raw ambition, greed, and instability they thought characterized American society. Others saw the same behavior and were captivated by it completely. Some foreign authors seemed motivated by little more than curiosity, while others proved shamelessly driven by their own pursuit of the main chance. Never so simple or innocent as their narrative voices pretended to be, these wandering critics nevertheless crafted extraordinary word portraits of an experimental

---

[3]For surveys of this rapid development see John Mayfield, *The New Nation, 1800–1845*, rev. ed. (New York, 1982); Edward Pessen, *Jacksonian America: Society, Personality, and Politics*, rev. ed. (Homewood, Ill., 1978); Robert H. Wiebe, *The Opening of American Society, from the Adoption of the Constitution to the Eve of Disunion* (New York, 1984).

people-in-the-making, without which later historians would find it hard to gain perspective on the accomplishments of these very self-conscious early Americans.

*   *   *   *   *

Frances Trollope was not yet a writer by profession when she began her adventure in the United States. She was an English "lady," one of that class of leisured Europeans who did not work for a living but instead pursued amusement, comfort, and the society of "refined" persons. The wife of a not-too-successful barrister, Thomas Anthony Trollope, Frances presided until 1828 over a lively country estate in Harrow, England, where her husband wrecked the fortune he possessed as a gentleman farmer and where Frances herself associated with glittering personalities, entertained friends with amateur theatricals, and annually spent more than the family took in. Such profligate habits worried nobody, for Mr. Trollope stood to inherit a comfortable estate from a childless uncle. The family's prospects sank, however, when Trollope's uncle abruptly married and sired an heir, leaving Thomas dependent on his own inadequate income. The family slipped steadily toward bankruptcy.[4]

Just as the crisis approached, an old family friend, the free-thinking English radical Fanny Wright, appeared at the Trollope's house in Harrow, recently returned from her second visit to America, full of tales of rich opportunities, and especially consumed with her experimental free-love anti-slavery commune, Nashoba. According to the traditional story, based on daughter-in-law Frances Eleanor Trollope's 1895 biography of Frances, the Trollopes were not quite tempted by the scandalous promise of Fanny's frontier paradise but decided instead to mend the family fortune by a commercial venture in the booming frontier economy of the American West. More recent scholarship suggests that Nashoba was indeed Mrs. Trollope's intended destination and that her commercial investments in Cincinnati, which failed utterly and colored much of her experi-

---

[4]The best sketch of Mrs. Trollope's personal adventures is Donald Smalley, "Introduction: Mrs. Trollope in America," in *Domestic Manners of the Americans*, ed. Donald Smalley (1949, rpt. Gloucester, Mass., 1974), especially viii–xix (hereafter cited as Smalley, "Introduction").

ence in America, were expedients born of her stunning disappointment with Nashoba.[5]

Nashoba was the latest of Fanny Wright's wild, idealistic experiments. On her recent trip to America, she had purchased near Memphis, Tennessee, a model plantation on which she hoped to establish a white communitarian society dedicated to free thinking (and free love). While this enlightened community perfected right relations among people and property they intended gradually to educate and emancipate their black slave labor force—thereby performing two good works simultaneously![6] It was to this romantic center of philanthropy and freedom, urged on by Fanny's irrepressible descriptions, that Frances Trollope determined to relocate with her son, Henry, and two daughters, Cecilia and Emily, to escape the poverty that awaited them in the English countryside. In high hopes the little party—comprising four Trollopes, a French painter named August Hervieu (who had attached himself to Mrs. Trollope's household), Fanny Wright, and a few others—sailed from London November 4, 1827, arriving at New Orleans (where the narrative begins) on Christmas Day and continuing by steamboat to Memphis on the first day of the New Year.

The reality of Nashoba proved "infinitely more dreadful" than anything Mrs. Trollope had imagined. Virtually nothing had been prepared. No assembly of happy communitarians greeted Fanny's return. The only white couple in residence (Fanny's sister and her husband) looked "like spectres from fever and ague." There was no beauty, no philanthropy, only bad air, bad water, no wholesome food, and no future there for Mrs. Trollope and her children. "I almost immediately decided upon not suffering my children to breathe the pestilential atmosphere more than a day or two," she confided to a friend; "it is impossible to give you an idea of their miserable and melancholy mode of life while I was there."[7]

[5]See Helen L. Heineman, " 'Starving in that Land of Plenty': New Backgrounds to Frances Trollope's *Domestic Manners of the Americans*," *American Quarterly* 24 (Dec. 1972), 643–60; see also Heineman, *Mrs. Trollope: The Triumphant Feminine in the Nineteenth Century* (Athens, Ohio, 1979).

[6]See Celia Morris Eckhardt, *Fanny Wright: Rebel in America* (Cambridge, Mass., 1984), 108–40; A. J. G. Perkins and Theresa Wolfson, *Frances Wright: Free Enquirer* (New York, 1939), 182–204.

[7]Frances Trollope to Harriet Garnett, 7 Dec. 1828, quoted in Heineman, " 'Starving,' " 650.

Mrs. Trollope's revulsion at the sight of Nashoba over-turned her entire plan. Out of travel money, yet determined to escape the deathly scene, she borrowed $300 from Nashoba's trustees, returned to Memphis, shipped son Henry off to a utopian community at New Harmony, Indiana, and booked passage for herself and daughters and the faithful Hervieu on the first steamboat to Cincinnati—rumored to be the most bustling "metropolis" on the western rivers. Thus the venue for her most impressive observations about life in the United States owed more to improvisation under extreme duress than to commercial premeditation. Mrs. Trollope probably entered Cincinnati badly shaken—much relieved to have eluded a disastrous end yet profoundly unsure how to proceed and what to do next.

Cincinnati in 1828 was indeed a bustling commercial port at the center of a fast-growing frontier region. Founded in 1788 on the Ohio River's north shore, opposite the Licking River of Kentucky, Cincinnati quickly became the "grand depot" for the farm produce of the newly organized Northwest Territory. By 1795, when Indian titles to land north of the Ohio River finally were extinguished by the Treaty of Greenville, some five hundred residents occupied the little village of Cincinnati, eager to serve the interests of the coming pioneers. Population grew almost exponentially, to 2,500 in 1810, six thousand in 1816, and nearly 20,000 in 1828, when Mrs. Trollope arrived.[8]

Before the advent of steamboat navigation, Cincinnatians made their living organizing the downstream export of grain, wool, livestock, and whiskey. These surplus products, hauled or driven into town by hundreds of pioneer farmers and country storekeepers, were loaded onto flatboats and rafted down the Ohio to New Orleans and the markets of the world. What this country trade needed in return was common manufactures— crockery, cooking pots, tools of iron and steel, nails, guns, powder, and ball, textiles, shoes, salt, coffee, and window glass. Most of these goods traveled laboriously from the East, overland to Pittsburgh and down the Ohio River to Cincinnati, at an expense that was only exceeded by the grueling keelboat trip

[8]On early Cincinnati, see Richard C. Wade, *The Urban Frontier: The Rise of Western Cities, 1790–1830* (Cambridge, Mass., 1959), especially 22–27, 53–59; R. Carlyle Buley, *The Old Northwest: Pioneer Period, 1815–1840*, 2 vols. (Bloomington, Ind., 1950), *passim.*; Smalley, "Introduction," xix–xx.

from New Orleans, nearly fifteen hundred miles upstream against the current. For twenty-five years the town's merchants struggled to attract skilled artisans and investment capital to offset with local manufacturing the high costs of delivering merchandise to the heart of the western forests.

Steamboat navigation, which began in Cincinnati in 1815, drastically reduced the costs of importing manufactured goods and stimulated an extraordinary burst of growth in commercial towns throughout the western river system. First demonstrated in 1807 on Atlantic coastal waters, steamboats soon acquired a special western design—shallow drafts, flat bottoms, stern-mounted paddlewheels, and ever-more-towering superstructures above the deck—that perfectly suited them to the twisting, snag-ridden, and unpredictable waters of the Ohio and Mississippi rivers. Encouraged by better transportation, brisk markets, and more affordable household consumables, settlers poured into Kentucky, Ohio, and Indiana, carved out pioneer farms, and swelled Cincinnati's country trade proportionately. By the time of Mrs. Trollope's sojourn there, the "Queen City" (as Cincinnati's boosters loved to call their town) had found its economic balance as a center of country commerce, steamboat construction, milling, manufacturing, and especially pork packing. So notorious was the butchering business that the "Queen City" earned another nickname more reflective of its leading industry: "Porkopolis."[9]

In addition to the normal accoutrements of business, Cincinnati by 1828 boasted certain evidences of urban refinement—a boast Mrs. Trollope would demolish. Dr. Daniel Drake, for a generation Cincinnati's leading citizen and indefatigable booster, had established a medical college and hospital. Residents (and visitors such as Mrs. Trollope) might worship in a wide variety of churches, attend various schools, read all kinds of local publications (religious periodicals, medical journals, nine newspapers), educate themselves at circulating libraries and reading rooms, take their leisure at the theater, and culti-

[9]On steamboating see Louis C. Hunter, *Steamboats on the Western Rivers: An Economic and Technological History* (Cambridge, Mass., 1949); Erik F. Haites, James Mak, and Gary M. Walton, *Western River Transportation: The Era of Early Internal Development, 1810–1860* (Baltimore, 1975). The nickname "Porkopolis" is quoted in Buley, *The Old Northwest*, I, 533.

vate their tastes at the Academy of Fine Arts or the Western Museum. Booming good fortune also produced in Cincinnati some familiar urban problems that would only grow worse for a generation: water and sanitary systems failed to meet the need; streets mostly were unpaved, filthy, and dark (private haphazard street lights appeared in 1810 but probably contributed more to the danger of fire than to the illumination of the city); police and fire protection faltered; housing fell short of demand. In sum, Cincinnati was precisely the booming frontier marketplace Mrs. Trollope had been told to expect, but she would discover that her English expectations did not square with what western Americans in the age of Jackson liked to call, among themselves, progress.

Frances Trollope proved to be a keen observer of others but a pretty poor judge of her own situation and best interests. Her two years' residence in Cincinnati was marked by extraordinary misadventures that ruined her family's fortunes, astonished and bewildered her American neighbors, and embittered the poor woman irrevocably. About the only enduring fruits of her misery were the notebooks filled with stories that made up the text of *Domestic Manners*. She had arrived practically penniless and lived for some time off the savings of August Hervieu (whose patronness she still perceived herself to be!). Groomed exclusively for the ornamental life of the English leisured class, Mrs. Trollope had little to offer an American frontier city-on-the-make, although her own inappropriateness seemed only to verify her sense that Cincinnati lacked culture most grievously. Her son, Henry, who had collapsed under the regimen of labor at New Harmony, rejoined the family and tried to turn a dollar teaching Latin in a city of tradesmen, with predictable results. Hervieu the artist quickly found a faculty position at the Academy of Fine Arts and just as quickly bolted to establish his own school. It was Hervieu's brushes, guided by Frances Trollope's flair for public spectacle and amusement, that finally brought this band of exiles into a successful connection with the Western Museum.[10]

Cincinnati's Western Museum was a failed center for natu-

[10]My account of Mrs. Trollope's Cincinnati adventures condenses material found in Smalley, "Introduction," xx–li, and Heineman, " 'Starving,' " 652–56.

ral history and archaeology that by 1828 had drifted toward bizarre and spectacular exhibits in a desperate effort to drum up business. By April 1828, animal monstrosities (a two-headed pig, for instance), back-lit transparent paintings, and wax figures already had brought the institution well into the entertainment business when Mrs. Trollope introduced "The Invisible Girl," a multi-media charade featuring a special chamber decorated with mysterious transparencies by Hervieu, in which an audience of twelve posed questions to an "Invisible Girl" (Henry Trollope), who delighted them with learned and obtuse pronouncements. Joseph Dorfeuille, proprietor of the Western Museum, enjoying his greatest success in years, warmly embraced Mrs. Trollope's next extravagant show, the "Infernal Regions" exhibit that became a trademark of the institution for generations. Groans, shrieks, and moanings accompanied vivid wax figures by Hiram Powers, set before Hervieu's back-lit transparencies, all depicting scenes from Dante's *Inferno*. For Mrs. Trollope, the success of Dorfeuille's "Infernal Regions" may have been her undoing, for it seems to have convinced her that Cincinnatians required her services as an arbiter of culture and that they would flock to whatever she prepared for them. Guided by these two smug and disastrous assumptions, she took up the project that would ruin her: the Bazaar.

Had the Bazaar been Frances Trollope's original reason for coming to America, the story of its weird conception and reckless execution would stand as a monument to commercial incompetence. Seen as another improvisation, however, conceived on the fly by an irrepressibly creative but headstrong individual, flush with her own sense of cultural superiority and eager to combine quick profits with extravagant display, the enterprise becomes brave in its failure. Mrs. Trollope designed a hideously gaudy building that was to house the finest merchandise for sale in the West as well as cultural exhibits, meeting rooms, a stock market-coffee house, a ballroom, and a rotunda with fifteen hundred feet of panoramic painting. Thomas A. Trollope, who had joined his wife and children for a few months in the winter of 1828–29, returned to England to buy the goods that were to astound Cincinnati buyers and set new standards of consumer taste. Workmen raised the incredible building in the spring and summer of 1829, but the money ran short, malaria threatened Mrs. Trollope's life (she lay in bed, by her own account, eleven weeks!), Mr. Trollope's $10,000 worth of merchandise proved unsalable (less appealing even than that already on the market in town), and it was seized almost immediately to satisfy the claims of unpaid contractors. With her capital exhausted, Frances Trollope could not finish or restock the Bazaar, and despite heroic efforts to raise money with artistic exhibits and theatricals, she failed. Before she could leave town, the sheriff seized the last of her household property; by March 1830 her welcome in Cincinnati had expired.

For the duration of her stay in America, Frances Trollope lived more as a refugee than as a tourist, dependent on the kindness of others yet determined to keep up appearances. Finding poverty in America more endurable and less embarrassing than it would have been in England, and lacking ready cash for an Atlantic voyage, she fled Cincinnati for the Atlantic seaboard with her children and August Hervieu. Her trip eastward by steamboat and stage generated yet another collection of keen images and anecdotes that would find their way into *Domestic Manners*. Arriving in Washington, D.C. via Wheeling and Baltimore, she took refuge with a relative of close English friends, living outside the city in Stonington, Maryland, whose own poverty required Mrs. Trollope to pay board which she borrowed from her *artiste*-for-hire, Hervieu. Thus situated, she began arranging her many notebooks with the recent, serious intention of writing a book to make money. Still subsidized by Hervieu's paintings and exhibitions, Mrs. Trollope structured the balance of her time in America according to the needs of her travel narrative. Struck down again by malaria in September 1831, she moved to Alexandria, Virginia, which offered a better physician—and a season's close observations of American slavery. The following spring, an extended tour of New York, including Niagara Falls, completed the writer's itinerary. With her material all collected and Hervieu's resources somewhat restored, the entire party set sail for England in late June, arriving back home on August 5, 1831. In March 1832, exactly two years after her ignominious departure from Cincinnati, Frances Trollope published *Domestic Manners of the Americans* to instant critical and popular acclaim. From the ashes of a brutal adventure she had raked a bit of fame and fortune after all.[11]

*   *   *   *   *

What, exactly, did Frances Trollope observe about the manners of the Americans that made her two volume narrative so popular in Europe and notorious in the United States? In a word, she found their manners to be bad. In anecdote after scorching anecdote, she portrayed the Americans as crude, rough, slovenly, greedy, vain, ignorant, untutored, silly, provincial, proud, and self-satisfied, lacking all evidence of grace, honor, or refinement. Mrs. Trollope's indictment blamed America's social and cultural shortcomings on the young republic's proudest achievements: equality and liberation. She made none of the allowances for the newness of the country or the untamed environment with which European critics customarily softened their dismay. Not simply disappointed with a culture that was not yet mature, Mrs. Trollope accused the Americans of embracing vice and calling it virtue, of marching boldly in the wrong direction and daring anyone (especially Frances Trollope) to find fault with the results. American society was a disgrace growing worse, she concluded; freedom and equality were the cause. To Americans who were just taking tentative pride in the "progress" of their democratic culture, Mrs. Trollope offered no encouragement.

Social equality bothered Mrs. Trollope inordinately. Time and again she reported encounters with Americans who refused to yield to her pretensions of gentility. She correctly observed that the elaborate rules that governed class relations in England had disappeared completely in the American West. Servants would not defer to their masters but displayed instead the smug indifference of independent contractors whose services the employer scarcely could do without. (As often was the case, Mrs. Trollope's resentment here cut unwittingly close to the truth: she *was* dependent on hired hands to do things that her own culture said a "lady" must not do herself!) The status she enjoyed in England despite her precarious financial situation meant

---

[11]See Smalley, "Introduction," li–lxi; Heineman, " 'Starving,' " 656–60.

xvii

nothing on an American steamboat, and it deteriorated exactly as her fortune disappeared. To be judged without reference to breeding and background, to be ranked crudely by the contents of her purse, seemed to Mrs. Trollope to contradict all that separated civilization from the savage condition.

Equality was quite disturbing in itself. The American preoccupation with equality had fostered a set of manners that Frances Trollope found aggressively offensive. Men (whether gentlemen or tradesmen) ate like animals at table, stuffing their mouths with food, hardly bothering to chew, pausing not to converse but only to wash down their crude repast with vile corn whiskey. Everywhere men chewed tobacco; and wherever they chewed, they spat. No single observation recurs in Mrs. Trollope's narrative so regularly as her revulsion at the public expectoration of tobacco juice. After dinner at hotels, in steamboat salons, at the theater, at court—in virtually any public place—American men slouched, leaning back in their seats, heels above their heads, exposing their posteriors to view in the most scandalous fashion. Pretending to have examined the cause of these barbarous displays, Mrs. Trollope invariably traced it to claims of individual liberty under the American Constitution, that guaranteed each citizen the right to sit, spit, and eat as he saw fit! That such revolting habits repulsed many Americans she did not notice, while the possibility that her undisguised horror might have encouraged teasing or brought out the worst in her companions seems never to have occurred to her.

The entrepreneurial character of American society struck Mrs. Trollope as rather more grasping and competitive than ought to be necessary in a civilized country. The privileged English classes always engaged in commerce at a safe and sanitized distance because tradition dictated that gentlemen did not work. Americans had abandoned their pretensions to genteel leisure around the time of the Revolution (they had long since lost the reality of leisure to the rough conditions of colonial and frontier life), and so Americans embraced both labor and competition with a frank and violent enthusiasm. Mrs. Trollope, who blamed so many unpleasant American habits on this preoccupation with getting ahead, was herself exactly so preoccupied throughout her residence in the United States. It was, moreover, the capitalism of the English civilization so precious to Mrs. Trollope which had given birth to the enterprising colonies that became the United States, and English capitalism in 1830 still led the world in economic "progress." What she found so terribly wanting in the material ambitions of the Americans was that ritual disclaimer by which the better class of English merchants and landlords disguised their reliance on market transactions—a pose Americans did not bother to assume.

The place of women in American society struck Frances Trollope as peculiarly retrograde and disappointing. Men and women, she complained, seldom mingled in public. Men and women dined separately at parties, withdrew into segregated clusters at receptions, and seemed to honor a code of gender discrimination that supposedly protected female delicacy but merely, in Mrs. Trollope's view, perpetuated female exclusion. An exaggerated prudery and almost comic discomfort came over American women and girls when confronted with men in public, which Mrs. Trollope shrewdly attributed not to genuine piety and decorum but to a learned defense against the male determination to indulge vulgar passions (such as spitting) without reproach. In their own homes, American women did the work of domestic servants without the benefit of "help"— another hollow victory for social equality! Outside the home, women's primary sphere of influence lay in religion, toward which practically all female emotional and intellectual energies seemed to be directed.

What stood out in Mrs. Trollope's study of religion in America was its overwhelmingly feminine orientation. As American men had claimed the marketplace for their domain, so American women seemed attached to sanctuaries of the spirit. Mrs. Trollope attended the services of a variety of different sects and denominations, visited a frontier revival, a protracted camp meeting, and several large urban churches in Baltimore, Washington, and New York. Preferring the well-ordered rituals of the English church, she found enthusiastic frontier Protestantism somewhat alarming, especially the disorderly emotional tempests of the camp meeting that placed spiritually distraught young women almost completely in the power of male preachers of unknown integrity. Although she never ventured a thorough analysis of American religion and its oddly

xix

sexual distortions, Mrs. Trollope registered a certain distrust of American piety that proved significantly insightful.

American slavery, of course, held a central place in the eyes of all European visitors, in part because by 1830 Europe's powers were in the process of abolishing slavery while Americans seemed eager to extend their own slave empire. Most English tourists, including Frances Trollope, harbored strong antislavery sentiments, and they approached the American South as a relic of some former civilization. Of course European abolitionists, whose slaves inhabited distant colonies, could freely indulge liberal plans of emancipation without contemplating the dependence of their own society on exploitation of workers at home and abroad. Until her final year in and around Washington, D.C., Mrs. Trollope had experienced only a fleeting glimpse of bondsmen at Nashoba and occasional encounters with free blacks in Cincinnati. Once confronted with Virginia-style slavery, she reported with typical dismay its ill effects on the sensibilities of *white* people, and in one story she featured herself cradling a slave girl who had taken a poison while other whites recoiled in horror—a scene almost too romantic to be believed. Mrs. Trollope's sympathy for the Africans in bondage was both sensitive and sincere and her descriptive observations of slavery as acute as any, but her contact with American free blacks, slaves, and slaveholders was too superficial to yield quite the penetrating insights she developed about such things as religion, women's lives, or the habit of chewing tobacco.

The careful reader of *Domestic Manners of the Americans* will detect a significant change in the tone and character of Mrs. Trollope's observations after her departure from Cincinnati. Both textual clues and supporting evidence suggest that her notebooks up through the Cincinnati period recorded impressions without premeditated purpose while those collected afterward in the East filled out a conscious writer's design for a marketable travel narrative.[12] It is therefore the Cincinnati material that contains the most extraordinary sparks of recognition about minute details of ordinary life. Mrs. Trollope's later trips through Baltimore, Washington, D.C., New York, and Niagara yielded very conventional notices of monuments,

[12]See Helen Heineman, "Frances Trollope in the New World: *Domestic Manners of the Americans*," *American Quarterly* 21 (Fall 1969), 544–59.

churches, natural wonders, and the public faces of the communities. She liked a great deal more of what she saw in the East—perhaps because the Atlantic cities were more sophisticated and more European in flavor, but also because her authorial purpose had found conscious form. Whatever the explanation, the second half of *Domestic Manners* delivers a less biting, more conventional tourist's view more clearly influenced by literary designs. Of course, no part of the text should be accepted as the plain, unvarnished truth; but there remains a spontaneity and candor in the Cincinnati material that sustains Mrs. Trollope's unique credibility and gradually disappears in later chapters of the work.

Mrs. Trollope did not like the United States, and she said so unambiguously at the end of her book. In answering her own question why, she settled on a closing observation that represents her most penetrating insight. The Americans had not yet, she concluded, produced the best place on earth to live, but no one among them would admit as much. She found their manners disappointing, their self-righteousness delusionary. She could not engage Americans in critical dialogue about the relative merits of her universe and theirs; and while Frances Trollope could be insufferably blinded by her own prejudices, she rightly found the Americans addicted to fantasy and projection. She concluded that their culture aptly conspired to prevent the evolution of great people and institutions, and that therefore Americans had little to fear—no future improvements would ruin their egalitarian wasteland. Then, as a parting overture of peace, she delivered what could only be received as the final insult: As soon as Americans abandoned their very nature and learned to "cling to the graces, the honours, the chivalry of life," then Mrs. Trollope would gladly say "farewell to American equality, and welcome to European fellowship one of the finest countries on the earth."[13] For good or ill, that day has never come.

[13]See p. 210 below.

A Note on the Abridgement

This edition of *Domestic Manners of the Americans* contains about two-thirds of the text of the original publication. Deletions of a few words or a single sentence are indicated in this edition by an ellipsis (. . . .) in the text. Deletions of two or more sentences are indicated by a row of asterisks (* * * * *) across the page. Where Mrs. Trollope divided her original text there is printed in this edition a row of "plus" signs (+ + + + + +) across the page. Three chapters have been deleted entirely, although the chapter numbers remain for the sake of clarity. What remains of the text is unaltered and nothing has been added or rearranged. For a complete, modern, critical edition of *Domestic Manners* with excellent scholarly annotations, see Frances Trollope, *Domestic Manners of the Americans,* ed. Donald Smalley (1949; rpt. Gloucester, Mass., 1974).

CHAPTER I

Entrance of the Mississippi . . .

On the 4th of November, 1827, I sailed from London, accompanied by my son and two daughters; and after a favourable, though somewhat tedious voyage, arrived on Christmas-day at the mouth of the Mississippi.

The first indication of our approach to land was the appearance of this mighty river pouring forth its muddy mass of waters, and mingling with the deep blue of the Mexican Gulf. The shores of this river are so utterly flat, that no object upon them is perceptible at sea, and we gazed with pleasure on the muddy ocean that met us, for it told us we were arrived, and seven weeks of sailing had wearied us; yet it was not without a feeling like regret that we passed from the bright blue waves, whose varying aspect had so long furnished our chief amusement, into the murky stream which now received us.

*　　*　　*　　*　　*

CHAPTER II

New Orleans . . . Society . . .
Creoles and Quadroons . . .
Voyage up the Mississippi . . .

On first touching the soil of a new land, of a new continent, of a new world, it is impossible not to feel considerable excitement and deep interest in almost every object that meets us. New Orleans presents very little that can gratify the eye of taste, but nevertheless there is much of novelty and interest for a newly arrived European. The large proportion of blacks seen in the streets, all labour being performed by them; the grace and beauty of the elegant Quadroons, the occasional groups of wild and savage looking Indians, the unwonted aspect of the vegetation, the huge and turbid river, with its low and slimy shore, all help to afford that species of amusement which proceeds from looking at what we never saw before.

The town has much the appearance of a French Ville de Province, and is, in fact, an old French colony taken from Spain by France. The names of the streets are French, and the language about equally French and English. The market is handsome and well supplied, all produce being conveyed by the river. We were much pleased by the chant with which the Negro boatmen regulate and beguile their labour on the river; it consists but of very few notes, but they are sweetly harmonious, and the Negro voice is almost always rich and powerful.

By far the most agreeable hours I passed at New Orleans were those in which I explored with my children the forest near the town. It was our first walk in "the eternal forests of the western world," and we felt rather sublime and poetical. The trees, generally speaking, are much too close to be either large or well grown; and, moreover, their growth is often stunted by a parasitical plant, for which I could learn no other name than "Spanish moss;" it hangs gracefully from the boughs, converting the outline of all the trees it hangs upon into that of weeping willows. The chief beauty of the forest in this region is from the luxuriant under-growth of palmettos, which is decidedly the loveliest coloured and most graceful plant I know. The pawpaw, too, is a splendid shrub, and in great abundance. We here, for the first time, saw the wild vine, which we afterwards found growing so profusely in every part of America, as naturally to suggest the idea that the natives ought to add wine to the numerous productions of their plenty-teeming soil. The strong pendant festoons made safe and commodious swings, which some of our party enjoyed, despite the sublime temperament above-mentioned.

Notwithstanding it was mid-winter when we were at New Orleans, the heat was much more than agreeable, and the attacks of the mosquitos incessant, and most tormenting; yet I suspect that, for a short time, we would rather have endured it, than not have seen oranges, green peas, and red pepper, growing in the open air at Christmas. In one of our rambles we ventured to enter a garden, whose bright orange hedge attracted our attention; here we saw green peas fit for the table, and fine crop of red pepper ripening in the sun. A young Negress was employed on the steps of the house; that she was a slave made her an object of interest to us. She was the first slave we had ever spoken to, and I believe we all felt that we could hardly address her with sufficient gentleness. She little dreamed, poor girl, what deep sympathy she excited; she answered us civilly and gaily, and seemed amused at our fancying there was something unusual in red pepper pods; she gave us several of them, and I felt fearful lest a hard mistress might blame her for it. How very childish does ignorance make us! and how very ignorant we are upon almost every subject, where hear-say evidence is all we can get!

I left England with feelings so strongly opposed to slavery, that it was not without pain I witnessed its effects around me. At the sight of every Negro man, woman, and child that passed, my fancy wove some little romance of misery, as belonging to each of them; since I have known more on the subject, and become better acquainted with their real situation in America, I have often smiled at recalling what I then felt.

*   *   *   *   *

Our stay in New Orleans was not long enough to permit our entering into society, but I was told that it contained two distinct sets of people, both celebrated, in their way, for their social meetings and elegant entertainments. The first of these is composed of Creole families, who are chiefly planters and merchants, with their wives and daughters; these meet together, eat together, and are very grand and aristocratic.... The other set consists of the excluded but amiable Quadroons, and such of the gentlemen of the former class as can by any means escape from the high places, where pure Creole blood swells the veins at the bare mention of any being tainted in the remotest degree with the Negro stain.

Of all the prejudices I have ever witnessed, this appears to me the most violent, and the most inveterate. Quadroon girls, the acknowledged daughters of wealthy American or Creole fathers, educated with all of style and accomplishments which money can procure at New Orleans, and with all the decorum that care and affection can give; exquisitely beautiful, graceful, gentle, and amiable, these are not admitted, nay, are not on any terms admissible, into the society of the Creole families of Louisiana. They cannot marry; that is to say, no ceremony can render an union with them legal or binding; yet such is the powerful effect of their very peculiar grace, beauty, and sweetness of manner, that unfortunately they perpetually become the objects of choice and affection. If the Creole ladies have privilege to exercise the awful power of repulsion, the gentle Quadroon has the sweet but dangerous vengeance of possessing that of attraction. The unions formed with this unfortunate race are said to be often lasting and happy, as far as any unions can be so, to which a certain degree of disgrace is attached.

*   *   *   *   *

Miss Wright,* then less known (though the author of more than one clever volume) than she has since become, was the

*Frances Wright. See introduction pp. xii–xiii.

companion of our voyage from Europe; and it was my purpose to have passed some months with her and her sister at the estate she had purchased in Tennessee. This lady, since become so celebrated as the advocate of opinions that make millions shudder, and some half-score admire, was, at the time of my leaving England with her, dedicated to a pursuit widely different from her subsequent occupations. Instead of becoming a public orator in every town throughout America, she was about, as she said, to seclude herself for life in the deepest forests of the western world, that her fortune, her time, and her talents might be exclusively devoted to aid the cause of the suffering Africans. Her first object was to shew that nature had made no difference between blacks and whites, excepting in complexion; and this she expected to prove by giving an education perfectly equal to a class of black and white children. Could this fact be once fully established, she conceived that the Negro cause would stand on firmer ground than it had yet done, and the degraded rank which they have ever held amongst civilized nations would be proved to be a gross injustice.

This question of the mental equality, or inequality between us, and the Negro race, is one of great interest, and has certainly never yet been fairly tried; and I expected for my children and myself both pleasure and information from visiting her establishment, and watching the success of her experiment.

The innumerable steam boats, which are the stage coaches and fly waggons of this land of lakes and rivers, are totally unlike any I had seen in Europe, and greatly superior to them. The fabrics which I think they most resemble in appearance, are the floating baths (les bains Vigier) at Paris. . . . The room to which the double line of windows belongs, is a very handsome apartment; before each window a neat little cot is arranged in such a manner as to give its drapery the air of a window curtain. This room is called the gentlemen's cabin, and their exclusive right to it is somewhat uncourteously insisted upon. The breakfast, dinner, and supper are laid in this apartment, and the lady passengers are permitted to take their meals there.

On the first of January, 1828, we embarked on board the Belvidere, a large and handsome boat; though not the largest or handsomest of the many which displayed themselves along the wharfs; but she was going to stop at Memphis, the point of the river nearest to Miss Wright's residence, and she was the first that departed after we had got through the customhouse, and finished our sight-seeing. We found the room destined for the use of the ladies dismal enough, as its only windows were below the stern gallery; but both this and the gentlemen's cabin were handsomely fitted up, and the former well carpeted; but oh! I will not, I may not describe its condition; indeed it requires the pen of a Swift to do it justice. Let no one who wishes to receive agreeable impressions of American manners, commence their travels in a Mississippi steam boat; for myself, it is with all sincerity I declare, that I would infinitely prefer sharing the apartment of a party of well conditioned pigs to the being confined to its cabin.

I hardly know any annoyance so deeply repugnant to English feelings, as the incessant, remorseless spitting of Americans. I feel that I owe my readers an apology for the repeated use of this, and several other odious words; but I cannot avoid them, without suffering the fidelity of description to escape me. It is possible that in this phrase, "Americans," I may be too general. The United States form a continent of almost distinct nations, and I must now, and always, be understood to speak only of that portion of them which I have seen. In conversing with Americans I have constantly found that if I alluded to any thing which they thought I considered as uncouth, they would assure me it was local, and not national; the accidental peculiarity of a very small part, and by no means a specimen of the whole. "That is because you know so little of America," is a phrase I have listened to a thousand times, and nearly as many different places. *It may be so*—and having made this concession, I protest against the charge of injustice in relating what I have seen.

CHAPTER III

Company on board the Steam Boat...
Scenery of the Mississippi...
Crocodiles... Arrival at Memphis...
Nashoba...

The weather was warm and bright, and we found the guard of the boat, as they call the gallery that runs round the cabins, a very agreeable station; here we all sat as long as light lasted, and sometimes wrapped in our shawls, we enjoyed the clear bright beauty of American moonlight long after every passenger but ourselves had retired. We had a full complement of passengers on board. The deck, as is usual, was occupied by the Kentucky flat-boat men, returning from New Orleans, after having disposed of the boat and cargo which they had conveyed thither, with no other labour than that of steering her, the current bringing her down at the rate of four miles an hour. We had about two hundred of these men on board, but the part of the vessel occupied by them is so distinct from the cabins, that we never saw them, except when we stopped to take in wood; and then they ran, or rather sprung and vaulted over each other's heads to the shore, whence they all assisted in carrying wood to supply the steam engine; the performance of this duty being a stipulated part of the payment of their passage.

From the account given by a man servant we had on board, who shared their quarters, they are a most disorderly set of persons, constantly gambling and wrangling, very seldom sober, and never suffering a night to pass without giving practical proof of the respect in which they hold the doctrines of equality, and community of property. The clerk of the vessel was kind enough to take our man under his protection, and assigned him a berth in his own little nook; but as this was not inaccessible, he told him by no means to detach his watch or money from his person during the night. Whatever their moral characteristics may be, these Kentuckians are a very noble-looking race of men; their average height considerably exceeds that of Europeans, and their countenances, excepting when disfigured by red hair, which is not unfrequent, extremely handsome.

The gentlemen in the cabin (we had no ladies) would certainly neither, from their language, manners, nor appearance, have received that designation in Europe; but we soon found their claim to it rested on more substantial ground, for we heard them nearly all addressed by the titles of general, colonel, and major. On mentioning these military dignities to an English friend some time afterwards, he told me that he too had made the voyage with the same description of company, but remarking that there was not a single captain among them; he made the observation to a fellow-passenger, and asked how he accounted for it. "Ho, sir, the captains are all on deck," was the reply.

Our honours, however, were not all military, for we had a judge among us. I know it is equally easy and invidious to ridicule the peculiarities of appearance and manner in people of a different nation from ourselves; we may, too, at the same moment, be undergoing the same ordeal in their estimation; and, moreover, I am by no means disposed to consider whatever is new to me as therefore objectionable; but, nevertheless, it was impossible not to feel repugnance to many of the novelties that now surrounded me.

The total want of all the usual courtesies of the table, the voracious rapidity with which the viands were seized and devoured, the strange uncouth phrases and pronunciation; the loathsome spitting, from the contamination of which it was absolutely impossible to protect our dresses; the frightful manner of feeding with their knives, till the whole blade seemed to enter into the mouth; and the still more frightful manner of cleaning the teeth afterwards with a pocket knife, soon forced us to feel that we were not surrounded by the generals, colonels, and majors of the old world; and that the dinner hour was to be any thing rather than an hour of enjoyment.

The little conversation that went forward while we

remained in the room, was entirely political, and the respective claims of Adams and Jackson to the presidency were argued with more oaths and more vehemence than it had ever been my lot to hear. Once a colonel appeared on the verge of assaulting a major, when a huge seven-foot Kentuckian gentleman horse-dealer, asked of the heavens to confound them both, and bade them sit still and be d-d. We too thought we should share this sentence; at least sitting still in the cabin seemed very nearly to include the rest of it, and we never tarried there a moment longer than was absolutely necessary to eat.

The unbroken flatness of the banks of the Mississippi continued unvaried for many miles above New Orleans; but the graceful and luxuriant palmetto, the dark and noble ilex, the bright orange, were every where to be seen, and it was many days before we were weary of looking at them. We occasionally used the opportunity of the boat's stopping to take in wood for a ten minutes' visit to the shore; we in this manner explored a field of sugar canes, and loaded ourselves with as much of the sweet spoil as we could carry. Many of the passengers seemed fond of the luscious juice that is easily expressed from the canes, but it was too sweet for my palate. We also visited, in the same rapid manner, a cotton plantation. A handsome spacious building was pointed out to us as a convent, where a considerable number of young ladies were educated by the nuns.

At one or two points the wearisome level line of forest is relieved by *bluffs*, as they call the short intervals of high ground. The town of Natches is beautifully situated on one of these high spots; the climate here, in the warm season, is as fatal as that of New Orleans; were it not for this, Natches would have great attractions to new settlers. The beautiful contrast that its bright green hill forms with the dismal line of black forest that stretches on every side, the abundant growth of pawpaw, palmetto and orange, the copious variety of sweet-scented flowers that flourish there, all make it appear like an oasis in the desert. Natches is the furthest point to the north at which oranges ripen in the open air, or endure the winter without shelter. With the exception of this sweet spot, I thought all the little towns and villages we passed, wretched looking, in the extreme. As the distance from New Orleans increased, the air of wealth and comfort exhibited in its immediate neighbourhood disappeared, and but for one or two clusters of wooden houses, calling themselves towns, and borrowing some pompous name, generally from Greece or Rome, we might have thought ourselves the first of the human race who had ever penetrated into this territory of bears and alligators. But still from time to time appeared the hut of the wood-cutter, who supplies the steam-boats with fuel, at the risk, or rather with the assurance of early death, in exchange for dollars and whiskey. These sad dwellings are nearly all of them inundated during the winter, and the best of them are constructed on piles, which permit the water to reach its highest level without drowning the wretched inhabitants. These unhappy beings are invariably the victims of ague, which they meet recklessly, sustained by the incessant use of ardent spirits. The squalid look of the miserable wives and children of these men was dreadful, and often as the spectacle was renewed I could never look at it with indifference. Their complexion is of a blueish white, that suggests the idea of dropsy; this is invariable, and the poor little ones wear exactly the same ghastly hue. A miserable cow and a few pigs standing knee-deep in water, distinguish the more prosperous of these dwellings, and on the whole I should say that I never witnessed human nature reduced so low, as it appeared in the wood-cutters' huts on the unwholesome banks of the Mississippi.

It is said that at some points of this dismal river, crocodiles are so abundant as to add the terror of their attacks to the other sufferings of a dwelling there. We were told a story of a squatter, who having "located" himself close to the river's edge, proceeded to build his cabin. This operation is soon performed, for social feeling and the love of whiskey bring all the scanty neighbourhood round a new comer, to aid him in cutting down trees, and in rolling up the logs, till the mansion is complete. This was done; the wife and five young children were put in possession of their new home, and slept soundly after a long march. Towards day-break the husband and father was awakened by a faint cry, and looking up, beheld relics of three of his children scattered over the floor, and an enormous crocodile, with several young ones around her, occupied in devouring the remnants of their horrid meal. He looked round for a weapon, but finding none, and aware that unarmed he could do nothing, he raised himself gently on his bed, and contrived to crawl from thence through a window, hoping that his wife, whom he left sleeping, might with the remaining children rest undiscovered till his return. He flew to his nearest neighbour and besought his aid; in less than half an hour two men returned with him, all three well armed; but alas! they were too late! the wife and her two babes lay mangled on their bloody bed. The gorged reptiles fell an easy prey to their assailants, who, upon examining the place, found the hut had been constructed close to the mouth of a large hole, almost a cavern, where the monster had hatched her hateful brood.*

Among other sights of desolation which mark this region, condemned of nature, the lurid glare of a burning forest was almost constantly visible after sun-set, and when the wind so willed, the smoke arising from it floated in heavy vapour over our heads. Not all the novelty of the scene, not all its vastness, could prevent its heavy horror wearying the spirits. Perhaps the dinners and suppers I have described may help to account for this; but certain it is, that when we had wondered for a week at the ceaseless continuity of forest; had first admired, and then wearied of the festooned drapery of Spanish moss; when we had learned to distinguish the different masses of timber that passed us, or that we passed, as a "snag," a "log," or a "sawyer;" when we had finally made up our minds that the gentlemen of the Kentucky and Ohio military establishments, were not of the same genus as those of the Tuilleries and St. James's, we began to wish that we could sleep more hours away. As we advanced to the northward we were no longer cheered by the beautiful border of palmettos; and even the amusement of occasionally spying out a sleeping crocodile was over.

Just in this state, when we would have fain believed that every mile we went, carried us two towards Memphis, a sudden and violent shock startled us frightfully.

"It is a sawyer!" said one.

"It is a snag!" cried another.

"We are aground!" exclaimed the captain.

"Aground? Good heavens! and how long shall we stay here?"

"The Lord in his providence can only tell, but long enough to tire my patience, I expect."

*Mrs. Trollope seems not to have recognized this as an example of a Mississippi River "tall tale."

11

And the poor English ladies, how fared they the while?

Two breakfasts, two dinners, and a supper did they eat, with the Ohio and Kentucky gentlemen, before they moved an inch. Several steam-boats passed while we were thus enthralled; but some were not strong enough to attempt drawing us off, and some attempted it, but were not strong enough to succeed; at length a vast and mighty "thing of life" approached, threw out grappling irons; and in three minutes the business was done; again we saw the trees and mud slide swiftly past us; and a hearty shout from every passenger on deck declared their joy.

At length we had the pleasure of being told that we had arrived at Memphis; but this pleasure was considerably abated by the hour of our arrival, which was mid-night, and by the rain, which was falling in torrents.

Memphis stands on a high bluff, and at the time of our arrival was nearly inaccessible. The heavy rain which had been falling for many hours would have made any steep ascent difficult, but unfortunately a new road had been recently marked out, which beguiled us into its almost bottomless mud, from the firmer footing of the unbroken cliff. Shoes and gloves were lost in the mire, for we were glad to avail ourselves of all our limbs, and we reached the grand hotel in a most deplorable state.

Miss Wright was well known there, and as soon as her arrival was announced, every one seemed on the alert to receive her, and we soon found ourselves in possession of the best rooms in the hotel. The house was new, and in what appeared to me a very comfortless condition, but I was then new to Western America, and unaccustomed to their mode of "getting along," as they term it. This phrase is eternally in use among them, and seems to mean existing with as few of the comforts of life as possible.

We slept soundly however, and rose in the hope of soon changing our mortar-smelling quarters for Miss Wright's Nashoba.

But we presently found that the rain which had fallen during the night would make it hazardous to venture through the forests of Tennessee in any sort of carriage; we therefore had to pass the day at our queer comfortless hotel. The steam-boat had wearied me of social meals, and I should have been thankful to

12

have eaten our dinner of hard venison and peach-sauce in a private room; but this, Miss Wright said was impossible, the lady of the house would consider the proposal as a personal affront, and, moreover, it would be assuredly refused. This latter argument carried weight with it, and when the great bell was sounded from an upper window of the house, we proceeded to the dining-room. The table was laid for fifty persons, and was already nearly full. Our party had the honour of sitting near "the lady," but to check the proud feelings to which such distinction might give birth, my servant, William, sat very nearly opposite to me. The company consisted of all the shop-keepers (store-keepers as they are called throughout the United States) of the little town. The mayor also, who was a friend of Miss Wright's, was of the party; he is a pleasing gentlemanlike man, and seems strangely misplaced in a little town on the Mississippi. We were told that since the erection of this hotel, it has been the custom for all the male inhabitants of the town to dine and breakfast there. They ate in perfect silence, and with such astonishing rapidity that their dinner was over literally before our's was began; the instant they ceased to eat, they darted from the table in the same moody silence which they had preserved since they entered the room, and a second set took their places, who performed their silent parts in the same manner. The only sounds heard were those produced by the knives and forks, with the unceasing chorus of coughing, &c. No women were present except ourselves and the hostess; the good women of Memphis being well content to let their lords partake of Mrs. Anderson's turkeys and venison, (without their having the trouble of cooking for them), whilst they regale themselves on mush and milk at home.

The remainder of the day passed pleasantly enough in rambling round the little town, which is situated at the most beautiful point of the Mississippi; the river is here so wide as to give it the appearance of a noble lake; an island, covered with lofty forest trees divides it, and relieves by its broad mass of shadow the uniformity of its waters. The town stretches in a rambling irregular manner along the cliff, from the Wolf River, one of the innumerable tributaries to the Mississippi, to about a mile below it. Half a mile more of the cliff beyond the town is cleared of trees, and produces good pasture for horses, cows, and pigs; sheep

13

they had none. At either end of this space the forest again rears its dark wall, and seems to say to man, "so far shalt thou come, and no farther!" Courage and industry, however, have braved the warning. Behind this long street the town straggles back into the forest, and the rude path that leads to the more distant log dwellings becomes wilder at every step. The ground is broken by frequent water-courses, and the bridges that lead across them are formed by trunks of trees thrown over the stream, which support others of smaller growth, that are laid across them. These bridges are not very pleasant to pass, for they totter under the tread of a man, and tremble most frightfully beneath a horse or a waggon; they are, however, very picturesque. The great height of the trees, the quantity of pendant vine branches that hang amongst them; and the variety of gay plumaged birds, particularly the small green parrot, made us feel we were in a new world; and a repetition of our walk the next morning would have pleased us well, but Miss Wright was anxious to get home, and we were scarcely less so to see her Nashoba. A clumsy sort of caravan drawn by two horses was prepared for us; and we set off in high spirits for an expedition of fifteen miles through the forest. To avoid passing one of the bridges above described, which was thought insecure, our negro driver took us through a piece of water, which he assured us was not deep "to matter," however we soon lost sight of our pole, and as we were evidently descending, we gently remonstrated with him on the danger of proceeding, but he only grinned, and flogged in reply; we soon saw the front wheels disappear, and the horses began to plunge and kick most alarmingly, but still without his looking at all disturbed. At length the splinter-bar gave way, upon which the black philosopher said very composedly, "I expect you'll best be riding out upon the horses, as we've got into an unhandsome fix here." Miss Wright, who sat composedly smiling at the scene, said, "Yes, Jacob, that is what we must do;" and with some difficulty we, in this manner, reached the shore, and soon found ourselves again assembled round Mrs. Anderson's fire.

It was soon settled that we must delay our departure till the waters had subsided, but Miss Wright was too anxious to reach home to endure this delay, and she set off again on horseback, accompanied by our man servant, who told me afterwards that they rode through places that might have daunted the boldest hunter, but that "Miss Wright took it quite easy."

The next day we started again, and the clear air, the bright sun, the novel wildness of the dark forest, and our keenly awakened curiosity, made the excursion delightful, and enabled us to bear without shrinking the bumps and bruises we encountered. We soon lost all trace of a road, at least so it appeared to us, for the stumps of the trees, which had been cut away to open a passage, were left standing three feet high. Over these, the high-hung Deerborn, as our carriage was called, passed safely; but it required some miles of experience to convince us that every stump would not be our last; it was amusing to watch the cool and easy skill with which the driver wound his horses and wheels among these stumps. I thought he might have been imported to Bond-street with great advantage. The forest became thicker and more dreary-looking every mile we advanced, but our ever-grinning negro declared it was a right good road, and that we should be sure to get to Nashoba.

And so we did . . . . and one glance sufficed to convince me that every idea I had formed of the place was as far as possible from the truth. Desolation was the only feeling—the only word that presented itself; but it was not spoken. I think, however, that Miss Wright was aware of the painful impression the sight of her forest home produced on me, and I doubt not that the conviction reached us both at the same moment, that we had erred in thinking that a few months passed together at this spot could be productive of pleasure to either. But to do her justice, I believe her mind was so exclusively occupied by the object she had then in view, that all things else were worthless, or indifferent to her. I never heard or read of any enthusiasm approaching her's, except in some few instances, in ages past, of religious fanaticism.

It must have been some feeling equally powerful which enabled Miss Wright, accustomed to all the comfort and refinement of Europe, to imagine not only that she herself could exist in this wilderness, but that her European friends could enter there, and not feel dismayed at the savage aspect of the scene. . . . Each building consisted of two large rooms furnished in the most simple manner; nor had they as yet collected round them any of those minor comforts which ordinary minds class among the necessaries of life. But in this our philosophical friend seemed to see no evil; nor was there any mixture of affectation in this indifference; it was a circumstance really and truly beneath her notice. Her whole heart and soul were occupied by the hope of raising the African to the level of European intellect; and even now, that I have seen this favourite fabric of her imagination fall to pieces beneath her feet, I cannot recall the self-devotion with which she gave herself to it, without admiration.

The only white persons we found at Nashoba were my amiable friend, Mrs. W****, the sister of Miss Wright, and her husband. I think they had between thirty and forty slaves, including children, but when I was there no school had been established. Books and other materials for the great experiment had been collected, and one or two professors engaged, but nothing was yet organized. I found my friend Mrs. W**** in very bad health, which she confessed she attributed to the climate. This naturally so much alarmed me for my children, that I decided upon leaving the place with as little delay as possible, and did so at the end of ten days.

I do not exactly know what was the immediate cause which induced Miss Wright to abandon a scheme which had taken such possession of her imagination, and on which she had expended so much money; but many months had not elapsed before I learnt, with much pleasure, that she and her sister had also left it. I think it probable that she became aware upon returning to Nashoba, that the climate was too hostile to their health. All I know farther of Nashoba is, that Miss Wright having found (from some cause or other) that it was impossible to pursue her object, herself accompanied her slaves to Hayti, and left them there, free, and under the protection of the President.

I found no beauty in the scenery round Nashoba, nor can I conceive that it would possess any even in summer. The trees were so close to each other as not to permit the growth of underwood, the great ornament of the forest at New Orleans, and still less of our seeing any openings, where the varying effects of light and shade might atone for the absence of other objects. The clearing round the settlement appeared to me inconsiderable and imperfect; but I was told that they had grown good crops of cotton and Indian corn. The weather was dry and agreeable, and the aspect of the heavens by night surprisingly beautiful. I never saw moonlight so clear, so pure, so powerful.

We returned to Memphis on the 26th of January, 1828, and

16

found ourselves obliged to pass five days there, awaiting a steam-boat for Cincinnati, to which metropolis of the west, I was now determined to proceed with my family to await the arrival of Mr. Trollope. We were told by every one we spoke to at Memphis, that it was in all respects the finest situation west of the Alleghanies. We found many lovely walks among the broken forest glades around Memphis, which, together with a morning and evening enjoyment of the effects of a glowing horizon on the river, enabled us to wait patiently for the boat that was to bear us away.

* * * * *

CHAPTER IV

Departure from Memphis . . . Ohio River . . .
Louisville . . . Cincinnati . . .

On the 1st of February, 1828, we embarked on board the Criterion, and once more began to float on the "father of waters," as the poor banished Indians were wont to call the Mississippi. The company on board was wonderfully like what we had met in coming from New Orleans; I think they must have all been first cousins; and what was singular, they too had all arrived at high rank in the army. For many a wearisome mile above the Wolf River the only scenery was still forest—forest—forest; the only variety was produced by the receding of the river at some points, and its encroaching on the opposite shore. These changes are continually going on, but from what cause none could satisfactorily explain to me. Where the river is encroaching, the trees are seen growing in water many feet deep; after some time, the water undermines their roots, and they become the easy victims of the first hurricane that blows. This is one source of the immense quantities of drift wood that float into the gulf of Mexico. Where the river has receded, a young growth of cane-brake is soon seen starting up with the rapid vegetation of the climate; these two circumstances in some degree relieve the sameness of the thousand miles of vegetable wall. But we were now approaching the river which is emphatically called "the beautiful," La Belle Riviere of the New Orleans French; and a few days took us, I trust for ever, out of that murky stream which is as emphatically called "the deadly;" and well does it seem to merit the title; the air of its shores is mephitic, and it is said that noth-

18

ing that ever sunk beneath its muddy surface was known to rise again. As truly does "La Belle Riviere" deserve its name; the Ohio is bright and clear; its banks are continually varied, as it flows through what is called a rolling country, which seems to mean a district that cannot shew a dozen paces of level ground at a time. The primval forest still occupies a considerable portion of the ground, and hangs in solemn grandeur from the cliffs; but it is broken by frequent settlements, where we were cheered by the sight of herds and flocks. I imagine that this river presents almost every variety of river scenery; sometimes its clear wave waters a meadow of level turf; sometimes it is bounded by perpendicular rocks; pretty dwellings, with their gay porticos are seen, alternately with wild intervals of forest, where the tangled bear-brake plainly enough indicates what inhabitants are native there. Often a mountain torrent comes pouring its silver tribute to the stream, and were there occasionally a ruined abbey, or feudal castle, to mix the romance of real life with that of nature, the Ohio would be perfect.

So powerful was the effect of this sweet scenery, that we ceased to grumble at our dinners and suppers; nay, we almost learnt to rival our neighbours at table in their voracious rapidity of swallowing, so eager were we to place ourselves again on the guard, lest we might lose sight of the beauty that was passing away from us.

Yet these fair shores are still unhealthy. More than once we landed, and conversed with the families of the wood-cutters, and scarcely was there one in which we did not hear of some member who had "lately died of the fever."—They are all subject to ague, and though their dwellings are infinitely better than those on the Mississippi, the inhabitants still look like a race that are selling their lives for gold.

Louisville is a considerable town, prettily situated on the Kentucky, or south side of the Ohio; we spent some hours in seeing all it had to shew; and had I not been told that a bad fever often rages there during the warm season, I should have liked to pass some months there for the purpose of exploring the beautiful country in its vicinity. Frankfort and Lexington are both towns worth visiting though from their being *out of the way* places, I never got to either. The first is the seat of the state government of Kentucky, and the last is, I was told, the residence of several independent families, who, with more leisure than is usually enjoyed in America, have its natural accompaniment, more refinement.

The falls of the Ohio are about a mile below Louisville, and produce a rapid, too sudden for the boats to pass, except in the rainy season. The passengers are obliged to get out below them, and travel by land to Louisville, where they find other vessels ready to receive them for the remainder of the voyage. We were spared this inconvenience by the water being too high for the rapid to be much felt, and it will soon be altogether removed by the Louisville canal coming into operation, which will permit the steam-boats to continue their progress from below the falls to the town.

The scenery on the Kentucky side is much finer than on that of Indiana or Ohio. The State of Kentucky was the darling spot of many tribes of Indians, and was reserved among them as a common hunting ground; it is said that they cannot yet name it without emotion, and that they have a sad and wild lament that they still chaunt to its memory. But their exclusion thence is of no recent date; Kentucky has been longer settled than Illinois, Indiana, or Ohio, and it appears not only more highly cultivated, but more fertile and more picturesque than either. I have rarely seen richer pastures than those of Kentucky. The forest trees, where not too crowded, are of magnificent growth, and the crops are gloriously abundant where the thriftless husbandry has not worn out the soil by unvarying succession of exhausting crops. We were shewn ground which had borne abundant crops of wheat for twenty successive years; but a much shorter period suffices to exhaust the ground, if it were made to produce tobacco without the intermission of some other crop.

We reached Cincinnati on the 10th of February. It is finely situated on the south side of a hill that rises gently from the water's edge; yet it is by no means a city of striking appearance; it wants domes, towers, and steeples; but its landing place is noble, extending for more than a quarter of a mile; it is well paved, and surrounded by neat, though not handsome buildings. I have seen fifteen steam-boats lying there at once, and still half the wharf was unoccupied.

On arriving we repaired to the Washington Hotel, and

thought ourselves fortunate when we were told that we were just in time for dinner at the table d'hôte; but when the dining-room door was opened, we retreated with a feeling of dismay at seeing between sixty and seventy men already at table. We took our dinner with the females of the family, and then went forth to seek a house for our permanent accommodation.

We went to the office of an advertising agent, who professed to keep a register of all such information, and described the dwelling we wanted. He made no difficulty, but told us his boy should be our guide through the city, and shew us what we sought; we accordingly set out with him, and he led us up one street, and down another, but evidently without any determinate object; I therefore stopped, and asked him whereabout the houses were which we were going to see.

"I am looking for bills," was his reply.

I thought we could have looked for bills as well without him, and I told him so; upon which he assumed an air of great activity, and began knocking regularly at every door we passed, enquiring if the house was to be let. It was impossible to endure this long, and our guide was dismissed, though I was afterwards obliged to pay him a dollar for his services.

We had the good fortune, however, to find a dwelling before long, and we returned to our hotel, having determined upon taking possession of it as soon as it could be got ready. Not wishing to take our evening meal either with the three score and ten gentlemen of the dining-room, nor yet with the half dozed ladies of the bar-room, I ordered tea in my own chamber. A good-humoured Irish woman came forward with a sort of patronising manner, took my hand, and said, "Och, my honey, ye'll be from the old country. I'll see you will have your tay all to yourselves, honey." With this assurance we retired to my room, which was a handsome one as to its size and bed furniture, but it had no carpet, and was darkened by blinds of paper, such as rooms are hung with, which required to be rolled up, and then fastened with strings very awkwardly attached to the window-frames, whenever light or air were wished for. I afterwards met with these same uncomfortable blinds in every part of America.

Our Irish friend soon reappeared, and brought us tea, together with the never-failing accompaniments of American tea-drinking, hung beef, "chipped up" raw, and sundry sweetmeats of brown sugar hue and flavour. We took our tea, and were enjoying our family talk, relative to our future arrangements, when a loud sharp knocking was heard at our door. My "come in," was answered by the appearance of a portly personage, who proclaimed himself our landlord.

"Are any of you ill?" he began.

"No thank you, sir; we are all quite well," was my reply.

"Then, madam, I must tell you, that I cannot accommodate you on these terms; we have no family tea-drinkings here, and you must live either with me or my wife, or not at all in my house."

This was said with an air of authority that almost precluded reply, but I ventured a sort of apologistic hint, that we were strangers and unaccustomed to the manners of the country.

"Our manners ave very good manners, and we don't wish any changes from England." ... I made no farther remonstrance, but determined to hasten my removal. This we achieved the next day to our great satisfaction.

We were soon settled in our new dwelling, which looked neat and comfortable enough, but we speedily found that it was devoid of nearly all the accommodation that Europeans conceive necessary to decency and comfort. No pump, no cistern, no drain of any kind, no dustman's cart, or any other visible means of getting rid of the rubbish, which vanishes with such celerity in London, that one has no time to think of its existence; but which accumulated so rapidly at Cincinnati, that I sent for my landlord to know in what manner refuse of all kinds was to be disposed of.

"Your Help will just have to fix them all into the middle of the street, but you must mind, old woman, that it is the middle. I expect you don't know as we have got a law what forbids throwing such things at the sides of the streets; they must just all be cast right into the middle, and the pigs soon takes them off."

In truth the pigs are constantly seen doing Herculean service in this way through every quarter of the city; and though it is not very agreeable to live surrounded by herds of these unsavoury animals, it is well they are so numerous, and so active in their capacity of scavengers, for without them the streets would soon be choked up with all sorts of substances in every stage of decomposition.

We had heard so much of Cincinnati, its beauty, wealth, and unequalled prosperity, that when we left Memphis to go thither, we almost felt the delight of Rousseau's novice, "un voyage faire, et Paris au bout!"—As soon, therefore, as our little domestic arrangements were completed, we set forth to view this "wonder of the west," this "prophet's gourd of magic growth,"—this "infant Hercules;" and surely no travellers ever paraded a city under circumstances more favourable to their finding it fair to the sight. Three dreary months had elapsed since we had left the glories of London behind us; for nearly the whole of that time we had beheld no other architecture than what our ship and steam-boats had furnished, and excepting at New Orleans, had seen hardly a trace of human habitations. The sight of bricks and mortar was really refreshing, and a house of three stories looked splendid. Of this splendour we saw repeated specimens, and moreover a brick church, which, from its two little peaked spires, is called the two-horned church. But, alas! the flatness of reality after the imagination has been busy! I hardly know what I expected to find in this city, fresh risen from the bosom of the wilderness, but certainly it was not a little town, about the size of Salisbury, without even an attempt at beauty in any of its edifices, and with only just enough of the air of a city to make it noisy and bustling. The population is greater than the appearance of the town would lead one to expect. This is partly owing to the number of free Negroes who herd together in a obscure part of the city, called little Africa; and partly to the density of the population round the paper-mills and other manufactories. I believe the number of inhabitants exceeds twenty thousand.

We arrived in Cincinnati in February, 1828, and I speak of the town as it was then; several small churches have been built since, whose towers agreeably relieve its uninteresting mass of buildings. At that time I think Main-street, which is the principal avenue, (and runs through the whole town, answering to the High-street of our old cities), was the only one entirely paved. The *troittoir* is of brick, tolerable well laid, but it is inundated by every shower, as Cincinnati has no drains whatever. What makes this omission the more remarkable is, that the situation of the place is calculated both to facilitate their construction and to render them necessary. Cincinnati is built on the side of a hill that begins to rise at the river's edge, and were it furnished with drains of the simplest arrangement, the heavy showers of the climate would keep them constantly clean; as it is, these showers wash the higher streets, only to deposit their filth in the first level spot; and this happens to be in the street second in importance to Main-street, running at right angles to it, and containing most of the large warehouses of the town. This deposit is a dreadful nuisance, and must be productive of miasma during the hot weather.

The town is built, as I believe most American towns are, in squares, as they call them; but these squares are the reverse of our's, being solid instead of hollow. Each consists, or is intended to consist, when the plan of the city is completed, of a block of buildings fronting north, east, west, and south; each house communicating with an alley, furnishing a back entrance. This plan would not be a bad one were the town properly drained, but as it is, these alleys are horrible abominations, and must, I conceive, become worse with every passing year.

To the north, Cincinnati is bounded by a range of forest-covered hills, sufficiently steep and rugged to prevent their being built upon, or easily cultivated, but not sufficiently high to command from their summits a view of any considerable extent. Deep and narrow water-courses, dry in summer, but bringing down heavy streams in winter, divide these hills into many separate heights, and this furnishes the only variety the landscape offers for many miles round the town. The lovely Ohio is a beautiful feature wherever it is visible, but the only part of the city that has the advantage of its beauty is the street nearest to its bank. The hills of Kentucky, which rise at about the same distance from the river, on the opposite side, form the southern boundary to the basin in which Cincinnati is built.

On first arriving, I thought the many tree-covered hills around, very beautiful, but long before my departure, I felt so weary of the confined view, that Salisbury Plain would have been an agreeable variety. I doubt if any inhabitant of Cincinnati ever mounted these hills so often as myself and my children; but it was rather for the enjoyment of a freer air than for any beauty of prospect, that we took our daily climb. These hills afford neither shrubs nor flowers, but furnish the finest specimens of millepore in the world; and the water-courses are full of fossil productions.

The forest trees are neither large nor well grown, and so close as to be nearly knotted together at top; even the wild vine here loses its beauty, for its graceful festoons bear leaves only when they reach the higher branches of the tree that supports them, both air and light being too scantily found below to admit of their doing more than climbing with a bare stem till they reach a better atmosphere. The herb we call pennyroyal was the only one I found in abundance, and that only on the brows, where the ground had been partially cleared; vegetation is impossible elsewhere, and it is this circumstance which makes the "eternal forests" of America so detestable. Near New Orleans the undergrowth of palmetto and pawpaw is highly beautiful, but in Tennessee, Indiana, and Ohio, I never found the slightest beauty in the forest scenery. Fallen trees in every possible stage of decay, and congeries of leaves that have been rotting since the flood, cover the ground and infect the air. The beautiful variety of foliage afforded by evergreens never occurs, and in Tennessee, and that part of Ohio that surrounds Cincinnati, even the sterile beauty of rocks is wanting. On crossing the water to Kentucky the scene is greatly improved; beech and chesnut, of magnificent growth, border the beautiful river; the ground has been well cleared, and the herbage is excellent; the pawpaw grows abundantly, and is a splendid shrub, though it bears neither fruit nor flowers so far north. The noble tulip tree flourishes here, and blooms profusely.

The river Licking flows into the Ohio nearly opposite Cincinnati; it is a pretty winding stream, and two or three miles from its mouth has a brisk rapid, dancing among white stones, which, in the absence of better rocks, we found very picturesque.

CHAPTER V

Cincinnati . . . Forest Farm . . .

Though I do not quite sympathise with those who consider Cincinnati as one of the wonders of the earth, I certainly think it a city of extraordinary size and importance, when it is remembered that thirty years ago the aboriginal forest occupied the ground where it stands; and every month appears to extend its limits and its wealth.

Some of the native political economists assert that this rapid conversion of a bear-brake into a prosperous city, is the result of free political institutions; not being very deep in such matters, a more obvious cause suggested itself to me, in the unceasing goad which necessity applies to industry in this country, and in the absence of all resource for the idle. During nearly two years that I resided in Cincinnati, or its neighbourhood, I neither saw a beggar, nor a man of sufficient fortune to permit his ceasing his efforts to increase it; thus every bee in the hive is actively employed in search of that honey of Hybla, vulgarly called money; neither art, science, learning, nor pleasure can seduce them from its pursuit. This unity of purpose, backed by the spirit of enterprise, and joined with an acuteness and *total* absence of probity, where interest is concerned, which might set canny Yorkshire at defiance, may well go far towards obtaining its purpose.

The low rate of taxation, too, unquestionably permits a more rapid accumulation of individual wealth than with us; but till I had travelled through America, I had no idea how much of the money collected in taxes returns among the people, not only in the purchase of what their industry furnishes, but in the actual enjoyment of what is furnished. Were I an English legislator, instead of sending sedition to the Tower, I would send her to make a tour of the United States. I had a little leaning towards sedition myself when I set out, but before I had half completed my tour I was quite cured.

* * * * *

The "simple" manner of living in Western America was more distasteful to me from its levelling effects on the manners of the people, than from the personal privations that it rendered necessary; and yet, till I was without them, I was in no degree aware of the many pleasurable sensations derived from the little elegancies and refinements enjoyed by the middle classes in Europe. There were many circumstances, too trifling even for my gossiping pages, which pressed themselves daily and hourly upon us, and which forced us to remember painfully that we were not at home. It requires an abler pen than mine to trace the connection which I am persuaded exists between these deficiencies and the minds and manners of the people. All animal wants are supplied profusely at Cincinnati, and at a very easy rate; but, alas! these go but a little way in the history of a day's enjoyment. The total and universal want of manners, both in males and females, is so remarkable, that I was constantly endeavouring to account for it. It certainly does not proceed from want of intellect. I have listened to much dull and heavy conversation in America, but rarely to any that I could strictly call silly, (if I except the every where privileged class of very young ladies). They appear to me to have clear heads and active intellects; are more ignorant on subjects that are only of conventional value, than on such as are of intrinsic importance; but there is no charm, no grace in their conversation. I very seldom during my whole stay in the country heard a sentence elegantly turned, and correctly pronounced from the lips of an American. There is always something either in the expression or the accent that jars the feelings and shocks the taste.

I will not pretend to decide whether man is better or worse off for requiring refinement in the manners and customs of the society that surrounds him, and for being incapable of enjoyment without them; but in America that polish which removes the coarser and rougher parts of our nature is unknown and undreamed of. There is much substantial comfort, and some display in the larger cities; in many of the more obvious features they are as Paris or as London, being all large assemblies of active and intelligent human beings—but yet they are wonderfully unlike in nearly all their moral features. Now God forbid that any reasonable American, (of whom there are so many millions), should ever come to ask me what I mean; I should find it very difficult, nay, perhaps, utterly impossible, to explain myself; but, on the other hand, no European who has visited the Union, will find the least difficulty in understanding me. I am in no way competent to judge of the political institutions of America; and if I should occasionally make an observation on their effects, as they meet my superficial glance, they will be made in the spirit, and with the feeling of a woman, who is apt to tell what her first impressions may be, but unapt to reason back from effects to their causes. Such observations, if they be unworthy of much attention, are also obnoxious to little reproof: but there are points of national peculiarity of which women may judge as able as men,—all that constitutes the external of society may be fairly trusted to us.

*   *   *   *   *

Notwithstanding all this, the country is a very fine country, well worth visiting for a thousand reasons; nine hundred and ninety-nine of these are reasons founded on admiration and respect; the thousandth is, that we shall feel the more contented with our own. The more unlike a country through which we travel is to all we have left, the more we are likely to be amused; every thing in Cincinnati had this newness, and I should have thought it a place delightful to visit, but to tarry there was not to feel at home.

My home, however, for a time it was to be. We heard on every side, that of all the known places on "the globe called earth," Cincinnati was the most favourable for a young man to settle in; and I only awaited the arrival of Mr. T. to fix our son there, intending to continue with him till he should feel himself sufficiently established. We accordingly determined upon making ourselves as comfortable as possible. I took a larger house which, however, I did not obtain without considerable difficulty, as, notwithstanding fourteen hundred new dwellings had been erected the preceding year, the demand for houses greatly exceeded the supply. We became acquainted with several amiable people, and we beguiled the anxious interval that preceded Mr. T.'s joining us by frequent excursions in the neighbourhood, which not only afforded us amusement, but gave us an opportunity of observing the mode of life of the country people.

We visited one farm, which interested us particularly from its wild and lonely situation, and from the entire dependence of the inhabitants upon their own resources. It was a partial clearing in the very heart of the forest. The house was built on the side of a hill, so steep that a high ladder was necessary to enter the front door, while the back one opened against the hill side; at the foot of this sudden eminence ran a clear stream, whose bed had been deepened into a little reservoir, just opposite the house. A noble field of Indian-corn stretched away into the forest on one side, and a few half-cleared acres, with a shed or two upon them, occupied the other, giving accommodation to cows, horses, pigs, and chickens innumerable. Immediately before the house was a small potatoe garden, with a few peach and apple trees. The house was built of logs, and consisted of two rooms, besides a little shanty or lean-to, that was used as a kitchen. Both rooms were comfortably furnished with good beds, drawers, &c. The farmer's wife, and a young woman who looked like her sister, were spinning, and three little children were playing about. The woman told me that they spun and wove all the cotton and woollen garments of the family, and knit all the stockings; her husband, though not a shoe-maker by trade, made all the shoes. She manufactured all the soap and candles they used, and prepared her sugar from the sugar-trees on their farm. All she wanted with money, she said, was to buy coffee, tea, and whiskey, and she could "get enough any day by sending a batch of butter and chicken to market." They used no wheat, nor sold any of their corn, which, though it appeared a very large quantity, was not more than they required to make their bread and cakes of various kinds, and to feed all their live stock during the winter. She did not look in health, and said they had all had ague in "the fall;" but she seemed contented, and proud of her independence; though it was in somewhat a mournful accent that she said, " 'Tis strange to us to see company: I expect the sun may rise and set a hundred times before I shall see another human that does not belong to the family,"

I have been minute in the description of this forest farm, as I think it the best specimen I saw of the back-wood's independence, of which so much is said in America. These people were indeed independent, Robinson Crusoe was hardly more so, and they eat and drink abundantly; but yet it seemed to me that there was something awful and almost unnatural in their loneliness. No village bell ever summoned them to prayer, where they might meet the friendly greeting of their fellow-men. When they die, no spot sacred by ancient reverence will receive their bones—Religion will not breathe her sweet and solemn farewell upon their grave; the husband or the father will dig the pit that is to hold them, beneath the nearest tree; he will himself deposit them within it, and the wind that whispers through the boughs will be their only requiem. But then they pay neither taxes nor tythes, are never expected to pull off a hat or to make a curtsy, and will live and die without hearing or uttering the dreadful words, "God save the king."

* * * * *

CHAPTER VI

Servants . . . Society . . . Evening Parties . . .

The greatest difficulty in organising a family establishment in Ohio, is getting servants, or, as it is there called, "getting help," for it is more than petty treason to the Republic, to call a free citizen a *servant*. The whole class of young women, whose bread depends upon their labour, are taught to believe that the most abject poverty is preferable to domestic service. Hundreds of half-naked girls work in the paper-mills, or in any other manufactory, for less than half the wages they would receive in service; but they think their equality is compromised by the latter, and nothing but the wish to obtain some particular article of finery will ever induce them to submit to it. A kind friend, however, exerted herself so effectually for me, that a tall stately lass soon presented herself, saying, "I be come to help you." The intelligence was very agreeable, and I welcomed her in the most gracious manner possible, and asked what I should give her by the year.

"Oh Gimini!" exclaimed the damsel, with a loud laugh, "you be a downright Englisher, sure enough. I should like to see a young lady engage by the year in America! I hope I shall get a husband before many months, or I expect I shall be an outright old maid, for I be most seventeen already; besides, mayhap I may want to go to school. You must just give me a dollar and half a week, and mother's slave, Phillis, must come over once a week, I expect, from t'other side the water, to help me clean."

I agreed to the bargain, of course, with all dutiful submis-

31

sion; and seeing she was preparing to set to work in a yellow dress parsemé with red roses, I gently hinted, that I thought it was a pity to spoil so fine a gown, and that she had better change it.

" 'Tis just my best and my worst," she answered, "for I've got no other."

And in truth I found that this young lady had left the paternal mansion with no more clothes of any kind than what she had on. I immediately gave her money to purchase what was necessary for cleanliness and decency, and set to work with my daughters to make her a gown. She grinned applause when our labour was completed, but never uttered the slightest expression of gratitude for that, or for any thing else we could do for her. She was constantly asking us to lend her different articles of dress, and when we declined it, she said, "Well, I never seed such grumpy folks as you be; there is several young ladies of my acquaintance what goes to live out now and then with the old women about the town, and they and their gurls always lends them what they asks for; I guess you Inglish thinks we should poison your things, just as bad as if we was Negurs." And here I beg to assure the reader, that whenever I give conversations they were not made àloisir, but were written down immediately after they occurred, with all the verbal fidelity my memory permitted.

This young lady left me at the end of two months, because I refused to lend her money enough to buy a silk dress to go to a ball, saying, "Then 'tis not worth my while to stay any longer."

I cannot imagine it possible that such a state of things can be desirable, or beneficial to any of the parties concerned. I might occupy a hundred pages of the subject, and yet fail to give an adequate idea of the sore, angry, ever wakeful pride that seemed to torment these poor wretches. In many of them it was so excessive, that all feeling of displeasure, or even of ridicule, was lost in pity. One of these was a pretty girl, whose natural disposition must have been gentle and kind; but her good feelings were soured, and her gentleness turned to morbid sensitiveness, by having heard a thousand and a thousand times that she was as good as any other lady, that all men were equal, and women too, and that it was a sin and a shame for a free-born American to be treated like a servant.

When she found she was to dine in the kitchen, she turned up her pretty lip, and said, "I guess that's 'cause you don't think I'm good enough to eat with you. You'll find that won't do here." I found afterwards that she rarely ate any dinner at all, and generally passed the time in tears. I did every thing in my power to conciliate and make her happy, but I am sure she hated me. I gave her very high wages, and she staid till she had obtained several expensive articles of dress, and then, *un beau matin*, she came to me full dressed, and said, "I must go." "When shall you return, Charlotte?" "I expect you'll see no more of me." And so we parted. Her sister was also living with me, but her wardrobe was not yet completed, and she remained some weeks longer, till it was.

I fear it may be called bad taste to say so much concerning my domestics, but, nevertheless, the circumstances are so characteristic of America that I must recount another history relating to them. A few days after the departure of my ambitious belle, my cries for "Help" had been so effectual that another young lady presented herself, with the usual preface "I'm come to help you." I had been cautioned never to ask for a reference for character, as it would not only rob me of that help, but entirely prevent my ever getting another; so, five minutes after she entered she was installed, bundle and all, as a member of the family. She was by no means handsome, but there was a air of simple frankness in her manner that won us all. For my own part, I thought I had got a second Jeanie Deans; for she recounted to me histories of her early youth, wherein her plain good sense and strong mind had enabled her to win her way through a host of cruel step-mothers, faithless lovers, and cheating brothers. Among other things, she told me, with the appearance of much emotion, that she had found, since she came to town, a cure for all her sorrows, "Thanks and praise for it, I have got religion!" and then she asked it I would spare her to go to Meeting every Tuesday and Thursday evening; "You shall not have to want me, Mrs. Trollope, for our minister knows that we have all our duties to perform to man, as well as to God, and he makes the Meeting late in the evening that they may not cross one another." Who could refuse? Not I, and Nancy had leave to go to Meeting two evenings in the week, besides Sundays.

One night, that the mosquitoes had found their way under

my net, and prevented my sleeping, I heard some one enter the house very late; I got up, went to the top of the stairs, and, by the help of a bright moon, recognised Nancy's best bonnet. I called to her; "You are very late," said I, "what is the reason of it?" "Oh, Mrs. Trollope," she replied, "I am late, indeed! We have this night had seventeen souls added to our flock. May they live to bless this night! But it has been a long sitting, and very warm; I'll just take a drink of water, and get to bed; you shan't find me later in the morning for it." Nor did I. She was an excellent servant, and performed more than was expected from her; moreover, she always found time to read the Bible several times in the day, and I seldom saw her occupied about any thing without observing that she had placed it near her.

At last she fell sick with the cholera, and her life was despaired of. I nursed her with great care, and sat up the greatest part of two nights with her. She was often delirious, and all her wandering thoughts seemed to ramble to heaven. "I have been a sinner," she said, "but I am safe in the Lord Jesus." When she recovered, she asked me to let her go into the country for a few days, to change the air, and begged me to lend her three dollars.

While she was absent a lady called on me, and enquired, with some agitation, if my servant, Nancy Fletcher, were at home. I replied that she was gone into the country. "Thank God," she exclaimed, "never let her enter your doors again, she is the most abandoned woman in the town: a gentleman who knows you, has been told that she lives with you, and that she boasts of having the power of entering your house at any hour of the night." She told many other circumstances, unnecessary to repeat, but all tending to prove that she was a very dangerous inmate.

I expected her home the next evening, and I believe I passed the interval in meditating how to get rid of her without an *eclaircissement*. At length she arrived, and all my study having failed to supply me with any other reason than the real one for dismissing her, I stated it at once. Not the slightest change passed over her countenance, but she looked steadily at me, and said, in a very civil tone, "I should like to know who told you." I replied that it could be of no advantage to her to know, and that I wished her to go immediately. "I am ready to go," she said, in the same quiet tone, "but what will you do for your three dollars?" "I must do without them, Nancy; good morning to you." "I must just put up my things," she said, and left the room. About half an hour afterwards, when we were all assembled at dinner, she entered with her usual civil composed air, "Well, I am come to wish you all good bye," and with a friendly good-humoured smile she left us.

This adventure frightened me so heartily, that, notwithstanding I had the dread of cooking my own dinner before my eyes, I would not take any more young ladies into my family without receiving some slight sketch of their former history. At length I met with a very worthy French woman, and soon after with a tidy English girl to assist her; and I had the good fortune to keep them till a short time before my departure: so, happily, I have no more misfortunes of this nature to relate.

Such being the difficulties respecting domestic arrangements, it is obvious, that the ladies who are brought up amongst them cannot have leisure for any great developement of the mind: it is, in fact, out of the question; and, remembering this, it is more surprising that some among them should be very pleasing, than that none should be highly instructed.

Had I passed as many evenings in company in any other town that I ever visited as I did in Cincinnati, I should have been able to give some little account of the conversations I had listened to; but, upon reading over my notes, and then taxing my memory to the utmost to supply the deficiency, I can scarcely find a trace of any thing that deserves the name. Such as I have, shall be given in their place. But, whatever may be the talents of the persons who meet together in society, the very shape, form, and arrangement of the meeting is sufficient to paralyze conversation. The women invariably herd together at one part of the room, and the men at the other; but, in justice to Cincinnati, I must acknowledge that this arrangement is by no means peculiar to that city, or to the western side of the Alleghanies. Sometimes a small attempt at music produces a partial reunion; a few of the most daring youths, animated by the consciousness of curled hair and smart waistcoats, approach the piano-forte, and begin to mutter a little to the half-grown pretty things, who are comparing with one another "how many quarters' music they have had." Where the mansion is of sufficient dignity to have two drawing-rooms, the piano, the little ladies, and the slender gentlemen are left to themselves, and on such occasions the sound of laughter is often heard to issue from among them. But the fate of the more dignified personages, who are left in the other room, is extremely dismal. The gentlemen spit, talk of elections and the price of produce, and spit again. The ladies look at each other's dresses till they know every pin by heart; talk of Parson Somebody's last sermon on the day of judgment, on Dr. T'otherbody's new pills for dyspepsia, till the "tea" is announced, when they all console themselves together for whatever they may have suffered in keeping awake, by taking more tea, coffee, hot cake and custard, hoe cake, johny cake, waffle cake, and dodger cake, pickled peaches, and preserved cucumbers, ham, turkey, hung beef, apple sauce, and pickled oysters than ever were prepared in any other country of the known world. After this massive meal is over, they return to the drawing-room, and it always appeared to me that they remained together as long as they could bear it, and then they rise *en masse*, cloak, bonnet, shawl, and exit.

CHAPTER VII

Market . . . Museum . . .
Phrenological Society . . .
Miss Wright's Lecture . . .

Perhaps the most advantageous feature in Cincinnati is its market, which, for excellence, abundance, and cheapness, can hardly, I should think, be surpassed in any part of the world, if I except the luxury of fruits, which are very inferior to any I have seen in Europe. There are no butchers, fishmongers, or indeed any shops for eatables, except *bakeries*, as they are called, in the town; every thing must be purchased at market; and to accomplish this, the busy housewife must be stirring betimes, or, 'spite of the abundant supply, she will find her hopes of breakfast, dinner, and supper for the day defeated, the market being pretty well over by eight o'clock.

The beef is excellent, and the highest price when we were there, four cents (about two-pence) the pound. The mutton was inferior, and so was veal to the eye, but it ate well, though not very fat; the price was about the same. The poultry was excellent; fowls or full-sized chickens, ready for table, twelve cents, but much less if bought alive, and not quite fat; turkeys about fifty cents, and geese the same. The Ohio furnishes several sorts of fish, some of them very good, and always to be found cheap and abundant in the market. Eggs, butter, nearly all kinds of vegetables, excellent, and at moderate prices. From June till December tomatoes (the great luxury of the American table in the opinion of most Europeans) may be found in the highest perfection in the market for about sixpence the peck. They have a great variety of beans unknown in England, particularly the

37

lima bean, the seed of which is dressed like the French harrico; it furnishes a very abundant crop, and is a most delicious vegetable: could it be naturalised with us it would be a valuable acquisition. The Windsor, or broad-bean, will not do well there: Mr. Bullock had them in his garden, where they were cultivated with much care; they grew about a foot high and blossomed, but the pod never ripened. All the fruit I saw exposed for sale in Cincinnati was most miserable. I passed two summers there, but never tasted a peach worth eating. Of apricots and nectarines I saw none; strawberries very small, raspberries much worse; gooseberries very few, and quite uneatable; currants about half the size of ours, and about double the price; grapes too sour for tarts; apples abundant, but very indifferent, none that would be thought good enough for an English table; pears, cherries, and plums most miserable bad. The flowers of these regions were at least equally inferior: whether this proceeds from want of cultivation or from peculiarity of soil I know not, but after leaving Cincinnati, I was told by a gentleman who appeared to understand the subject, that the state of Ohio had no indigenous flowers or fruits. The water-melons, which in that warm climate furnish a delightful refreshment, were abundant and cheap; but all other melons very inferior to those of France, or even of England, when ripened in a common hot-bed.

From the almost total want of pasturage near the city, it is difficult for a stranger to divine how milk is furnished for its supply, but we soon learnt that there are more ways than one of keeping a cow. A large proportion of the families in the town, particularly of the poorer class, have one, though apparently without any accommodation whatever for it. These animals are fed morning and evening at the door of the house with a good mess of Indian corn, boiled with water; while they eat, they are milked, and when the operation is completed the milk-pail and the meal-tub retreat into the dwelling, leaving the republican cow to walk away, to take her pleasure on the hills, or in the gutters, as may suit her fancy best. They generally return very regularly to give and take the morning and evening meal; though it more than once happened to us, before we were supplied by a regular milk cart, to have our jug sent home empty, with the sad news that "the cow was not come home, and it was too late to look for her to breakfast now." Once, I remember, the good woman told us that she had overslept herself, and that the cow had come and gone again, "not liking, I expect, to hanker about by herself for nothing, poor thing."

Cincinnati has not many lions to boast, but among them are two museums of natural history; both of these contain many respectable specimens, particularly that of Mr. Dorfeuille, who has, moreover, some highly interesting Indian antiquities. He is a man of taste and science, but a collection formed strictly according to their dictates, would by no means satisfy the western metropolis. The people have a most extravagant passion for wax figures, and the two museums vie with each other in displaying specimens of this barbarous branch of art. As Mr. Dorfeuille cannot trust to his science for attracting the citizens, he has put his ingenuity into requisition, and this has proved to him the surer aid of the two. He has constructed a pandæmonium in an upper story of his museum, in which he has congregated all the images of horror that his fertile fancy could devise; dwarfs that by machinery grow into giants before the eyes of the spectator; imps of ebony with eyes of flame; monstrous reptiles devouring youth and beauty; lakes of fire, and mountains of ice; in short, wax, paint and springs have done wonders. "To give the scheme some more effect,: he makes it visible only through a grate of massive iron bars, among which are arranged wires connected with an electrical machine in a neighbouring chamber; should any daring hand or foot obtrude itself within the bars, it receives a smart shock, that often passes through many of the crowd, and the cause being unknown, the effect is exceedingly comic; terror, astonishment, curiosity, are all set in action, and all contribute to make "Dorfeuille's Hell" one of the most amusing exhibitions imaginable.*

*   *   *   *   *

We had not been long at Cincinnati when Dr. Caldwell, the Spurzheim of America, arrived there for the purpose of delivering lectures on phrenology. I attended his lectures, and was introduced to him. He has studied Spurzheim and Combe diligently, and seems to understand the science to which he has devoted himself; but neither his lectures nor his conversation had that delightful truth of genuine enthusiasm, which makes

*See introduction, p. xvii.

39

listening to Dr. Spurzheim so great a treat. His lectures, however, produced considerable effect. Between twenty and thirty of the most erudite citizens decided upon forming a phrenological society. A meeting was called, and fully attended; a respectable number of subscribers' names was registered, the payment of subscriptions being arranged for a future day. President, vicepresident, treasurer, and secretary, where chosen; and the first meeting dissolved with every appearance of energetic perseverance in scientific research.

The second meeting brought together one-half of this learned body, and they enacted rules and laws, and passed resolutions, sufficient, it was said, to have filled three folios.

A third day of meeting arrived, which was an important one, as on this occasion the subscriptions were to be paid. The treasurer came punctually, but found himself alone. With patient hope, he waited two hours for the wise men of the west, but he waited in vain: and so expired the Phrenological Society of Cincinnati.

I had often occasion to remark that the spirit of enterprise or improvement seldom glowed with sufficient ardour to resist the smothering effect of a demand for dollars. The Americans love talking. All great works, however, that promise a profitable result, are sure to meet support from men who have enterprise and capital sufficient to await the return; but where there is nothing but glory, or the gratification of taste to be expected, it, I believe, very rarely that they give any thing beyond "their most sweet voices."

Perhaps they are right. In Europe we see fortunes crippled by a passion for statues, or for pictures, or for books, or for gems; for all and every of the artificial wants that give grace to life, and tend to make man forget that he is a thing of clay. They are wiser in their generation on the other side of the Atlantic; I rarely saw any thing that led to such oblivion there.

Soon after Dr. Caldwell's departure, another lecturer appeared upon the scene, whose purpose of publicly addressing the people was no sooner made known, than the most violent sensation was excited.

That a lady of fortune, family, and education, whose youth had been passed in the most refined circles of private life, should present herself to the people as a public lecturer, would naturally excite surprise any where, and the *nil admirari* of the old world itself, would hardly be sustained before such a spectacle; but in America, where women are guarded by a seven-fold shield of habitual insignificance, it caused an effect that can hardly be described. "Miss Wright, of Nashoba, is going to lecture at the court-house," sounded from street to street, and from house to house. I shared the surprise, but not the wonder; I knew her extraordinary gift of eloquence, her almost unequalled command of words, and the wonderful power of her rich and thrilling voice; and I doubted not that if it was her will to do it, she had the power of commanding the attention, and enchanting the ear of any audience before whom it was her pleasure to appear. I was most anxious to hear her, but was almost deterred from attempting it, by the reports that reached me of the immense crowd that was expected. After many consultations, and hearing that many other ladies intended going, my friend Mrs. P****, and myself, decided upon making the attempt, accompanied by a party of gentlemen, and found the difficulty less than we anticipated, though the building was crowded in every part. We congratulated ourselves that we had had the courage to be among the number, for all my expectations fell far short of the splendour, the brilliance, the overwhelming eloquence of this extraordinary orator.

Her lecture was upon the nature of true knowledge, and it contained little that could be objected to, by any sect or party; it was intended as an introduction to the strange and startling theories contained in her subsequent lectures, and could alarm only by the hints it contained that the fabric of human wisdom could rest securely on no other base than that of human knowledge.

There was, however, one passage from which common-sense revolted; it was one wherein she quoted that phrase of mischievous sophistry, "all men are born free and equal."

This false and futile axiom, which has done, is doing and will do so much harm to this fine country, came from Jefferson; and truly his life was a glorious commentary upon it. I pretend not to criticise his written works, but common-sense enables me to pronounce this, his favourite maxim, false.

Few names are held in higher estimation in America, than that of Jefferson; it is the touchstone of the democratic party, and all seem to agree that he was one of the greatest of men; yet I have heard his name coupled with deeds which would make the sons of Europe shudder. The facts I allude to are spoken openly by all, not whispered privately by a few; and in a country where religion is the tea-table talk, and its strict observance a fashionable distinction, these facts are recorded, and listened to, without horror, nay, without emotion.

Mr. Jefferson is said to have been the father of children by almost all his numerous gang of female slaves. These wretched offspring were also the lawful slaves of their father, and worked in his house and plantations as such; in particular, it is recorded that it was his especial pleasure to be waited upon by them at table, and the hospitable orgies for which his Montecielo [sic] was so celebrated, were incomplete, unless the goblet he quaffed were tendered by the trembling hand of his own slavish offspring.

I once heard it stated by a democratical adorer of this great man, that when, as it sometimes happened, his children by Quadroon slaves were white enough to escape suspicion of their origin, he did not pursue them if they attempted to escape, saying laughingly, "Let the rogues get off, if they can; I will not hinder them." This was stated in a large party, as a proof of his kind and noble nature, and was received by all with approving smiles.

If I know any thing of right or wrong, if virtue and vice be indeed something more than words, then was this great American an unprincipled tyrant, and most heartless libertine.*

But to return to Miss Wright,—it is impossible to imagine any thing more striking than her appearance. Her tall and majestic figure, the deep and almost solemn expression of her eyes, the simple contour of her finely formed head, unadorned, excepting by its own natural ringlets; her garment of plain white muslin, which hung around her in folds that recalled the drapery of a Grecian statue, all contributed to produce an effect, unlike any thing I had ever seen before, or ever expect to see again.

*These accusations against Jefferson originated in political slanders published by James Callender in 1802. Historians have neither proved nor disproved the charges.

CHAPTER VIII

*Absence of public and private
Amusement . . . Churches and Chapels . . .
Influence of the Clergy . . . A Revival . . .*

I never saw any people who appeared to live so much without amusement as the Cincinnatians. Billiards are forbidden by law, so are cards. To sell a pack of cards in Ohio subjects the seller to a penalty of fifty dollars. They have no public balls, excepting, I think, six, during the Christmas holidays. They have no concerts. They have no dinner parties.

They have a theatre, which is, in fact, the only public amusement of this triste little town; but they seem to care little about it, and either from economy or distaste, it is very poorly attended. Ladies are rarely seen there, and by far the larger proportion of females deem it an offence against religion to witness the representation of a play. It is in the churches and chapels of the town that the ladies are to be seen in full costume; and I am tempted to believe that a stranger from the continent of Europe would be inclined, on first reconnoitering the city, to suppose that the places of worship were the theatres and cafés of the place. No evening in the week but brings throngs of the young and beautiful to the chapels and meeting-houses, all dressed with care, and sometimes with great pretension; it is there that all display is made, and all fashionable distinction sought. The proportion of gentlemen attending these evening meetings is very small, but often, as might be expected, a sprinkling of smart young clerks make this sedulous display of ribbons and ringlets intelligible and natural. Were it not for the churches,

43

indeed, I think there might be a general bonfire of best bonnets, for I never could discover any other use for them.

The ladies are too actively employed in the interior of their houses to permit much parading in full dress for morning visits. There are no public gardens or lounging shops of fashionable resort, and were it not for public worship, and private tea-drinkings, all the ladies in Cincinnati would be in danger of becoming perfect recluses.

The influence which the ministers of all the innumerable religious sects throughout America, have on the females of their respective congregations, approaches very nearly to what we read of in Spain, or in other strictly Roman Catholic Countries. There are many causes for this peculiar influence. Where equality of rank is affectedly acknowledged by the rich, and clamorously claimed by the poor, distinction and pre-eminence are allowed to the clergy only. This gives them high importance in the eyes of the ladies. I think, also, that it is from the clergy only that the women of America receive that sort of attention which is so dearly valued by every female heart throughout the world. With the priests of America, the women hold that degree of influential importance which, in the countries of Europe, is allowed them throughout all orders and ranks of society, except, perhaps, the very lowest; and in return for this they seem to give their hearts and souls into their keeping. I never saw, or read, of any country where religion had so strong a hold upon the women, or a slighter hold upon the men.

I mean not to assert that I met with no men of sincerely religious feelings, or with no women of no religious feelings at all; but I feel perfectly secure of being correct as to the great majority in the statement I have made.

We had not been many months in Cincinnati when our curiosity was excited by hearing the "revival" talked of by every one we met throughout the town. "The revival will be very full"—"We shall be constantly engaged during the revival"—were the phrases we constantly heard repeated, and for a long time, without in the least comprehending what was meant; but at length I learnt that the un-national church of America required to be roused, at regular interval, to greater energy and exertion. At these seasons the most enthusiastic of the clergy travel the country, and enter the cities and towns by scores, or by hundreds, as the accommodation of the place may admit, and for a week or fortnight, or, if the population be large, for a month; they preach and pray all day, and often for a considerable portion of the night, in the various churches and chapels of the place. This is called a Revival.

I took considerable pains to obtain information on this subject; but in detailing what I learnt I fear that it is probable I shall be accused of exaggeration; all I can do is cautiously to avoid deserving it. The subject is highly interesting, and it would be a fault of no trifling nature to treat it with levity.

These itinerant clergymen are of all persuasions, I believe, except the Episcopalian, Catholic, Unitarian, and Quaker. I heard of Presbyterian of all varieties; of Baptists of I know not how many divisions; and of Methodists of more denominations than I can remember; whose innumerable shades of varying belief, it would require much time to explain, and more to comprehend. They enter all the cities, towns, and villages of the Union in succession; I could not learn with sufficient certainty to repeat, what the interval generally is between their visits. These itinerants are, for the most part, lodged in the houses of their respective followers, and every evening that is not spent in the churches and meeting-houses, is devoted to what would be called parties by others, but which they designate as prayer meetings. Here they eat, drink, pray, sing, hear confessions, and make converts. To these meetings I never got invited, and therefore I have nothing but hear-say evidence to offer, but my information comes from an eye-witness, and one on whom I believe I may depend. If one half of what I heard may be believed, these social prayer meetings are by no means the most curious, or the least important part of the business.

It is impossible not to smile at the close resemblance to be traced between the feelings of a first-rate Presbyterian or Methodist lady, fortunate enough to have secured a favourite Itinerant for her meeting, and those of a first-rate London Blue, equally blest in the presence of a fashionable poet. There is a strong family likeness among us all the world over.

The best rooms, the best dresses, the choicest refreshments solemnize the meeting. While the party is assembling, the loadstar of the hour is occupied in whispering conversations with the guests as they arrive. They are called brothers and sisters, and the greetings are very affectionate. When the room is full, the company, of whom a vast majority are always women, are invited, intreated, and coaxed to confess before their brothers and sisters, all their thoughts, faults, and follies.

These confessions are strange scenes; the more they confess, the more invariably are they encouraged and caressed. When this is over, they all kneel, and the Itinerant prays extempore. They then eat and drink; and then they sing hymns, pray, exhort, sing, and pray again, till the excitement reaches a very high pitch indeed. These scenes are going on at some house or other every evening during the revival, nay, at many at the same time, for the churches and meeting-houses cannot give occupation to half the Itinerants, though they are all open throughout the day, and till a late hour in the night, and the officiating ministers succeed each other in the occupation of them.

It was at the principal of the Presbyterian churches that I was twice witness to scenes that made me shudder; in describing one, I describe both, and every one; the same thing is constantly repeated.

It was in the middle of summer, but the service we were recommended to attend did not begin till it was dark. The church was well lighted, and crowded almost to suffocation. On entering, we found three priests standing side by side, in a sort of tribune, placed where the altar usually is, handsomely fitted up with crimson curtains, and elevated about as high as our pulpits. We took our places in a pew close to the rail which surrounded it.

The priest who stood in the middle was praying; the prayer was extravagantly vehement, and offensively familiar in expression; when this ended, a hymn was sung, and then another priest took the centre place, and preached. The sermon had considerable eloquence, but of a frightful kind. The preacher described, with ghastly minuteness, the last feeble fainting moments of human life, and then the gradual progress of decay after death, which he followed through every process up to the last loathsome stage of decomposition. Suddenly changing his tone, which had been that of sober accurate description, into the shrill voice of horror, he bent forward his head, as if to gaze on some object beneath the pulpit. And as Rebecca made known to Ivanhoe what she saw through the window, so the preacher made known to us what he saw in the pit that seemed to open before him. The device was certainly a happy one for giving effect to his description of hell. No image that fire, flame, brimstone, molten lead, or red-hot pincers could supply; with flesh, nerves, and sinews quivering under them, was omitted. The perspiration ran in streams from the face of the preacher; his eyes rolled, his lips were covered with foam, and every feature had the deep expression of horror it would have borne, had he, in truth, been gazing at the scene he described. The acting was excellent. At length he gave a languishing look to his supporters on each side, as if to express his feeble state, and then sat down, and wiped the drops of agony from his brow.

The other two priests arose, and began to sing a hymn. It was some seconds before the congregation could join as usual; every up-turned face looked pale and horror struck. When the singing ended, another took the centre place, and began in a sort of coaxing affectionate tone, to ask the congregation if what their dear brother had spoken had reached their hearts? Whether they would avoid the hell he had made them see? "Come, then!" he continued, stretching out his arms towards them "come to us, and tell us so, and we will make you see Jesus, the dear gentle Jesus, who shall save you from it. But you must come to him! You must not be ashamed to come to him! This night you shall tell him that you are not ashamed of him; we will make way for you; we will clear the bench for anxious sinners to sit upon. Come, then! come to the anxious bench, and we will shew you Jesus! Come! Come! Come!"

Again a hymn was sung, and while it continued, one of the three was employed in clearing one or two long benches that went across the rail, sending the people back to the lower part of the church. The singing ceased, and again the people were invited, and exhorted not to be ashamed of Jesus, but to put themselves upon "the anxious benches," and lay their heads on his bosom. "Once more we will sing," he concluded, "that we may give you time." And again they sung a hymn.

And now in every part of the church a movement was perceptible, slight at first, but by degrees becoming more decided.

Young girls arose, and sat down, and rose again; and then the pews opened, and several came tottering out, their hands clasped, their heads hanging on their bosoms, and every limb

47

trembling, and still the hymn went on; but as the poor creatures approached the rail their sobs and groans became audible. They seated themselves on the "anxious benches;" the hymn ceased, and two of the three priests walked down from the tribune, and going, one to the right, and the other to the left, began whispering to the poor tremblers seated there. These whispers were inaudible to us, but the sobs and groans increased to a frightful excess. Young creatures, with features pale and distorted, fell on their knees on the pavement, and soon sunk forward on their faces; the most violent cries and shrieks followed, while from time to time a voice was heard in convulsive accents, exclaiming, "Oh Lord!" "Oh Lord Jesus!" "Help me, Jesus!" and the like.

Meanwhile the two priests continued to walk among them; they repeatedly mounted on the benches, and trumpet-mouthed proclaimed to the whole congregation, "the tidings of salvation," and then from every corner of the building arose in reply, short sharp cries of "Amen!" "Glory!" "Amen!" while the prostrate penitents continued to receive whispered comfortings, and from time to time a mystic caress. More than once I saw a young neck encircled by a reverend arm. Violent hysterics and convulsions seized many of them, and when the tumult was at the highest, the priest who remained above, again gave out a hymn as if to drown it.

It was a frightful sight to behold innocent young creatures, in the gay morning of existence, thus seized upon, horror struck, and rendered feeble and enervated for ever. One young girl, apparently not more than fourteen, was supported in the arms of another, some years older; her face was pale as death; her eyes wide open, and perfectly devoid of meaning; her chin and bosom wet with slaver; she had every appearance of idiotism. I saw a priest approach her, he took her delicate hand, "Jesus is with her!" he said, and passed on.

Did the men of America value their women as men ought to value their wives and daughters, would such scenes be permitted among them?

It is hardly necessary to say that all who obeyed the call to place themselves on the "anxious benches" were women, and by far the greater number, very young women. The congregation was, in general, extremely well dressed, and the smartest and most fashionable ladies of the town were there; during the whole revival the churches and meeting-houses were every day crowded with well dressed people.

It is thus the ladies of Cincinnati amuse themselves; to attend the theatre is forbidden; to play cards is unlawful; but they work hard in their families, and must have some relaxation. For myself, I confess that I think the coarsest comedy ever written would be a less detestable exhibition for the eyes of youth and innocence than such a scene.

CHAPTER IX

Schools . . . Climate . . . Water Melons . . .
Fourth of July . . . Pigs . . .
Moving Houses . . .

Cincinnati contains many schools, but of their rank or merit I had very little opportunity of judging; the only one which I visited was kept by D. Lock, a gentleman who appears to have liberal and enlarged opinions on the subject of female education. Should his system produce practical results proportionably excellent, the ladies of Cincinnati will probably some years hence be much improved in their powers of companionship. I attended the annual public exhibition at this school, and perceived, with some surprise, that the higher branches of science were among the studies of the pretty creatures I saw assembled there. One lovely girl of sixteen *took her degree* in mathematics, and another was examined in moral philosophy. They blushed so sweetly, and looked so beautifully puzzled and confounded, that it might have been difficult for an abler judge than I was to decide how far they merited the diploma they received.

This method of letting young ladies graduate, and granting them diplomas on quitting the establishment, was quite new to me; at least, I do not remember to have heard of any thing similar elsewhere. I should fear that the time allowed to the fair graduates of Cincinnati for the acquirement of these various branches of education would seldom be sufficient to permit their reaching the eminence in each which their enlightened instructor anticipates. "A quarter's" mathematics, or "two quarters'" political economy, moral philosophy, algebra, and quadratic equations, would seldom, I should think, enable the

50

teacher and the scholar, by their joint efforts, to lay in such a stock of these sciences as would stand the wear and tear of half a score of children, and one help.

+   +   +   +   +

Towards the end of May we began to feel that we were in a climate warmer than any we had been accustomed to, and my son suffered severely from the effects of it. A bilious complaint, attended by a frightful degree of fever, seized him, and for some days we feared for his life. The treatment he received was, I have no doubt, judicious, but the quantity of calomel prescribed was enormous. I asked one day how many grains I should prepare, and was told to give half a teaspoonful. The difference of climate must, I imagine, make a difference in the effect of this drug, or the practice of the old and new world could hardly differ so widely as it does in the use of it. . . . Repeated and violent bleeding was also had recourse to in the case of my son, and in a few days he was able to leave his room, but he was dreadfully emaciated, and it was many weeks before he recovered his strength.

As the heat of the weather increased we heard of much sickness around us. The city is full of physicians, and they were all to be seen driving about in their cabs at a very alarming rate. One of these gentlemen told us, that when a medical man intended settling in a new situation, he always, if he knew his business, walked through the streets at night, before he decided. If he saw the dismal twinkle of the watch-light from many windows he might be sure that disease was busy, and that the "location" might suit him well. Judging, by this criterion, Cincinnati was far from healthy, I began to fear for our health, and determined to leave the city; but, for a considerable time I found it impossible to procure a dwelling out of it. There were many boarding-houses in the vicinity, but they were all overflowing with guests. We were advised to avoid, as much as possible, walking out in the heat of the day; but the mornings and evenings were delightful, particularly the former, if taken sufficiently early. For several weeks I was never in bed after four o'clock, and at this hour I almost daily accompanied my "help" to market, where the busy novelty of the scene afforded me much amusement.

Many waggon-loads of enormous water-melons were

brought to market every day, and I was sure to see groups of men, women, and children seated on the pavement round the spot where they were sold, sucking in prodigious quantities of this watery fruit. Their manner of devouring them is extremely unpleasant; the huge fruit is cut into half a dozen sections, of about a foot long, and then, dripping as it is with water, applied to the mouth, from either side of which pour copious streams of the fluid, while, ever and anon, a mouthful of the hard black seeds are shot out in all directions, to the great annoyance of all within reach. When I first tasted this fruit I thought it very vile stuff indeed, but before the end of the season we all learned to like it. When taken with claret and sugar it makes delicious wine and water.

It is the custom for the gentlemen to go to market at Cincinnati; the smartest men in the place, and those of the "highest standing" do not scruple to leave their beds with the sun, six days in the week, and, prepared with a mighty basket, to sally forth in search of meat, butter, eggs, and vegetables,. I have continually seen them returning, with their weighty basket on one arm and an enormous ham depending from the other.

And now arrived the 4th of July, that greatest of all American festivals. On the 4th of July, 1776, the declaration of their independence was signed, at the State-house in Philadelphia.

To me, the dreary coldness and want of enthusiasm in American manners is one of their greatest defects, and I therefore hailed the demonstrations of general feeling which this day elicits with real pleasure. On the 4th of July the hearts of the people seem to awaken from a three hundred and sixty-four days' sleep; they appear high-spirited, gay, animated, social, generous, or at least liberal in expense; and would they but refrain from spitting on that hallowed day, I should say, that on the 4th of July, at least, they appeared to be an amiable people. It is true that the women have but little to do with the pageantry, the splendour, or the gaiety of the day; but, setting this defect aside, it was indeed a glorious sight to behold a jubilee so heartfelt as this; and had they not the bad taste and bad feeling to utter an annual oration, with unvarying abuse of the mother country, to say nothing of the warlike manifesto called the Declaration of Independence, our gracious king himself might look upon the scene and say that it was good; nay, even rejoice, that twelve millions of bustling bodies, at four thousand miles distance from his throne and his altars, should make their own laws, and drink their own tea, after the fashion that pleased them best.

*   *   *   *   *

It seems hardly fair to quarrel with a place because its staple commodity is not pretty, but I am sure I should have liked Cincinnati much better if the people had not dealt so very largely in hogs. The immense quantity of business done in this line would hardly be believed by those who had not witnessed it. I never saw a newspaper without remarking such advertisements as the following:

"Wanted, immediately, 4,000 fat hogs."

"For sale, 2,000 barrels of prime pork."

But the annoyance came nearer than this; if I determined upon a walk up Main-street, the chances were five hundred to one against my reaching the shady side without brushing by a snout fresh dripping from the kennel; when we had screwed our courage to the enterprise of mounting a certain noble-looking sugar-loaf hill, that promised pure air and a fine view, we found the brook we had to cross, at its foot, red with the stream from a pig slaughter-house; while our noses, instead of meeting "the thyme that loves the green hill's breast," were greeted by odours that I will not describe, and which I heartily hope my readers cannot imagine; our feet, that on leaving the city had expected to press the flowery sod, literally got entangled in pigs' tails and jawbones: and thus the prettiest walk in the neighbourhood was interdicted for ever.

+   +   +   +   +

One of the sights to stare at in America is that of houses moving from place to place. We were often amused by watching this exhibition of mechanical skill in the streets. They make no difficulty of moving dwellings from one part of the town to another. Those I saw travelling were all of them frame-houses, that is, built wholly of wood, except the chimneys; but it is said that brick buildings are sometimes treated in the same manner. The largest dwelling that I saw in motion was one containing two stories of four rooms each; forty oxen were yoked to it. The

53

first few yards brought down the two stacks of chimneys, but it afterwards went on well. The great difficulties were the first getting it in motion and the stopping exactly in the right place. This locomotive power was extremely convenient at Cincinnati, as the constant improvements going on there made it often desirable to change a wooden dwelling for one of brick; and whenever this happened, we were sure to see the ex No. 100 of Main-street or the ex No. 55 of Second-street creeping quietly out of town, to take possession of a humble suburban station on the common above it.

*   *   *   *   *

CHAPTER X

Removal to the country . . .
Walk in the forest . . . Equality . . .

At length my wish of obtaining a house in the country was gratified. A very pretty cottage, the residence of a gentleman who was removing into town, for the convenience of his business as a lawyer, was to let, and I immediately secured it. It was situated in a little village about a mile and a half from the town, close to the foot of the hills formerly mentioned as the northern boundary of it. We found ourselves much more comfortable here than in the city. The house was pretty and commodious, our sitting-rooms were cool and airy; we had got rid of the detestable mosquitoes, and we had an ice-house that never failed. Besides all this, we had the pleasure of gathering our tomatoes from our own garden, and receiving our milk from our own cow. Our manner of life was infinitely more to my taste than before; it gave us all the privileges of rusticity, which are fully as incompatible with a residence in a little town of Western America as with a residence in London. We lived on terms of primæval intimacy with our cow, for if we lay down on our lawn she did not scruple to take a sniff at the book we were reading, but then she gave us her own sweet breathe in return. The verge of the cool-looking forest that rose opposite our windows was so near, that we often used it as an extra drawing-room, and there was no one to wonder if we went out with no other preparation than our parasols, carrying books and work enough to while away a long summer day in the shade; the meadow that divided us from it was covered with a fine short grass, that continued for a little way under the trees, making a beautiful carpet, while sundry logs and stumps furnished our sofas and tables. But even this was not enough to satisfy us when we first escaped from the city, and we determined upon having a day's enjoyment of the wildest forest scenery we could find. So we packed up books, albums, pencils, and sandwiches, and, despite a burning sun, dragged up a hill so steep that we sometimes fancied we could rest ourselves against it by only leaning forward a little. In panting and in groaning we reached the top, hoping to be refreshed by the purest breath of heaven; but to have tasted the breath of heaven we must have climbed yet farther, even to the tops of the trees themselves, for we soon found that the air beneath them stirred not, nor ever had stirred, as it seemed to us, since first it settled there, so heavily did it weigh upon our lungs.

Still we were determined to enjoy ourselves, and forward we went, crunching knee deep through aboriginal leaves, hoping to reach some spot less perfectly air-tight than our landing-place. Wearied with the fruitless search, we decided on reposing awhile on the trunk of a fallen tree; being all considerably exhausted, the idea of sitting down on this tempting log was conceived and executed simultaneously by the whole party, and the whole party sunk together through its treacherous surface into a mass of rotten rubbish that had formed part of the pith and marrow of the eternal forest a hundred years before.

We were by no means the only sufferers by the accident; frogs, lizards, locusts, katiedids, beetles, and hornets, had the whole of their various tenements disturbed, and testified their displeasure very naturally by annoying us as much as possible in return; we were bit, we were stung, we were scratched; and when, at last, we succeeded in raising ourselves from the venerable ruin, we presented as woeful a spectacle as can well be imagined. We shook our (not ambrosial) garments, and panting with heat, stings, and vexation, moved a few paces from the scene of our misfortune, and again sat down; but this time it was upon the solid earth.

We had no sooner began to "chew the cud" of the bitter fancy that had beguiled us to these mountain solitudes than a new annoyance assailed us. A cloud of mosquitoes gathered round, and while each sharp proboscis sucked our blood, they teased us with their humming chorus, till we lost all patience and started again on our feet, pretty firmly resolved never to try the *al fresco* joys of an American forest again. The sun was now in its meridian splendour, but our homeward path was short, and down hill, so again packing up our preparations for felicity, we started homeward, or, more properly speaking, we started, for in looking for an agreeable spot in this dungeon forest we had advanced so far from the verge of the hill that we had lost all trace of the precise spot where we had entered it. Nothing was to be seen but multitudes of tall, slender, melancholy stems, as like as peas, and standing within a foot of each other. The ground, as far as the eye could reach (which certainly was not far), was covered with an unvaried bed of dried leaves; no trace, no track, no trail, as Mr. Cooper would call it, gave us a hint which way to turn; and having paused for a moment to meditate, we remembered that chance must decide for us at last, so we set forward, in no very good mood, to encounter new misfortunes. We walked about a quarter of a mile, and coming to a steep descent, we thought ourselves extremely fortunate, and began to scramble down, nothing doubting that it was the same we had scrambled up. In truth, nothing could be more like, but, alas! things that are like are not the same; when we had slipped and stumbled down to the edge of the wood, and were able to look beyond it, we saw no pretty cottage with the shadow of its beautiful acacias coming forward to meet us: all was different; and, what was worse, all was distant from the spot where we had hoped to be. We had come down the opposite side of the ridge, and had now to win our weary way a distance of three miles round its base. I believe we shall none of us ever forget that walk. The bright, glowing, furnace-like heat of the atmosphere seems to scorch as I recal it. It was painful to tread, it was painful to breathe, it was painful to look round; every object glowed with the reflection of the fierce tyrant that glared upon us from above.

We got home alive, which agreeably surprised us; and when our parched tongues again found power of utterance, we promised each other faithfully never to propose any more parties of pleasure in the grim stove-like forests of Ohio.

We were now in daily expectation of the arrival of Mr. T.; but day after day, and week after week passed by, till we began to fear some untoward circumstance might delay his coming till the Spring; at last, when we had almost ceased to look out for him, on the road which led from the town, he arrived, late at night, by that which leads across the country from Pitzburgh. The pleasure we felt at seeing him was greatly increased by his bringing with him our eldest son, which was a happiness we had not hoped for. Our walks and our drives now became doubly interesting. The young men, fresh from a public school, found America so totally unlike all the nations with which their reading had made them acquainted, that it was indeed a new world to them. Had they visited Greece or Rome they would have encountered objects with whose images their minds had been long acquainted; or had they travelled to France or Italy they would have seen only what daily conversation had already rendered familiar; but at our public schools America (except perhaps as to her geographical position) is hardly better known than Fairy Land; and the American character has not been much more deeply studied than that of the Anthropophagi: all, therefore, was new, and every thing amusing.

The extraordinary familiarity of our poor neighbours startled us at first, and we hardly knew how to receive their uncouth advances, or what was expected of us in return; however, it sometimes produced very laughable scenes. Upon one occasion two of my children set off upon an exploring walk up the hills; they were absent rather longer than we expected, and the rest of our party determined upon going out to meet them; we knew the direction they had taken, but thought it would be as well to enquire at a little public-house at the bottom of the hill, if such a pair had been seen to pass. A woman, whose appearance more resembled a Covent Garden market-woman than any thing else I can remember, came out and answered my question with the most jovial good humour in the affirmative, and prepared to join us in our search. Her look, her voice, her manner, were so exceedingly coarse and vehement, that she almost frightened me; she passed her arm within mine, and to the inexpressible amusement of my young people, she dragged me on, talking and questioning me without ceasing. She lived but a short distance from us, and I am sure intended to be a very good neighbour; but her violent intimacy made me dread to pass her door; my children, including my sons, she always addressed by their Christian names, excepting when she substituted the word "honey;" this familiarity of address, however, I afterwards found was universal throughout all ranks in the United States.

My general appellation amongst my neighbours was "the English old woman," but in mentioning each other they constantly employed the term "lady;" and they evidently had a pleasure in using it, for I repeatedly observed, that in speaking of a neighbour, instead of saying Mrs. Such-a-one, they described her as "the lady over the way what takes in washing," or as "that there lady, out by the Gulley, what is making dip-candles." Mr. Trollope was as constantly called "the old man," while draymen, butchers' boys, and the labourers on the canal were invariably denominated "them gentlemen;" nay, we once saw one of the most gentlemanlike men in Cincinnati introduce a fellow in dirty shirt sleeves, and all sorts of detestable et cetera, to one of his friends, with this formula, "D***** let me introduce this gentleman to you."

Our respective titles certainly were not very important; but the eternal shaking hands with these ladies and gentlemen was really an annoyance, and the more so, as the near approach of the gentlemen was always redolent of whiskey and tobacco.

But the point where this republican equality was the most distressing was in the long and frequent visitations that it produced. No one dreams of fastening a door in Western America; I was told that it would be considered as an affront by the whole neighbourhood. I was thus exposed to perpetual, and most vexatious interruptions from people whom I had often never seen, and whose names still oftener were unknown to me.

Those who are native there, and to the manner born, seem to pass over these annoyances with more skill than I could ever acquire. More than once I have seen some of my acquaintance beset in the same way, without appearing at all distressed by it; they continued their employment or conversation with me, much as if no such interruption had taken place; when the visitor entered, they would say, "How do you do?" and shake hands.

"Tolerable, I thank ye, how be you?" was the reply.

If it was a female, she took off her hat; if a male, he kept it on, and then taking possession of the first chair in their way, they would retain it for an hour together, without uttering another word; at length, rising abruptly, they would again shake hands, with, "Well, now I must be going, I guess," and so take themselves off, apparently well contented with their reception.

I could never attain this philosophical composure; I could neither write or read, and I always fancied I must talk to them. I will give the minutes of a conversation which I once set down after one of their visits, as a specimen of their tone and manner of speaking and thinking. My visitor was a milkman.

"Well now, so you be from the old country? Ay—you'll see sights here, I guess."

"I hope I shall see many."

"That's a fact. I expect your little place of an island don't grow such dreadful fine corn as you sees here?"

"It grows no corn at all, sir."

"Possible! no wonder, then, that we reads such awful stories in the papers of your poor people being starved to death."

"We have wheat, however."

"Ay, for your rich folks, but I calculate the poor seldom gets a belly full."

"You have certainly much greater abundance here."

"I expect so. Why they do say, that if a poor body contrives to be smart enough to scrape together a few dollars, that your King George always comes down upon 'em, and takes it all away. Don't he?"

"I do not remember hearing of such a transaction."

"I guess they be pretty close about it. Your papers ben't like ourn, I reckon? Now we says and prints just what we likes."

"You spend a good deal of time in reading the newspapers."

"And I'd like you to tell me how we can spend it better. How should freemen spend their time, but looking after their government, and watching that them fellers as we gives offices to, doos their duty, and gives themselves no airs?"

"But I sometimes think, sir, that your fences might be in more thorough repair, and your roads in better order, if less time was spent in politics."

"The Lord! to see how little you knows of a free country! Why, what's the smoothness of a road, put against the freedom of a free-born American? And what does a broken zigzag signify, comparable to knowing that the men what we have been pleased to send up to Congress, speaks handsome and straight, as we chooses they should?"

"It is from a sense of duty, then, that you all go to the liquor store to read the papers?"

"To be sure it is, and he'd be no true born American as didn't. I don't say that the father of a family should always be after liquor, but I do say that I'd rather have my son drunk three times in a week, than not look after the affairs of his country."

+   +   +   +   +

Our autumn walks were delightful; the sun ceased to scorch; the want of flowers was no longer peculiar to Ohio: and the trees took a colouring, which in richness, brilliance, and variety, exceeded all description. I think it is the maple, or sugar-tree, that first sprinkles the forest with rich crimson; the beech follows, with all its harmony of golden tints, from pale yellow up to brightest orange. The dog-wood gives almost the purple colour of the mulberry; the chesnut softens all with its frequent mass of delicate brown, and the sturdy oak carries its deep green into the very lap of winter. These tints are too bright for the landscape painter; the attempt to follow nature in an American autumn scene must be abortive. The colours are in reality extremely brilliant, but the medium through which they are seen increases the effect surprisingly. Of all the points in which America has the advantage of England, the one I felt most sensibly was the clearness and brightness of the atmosphere. By day and by night this exquisite purity of air gives tenfold beauty to every object.

*   *   *   *   *

Our walks were, however, curtailed in several directions by my old Cincinnati enemies, the pigs; immense droves of them were continually arriving from the country by the road that led to most of our favourite walks; they were often fed and lodged in the prettiest valleys, and worse still, were slaughtered beside the prettiest streams. Another evil threatened us from the same quarter, that was yet heavier. Our cottage had an ample piazza, (a luxury almost universal in the country houses of America), which, shaded by a group of acacias, made a delightful sitting-room; from this favourite spot we one day perceived symptoms of building in a field close to it; with much anxiety we hastened to the spot, and asked what building was to be erected there.

" 'Tis to be a slaughter-house for hogs," was the dreadful

reply. As there were several gentlemen's houses in the neighbourhood, I asked if such an erection might not be indicted as a nuisance.

"A what?"

"A nuisance," I repeated, and explained what I meant.

"No, no," was the reply, "that may do very well for your tyrannical country, where a rich man's nose is more thought of than a poor man's mouth; but hogs be profitable produce here, and we be too free for such a law as that, I guess."

*　*　*　*　*

All the freedom enjoyed in America, beyond what is enjoyed in England, is enjoyed solely by the disorderly at the expense of the orderly; and were I a stout knight, either of the sword or of the pen, I would fearlessly throw down my gauntlet, and challenge the whole Republic to prove the contrary; but being, as I am, a feeble looker on, with a needle for my spear, and "I talk" for my device, I must be contented with the power of stating the fact, perfectly certain that I shall be contradicted by one loud shout from Maine to Georgia.

CHAPTER XI

Religion . . .

I had often heard it observed before I visited America, that one of the great blessings of its constitution was the absence of a national religion, the country being thus exonerated from all obligation of supporting the clergy; those only contributing to do so whose principles led them to it. My residence in the country has shewn me that a religious tyranny may be exerted very effectually without the aid of the government, in a way much more oppressive than the paying of tithe, and without obtaining any of the salutary decorum, which I presume no one will deny is the result of an established mode of worship.

As it was impossible to remain many weeks in the country without being struck with the strange anomalies produced by its religious system, my early notes contain many observations on the subject; but as nearly the same scenes recurred in every part of the country, I state them here, not as belonging to the west alone, but to the whole Union, the same cause producing the same effect every where.

The whole people appear to be divided into an almost endless variety of religious factions, and I was told, that to be well received in society, it was necessary to declare yourself as belonging to some one of these. Let your acknowledged belief be what it may, you are said to be *not a Christian*, unless you attach yourself to a particular congregation. Besides the broad and well-known distinctions of Episcopalian, Catholic, Presbyterian, Calvinist, Baptist, Quaker, Swedenborgian, Universalist,

Dunker, &c. &c. &c.; there are innumerable others springing out of these, each of which assumes a church government of its own; of this, the most intriguing and factious individual is invariably the head; and in order, as it should seem, to shew a reason for this separation, each congregation invests itself with some queer variety of external observance that has the melancholy effect of exposing *all* religious ceremonies to contempt.

It is impossible, in witnessing all these unseemly vagaries, not to recognise the advantages of an established church as a sort of head-quarters for quiet unpresuming Christians, who are contented to serve faithfully, without insisting upon having each a little separate banner, embroidered with a device of their own imagining.

The Catholics alone appear exempt from the fury of division and sub-division that has seized every other persuasion. Having the Pope for their common head, regulates, I presume, their movements, and prevents the outrageous display of individual whim which every other sect is permitted.

I had the pleasure of being introduced to the Catholic bishop of Cincinnati, and have never known in any country a priest of a character and bearing more truly apostolic. He was an American, but I should never have discovered it from his pronunciation or manner. He received his education partly in England, and partly in France. His manners were highly polished; his piety active and sincere, and infinitely more mild and tolerant than that of the factious Sectarians who form the great majority of the American priesthood.

I believe I am sufficiently tolerant; but this does not prevent my seeing that the object of all religious observances is better obtained, when the government of the church is confided to the wisdom and experience of the most venerated among the people, than when it is placed in the hands of every tinker and tailor who chooses to claim a share in it. Nor is this the only evil attending the want of a national religion, supported by the State. As there is no legal and fixed provision for the clergy, it is hardly surprising that their services are confined to those who can pay them. The vehement expressions of insane or hypocritical zeal, such as were exhibited during "the Revival," can but ill atone for the want of village worship, any more than the eternal talk of the admirable and unequalled government, can atone for the continual contempt of social order. Church and State hobble along, side by side, notwithstanding their boasted independence. Almost every man you meet will tell you, that he is occupied in labours most abundant for the good of his country; and almost every woman will tell you, that besides those things that are within (her house) she has coming upon her daily the care of all the churches. Yet spite of this universal attention to the government, its laws are half asleep; and spite of the old women and their Dorcas societies, atheism is awake and thriving.

In the smaller cities and towns prayer-meetings take the place of almost all other amusements; but as the thinly scattered population of most villages can give no parties, and pay no priests, they contrive to marry, christen, and bury without them. A stranger taking up his residence in any city in America must think the natives the most religious people upon earth; but if chance lead him among her western villages, he will rarely find either churches or chapels, prayer or preacher; except, indeed, at that most terrific saturnalia, "a camp-meeting." I was much struck with the answer of a poor woman, whom I saw ironing on a Sunday. "Do you make no difference in your occupations on a Sunday?" I said. "I beant a Christian, Ma'am; we have got no opportunity," was the reply. It occurred to me, that in a country where "all men are equal," the government would be guilty of no great crime, did it so far interfere as to give them all *an opportunity* of becoming Christians if they wished it. But should the federal government dare to propose building a church, and endowing it, in some village that has never heard "the bringing home of bell and burial," it is perfectly certain that not only the sovereign state where such an abomination was proposed, would rush into the Congress to resent the odious interference, but that all the other states would join the clamour, and such an intermeddling administration would run great risk of impeachment and degradation.

Where there is a church-government so constituted as to deserve human respect, I believe it will always be found to receive it, even from those who may not assent to the dogma of its creed; and where such respect exists, it produces a decorum in manners and language often found wanting where it does not. Sectarians will not venture to rhapsodise, nor infidels to scoff, in the common intercourse of society. Both are injurious to the cause of rational religion, and to check both must be advantageous.

*   *   *   *   *

It was not once, nor twice, nor thrice, but many many times, during my residence in America, that I was present when subjects which custom as well as principle had taught me to consider as fitter for the closet than the tea-table, were ... lightly discussed. I hardly know whether I was more startled at first hearing, in little dainty namby pamby tones, a profession of Atheism over a teacup, or at having my attention called from a Johnny cake, to a rhapsody on election and the second birth.

But, notwithstanding this revolting license, persecution exists to a degree unknown, I believe, in our well-ordered land since the days of Cromwell. I had the following anecdote from a gentleman perfectly well acquainted with the circumstances. A tailor sold a suit of clothes to a sailor a few moments before he sailed, which was on a Sunday morning. The corporation of New York prosecuted the tailor, and he was convicted, and sentenced to a fine greatly beyond his means to pay. Mr. F., a lawyer of New York, defended him with much eloquence, but in vain. His powerful speech, however, was not without effect, for it raised him such a host of Presbyterian enemies as sufficed to destroy his practice. Nor was this all: his nephew was at the time preparing for the bar, and soon after the above circumstance occurred his certificates were presented, and refused, with this declaration, "that no man of the name and family of F. should be admitted." I have met this young man in society; he is a person of very considerable talent, and being thus cruelly robbed of his profession, has become the editor of a newspaper.

CHAPTER XII

Peasantry, compared to that of England . . .
Early marriages . . . Charity . . .
Independence and equality . . .
Cottage prayer-meeting . . .

Mohawk, as our little village was called, gave us an excellent opportunity of comparing the peasants of the United States with those of England, and of judging the average degree of comfort enjoyed by each. I believe Ohio gives as fair a specimen as any part of the Union; if they have the roughness and inconveniences of a new state to contend with, they have higher wages and cheaper provisions; if I err in supposing it a mean state in point of comfort, it certainly is not in taking too low a standard.

Mechanics, if good workmen, are certain of employment, and good wages, rather higher than with us; the average wages of a labourer throughout the Union is ten dollars a month, with lodging, boarding, washing, and mending; if he lives at his own expense he has a dollar a day. It appears to me that the necessaries of life, that is to say, meat, bread, butter, tea, and coffee, (not to mention whiskey), are within the reach of every sober, industrious, and healthy man who chooses to have them; and yet I think that an English peasant, with the same qualifications, would, in coming to the United States, change for the worse. He would find wages somewhat higher, and provisions in Western America considerably lower; but this statement, true as it is, can lead to nothing but delusion if taken apart from other facts, fully as certain, and not less important, but which require more detail in describing, and which perhaps cannot be fully comprehended, except by an eye-witness. The American poor are accustomed to eat meat three times a day; I never enquired into the habits of any cottagers in Western America, where this was not the case. I found afterwards in Maryland, Pennsylvania, and other parts of the country, where the price of meat was higher, that it was used with more economy; yet still a much larger portion of the weekly income is thus expended than with us. Ardent spirits, though lamentable cheap, still cost something, and the use of them among the men, with more or less of discretion, according to the character, is universal. Tobacco also grows at their doors, and is not taxed; yet this too costs something, and the air of heaven is not in more general use among the men at America, than chewing tobacco. I am not now pointing out the evils of dram-drinking, but it is evident, that where this practice prevails universally, and often to the most frightful excess, the consequence must be, that the money spent to obtain the dram is less than the money lost by the time consumed in drinking it. Long, disabling, and expensive fits of sickness are incontestably more frequent in every part of America, than in England, and the sufferers have no aid to look to, but what they have saved, or what they may be enabled to sell. I have never seen misery exceed what I have witnessed in an American cottage where disease has entered.

But if the condition of the labourer be not superior to that of the English peasant, that of his wife and daughters is incomparably worse. It is they who are indeed the slaves of the soil. One has but to look at the wife of an American cottager, and ask her age, to be convinced that the life she leads is one of hardship, privation, and labour. It is rare to see a woman in this station who has reached the age of thirty, without losing every trace of youth and beauty. You continually see women with infants on their knee, that you feel sure are their grand-children, till some convincing proof of the contrary is displayed. Even the young girls, though often with lovely features, look pale, thin, and haggard. I do not remember to have seen in any single instance among the poor, a specimen of the plump, rosy, laughing physiognomy so common among our cottage girls. The horror of domestic service, which the reality of slavery, and the fable of equality, have generated, excludes the young women from that sure and most comfortable resource of decent English girls; and the consequence is, that with a most irreverent freedom of manner to the parents, the daughters are, to the full extent of the word, domestic slaves. This condition, which no periodical merry-making, no village *fete*, ever occurs to cheer, is only changed for the still sadder burdens of a teeming wife. They marry very young; in fact, in no rank of life do you meet with young women in that delightful period of existence between childhood and marriage, wherein, if only tolerably well spent, so much useful information is gained, and the character takes a sufficient degree of firmness to support with dignity the more important parts of wife and mother. The slender, childish thing, without vigour of mind or body, is made to stem a sea of troubles that dims her young eye and makes her cheek grow pale, even before nature has given it the last beautiful finish of the full-grown woman.

"We shall get along," is the answer in full, for all that can be said in way of advice to a boy and girl who take it into their heads to go before a magistrate and "get married." And they do get along, till sickness overtakes them, by means perhaps of borrowing a kettle from one and a tea-pot from another; but intemperance, idleness, or sickness will, in one week, plunge those who are even getting along well, into utter destitution; and where this happens, they are completely without resource.

The absence of poor-laws is, without doubt, a blessing to the country, but they have not that natural and reasonable dependence on the richer classes which, in countries differently constituted, may so well supply their place. I suppose there is less alms-giving in America than in any other Christian country on the face of the globe. It is not in the temper of the people either to give or to receive.

I extract the following pompous passage from a Washington paper of Feb. 1829, (a season of uncommon severity and distress,) which, I think, justifies my observation.

"Among the liberal evidences of sympathy for the suffering poor of this city, two have come to our knowledge which deserve to be especially noticed: the one a donation by the President of the United States to the committee of the ward in which he resides of fifty dollars; the other the donation by a few of the officers of the war department to the Howard and Dorcas Societies, of seventy-two dollars." When such mention is made of a gift of about nine pounds sterling from the sovereign magistrate

69

of the United States, and of thirteen pounds sterling as a contribution from one of the state departments, the inference is pretty obvious, that the sufferings of the destitute in America are not liberally relieved by individual charity.

I had not been three days at Mohawk-cottage before a pair of ragged children came to ask for medicine for a sick mother; and when it was given to them, the eldest produced a handful of cents, and desired to know what he was to pay. The superfluous milk of our cow was sought after eagerly, but every new comer always proposed to pay for it. When they found out that "the English old woman" did not sell any thing, I am persuaded they by no means liked her the better for it; but they seemed to think, that if she were a fool it was no reason they should be so too, and accordingly the borrowing, as they called it, became very constant, but always in a form that shewed their dignity and freedom. One woman sent to borrow a pound of cheese; another half a pound of coffee; and more than once an intimation accompanied the milk-jug, that the milk must be fresh, and unskimmed: on one occasion the messenger refused milk, and said, "Mother only wanted a little cream for her coffee."

I could never teach them to believe, during above a year that I lived at this house, that I would not sell the old clothes of the family; and so pertinacious were they in bargain-making, that often, when I had given them the articles which they wanted to purchase, they would say, "Well, I expect I shall have to do a turn of work for this; you may send for me when you want me." But as I never did ask for the turn of work, and as this formula was constantly repeated, I began to suspect that it was spoken solely to avoid uttering that most un-American phrase "I thank you."

There was one man whose progress in wealth I watched with much interest and pleasure. When I first became his neighbour, himself, his wife, and four children, were living in one room, with plenty of beef-steaks and onions for breakfast, dinner, and supper, but with very few other comforts. He was one of the finest men I ever saw, full of natural intelligence and activity of mind and body, but he could neither read or write. He drank but little whiskey, and but rarely chewed tobacco, and was therefore more free from that plague spot of spitting which rendered male colloquy so difficult to endure. He worked for us frequently, and often used to walk into the drawing-room and seat himself on the sofa, and tell me all his plans. He made an engagement with the proprietor of the wooded hill before mentioned, by which half the wood he could fell was to be his own. His unwearied industry made this a profitable bargain, and from the proceeds he purchased the materials for building a comfortable frame (or wooden) house; he did the work almost entirely himself. He then got a job for cutting rails, and, as he could cut twice as many in a day as any other man in the neighbourhood, he made a good thing of it. He then let half his pretty house, which was admirably constructed, with an ample portico, that kept it always cool. His next step was contracting for the building a wooden bridge, and when I left Mohawk he had fitted up his half of the building as an hotel and grocery store; and I have no doubt that every sun that sets sees him a richer man than when it rose. He hopes to make his son a lawyer, and I have little doubt that he will live to see him sit in congress; when this time arrives, the woodcutter's son will rank with any other member of congress, not of courtesy, but of right, and the idea that his origin is a disadvantage, will never occur to the imagination of the most exalted of his fellow-citizens.

This is the only feature in American society that I recognise as indicative of the equality they profess. Any man's son may become the equal of any other man's son, and the consciousness of this is certainly a spur to exertion; on the other hand, it is also a spur to that coarse familiarity, untempered by any shadow of respect, which is assumed by the grossest and the lowest in their intercourse with the highest and most refined. This is a positive evil, and, I think, more than balances its advantages.

And here again it may be observed, that the theory of equality may be very daintily discussed by English gentlemen in a London dining-room, when the servant, having placed a fresh bottle of cool wine on the table, respectfully shuts the door, and leaves them to their walnuts and their wisdom; but it will be found less palatable when it presents itself in the shape of a hard, greasy paw, and is claimed in accents that breathe less of freedom than on onions and whiskey. Strong, indeed, must be the love of equality in an English breast if it can survive a tour through the Union.

There was one house in the village which was remarkable

from its wretchedness. It had an air of *in*decent poverty about it, which long prevented my attempting an entrance; but at length, upon being told that I could get chicken and eggs there whenever I wanted them, I determined upon venturing. The door being opened to my knock, I very nearly abandoned my almost blunted purpose; I never beheld such a den of filth and misery: a woman, the very image of dirt and disease, held a squalid imp of a baby on her hip bone while she kneaded her dough with her right fist only. A great lanky girl, of twelve years old, was sitting on a barrel, gnawing a corn cob; when I made known my business, the woman answered, "No, not I; I got no chickens to sell, nor eggs neither; but my son will, plenty I expect. Here, Nick," (bawling at the bottom of a ladder), "here's an old woman what wants chickens." Half a moment brought Nick to the bottom of the ladder, and I found my merchant was one of a ragged crew, whom I had been used to observe in my daily walk, playing marbles in the dust, and swearing lustily; he looked about ten years old.

"Have you chicken to sell, my boy?"

"Yes, and eggs too, more nor what you'll buy."

Having enquired price, condition, and so on, I recollected that I had been used to give the same price at market, the feathers plucked, and the chicken prepared for the table, and I told him that he ought not to charge the same.

"Oh for that, I expect I can fix 'em as well as ever them was, what you got in market."

"You fix them?"

"Yes to be sure, why not?"

"I thought you were too fond of marbles."

He gave me a keen glance, and said, "You don't know I.— When will you be wanting the chickens?"

He brought them at the time directed, extremely well "fixed," and I often dealt with him afterwards. When I paid him, he always thrust his hand into his breeches pocket, which I presume, as being *the keep*, was fortified more strongly than the dilapidated outworks, and drew from thence rather more dollars, half-dollars, levies, and fips, than his dirty little hand could well hold. My curiosity was excited, and . . . I repeatedly conversed with him.

"You are very rich, Nick," I said to him one day, on his

making an ostentatious display of change, as he called it; he sneered with a most unchildish expression of countenance, and replied, "I guess 'twould be a bad job for I, if that was all I'd got to shew."

I asked him how he managed his business. He told me that he bought eggs by the hundred, and lean chicken by the score, from the waggons that passed their door on the way to market; that he fatted the latter in coops he had made himself, and could easily double their price, and that his eggs answered well too, when he sold them out by the dozen.

"And do you give the money to your mother?"

"I expect not," was the answer, with another sharp glance of his ugly blue eyes.

"What do you do with it, Nick?"

His look said plainly, what is that to you? but he only answered, quaintly enough, "I takes care of it."

How Nick got his first dollar is very doubtful; I was told that when he entered the village store, the person serving always called in another pair of eyes; but having obtained it, the spirit, activity, and industry, with which he caused it to increase and multiply, would have been delightful in one of Miss Edgeworth's dear little clean bright-looking boys, who would have carried all he got to his mother; but in Nick it was detestable. No human feeling seemed to warm his young heart, not even the love of self-indulgence, for he was not only ragged and dirty, but looked considerably more than half starved, and I doubt not his dinners and suppers half fed his fat chickens.

I by no means give this history of Nick, the chicken merchant, as an anecdote characteristic in all respects of America; the only part of the story which is so, is the independence of the little man, and is one instance out of a thousand, of the hard, dry, calculating character that is the result of it. Probably Nick will be very rich; perhaps he will be President. I once got so heartily scolded for saying, that I did not think all American citizens were equally eligible to that office, that I shall never again venture to doubt it.

Another of our cottage acquaintance was a market-gardener, from whom we frequently bought vegetables; from the wife of this man we one day received a very civil invitation to "please to come and pass the evening with them in prayer." The novelty of the circumstance, and its great dissimilarity to the way and manners of our own country, induced me to accept the invitation, and also to record the visit here.

We were received with great attention, and a place was assigned us on one of the benches that surrounded the little parlour. Several persons, looking like mechanics and their wives, were present; every one sat in profound silence, and with that quiet subdued air, that serious people assume on entering a church. At length, a long, black, grim-looking man entered; his dress, the cut of his hair, and his whole appearance, strongly recalled the idea of one of Cromwell's fanatics. He stepped solemnly into the middle of the room, and took a chair that stood there, but not to sit upon it; he turned the back towards him, on which he placed his hands, and stoutly uttering a sound between a hem and a cough, he deposited freely on either side of him a considerable portion of masticated tobacco. He then began to preach. His text was "Live in hope," and he continued to expound it for two hours in a drawling, nasal tone, with no other respite than what he allowed himself for expectoration. If I say that he repeated the words of his text a hundred times, I think I shall not exceed the truth, for that allows more than a minute for each repetition, and in fact the whole discourse was made up of it. The various tones in which he uttered it might have served as a lesson on emphasis; as a question—in accents of triumph—in accents of despair—of pity—of threatening—of authority—of doubt—of hope—of faith. Having exhausted every imaginable variety of tone, he abruptly said, "Let us pray," and twisting his chair round, knelt before it. Every one knelt before the seat they had occupied, and listened for another half hour to a rant of miserable, low, familiar jargon, that he presumed to *improvise* to his Maker as a prayer. In this, however, the cottage apostle only followed the example set by every preacher throughout the Union, excepting those of the Episcopalian and Catholic congregations; *they* only do not deem themselves privileged to address the Deity in strains of crude and unweighed opportunity. These ranters may sometimes be very much in earnest, but surely the least we can say of it is, that they
"Praise their God amiss."

I enquired afterwards of a friend, well acquainted with such matters, how the grim preacher of "Hope" got paid for his labours, and he told me that the trade was an excellent one, for that many a gude wife bestowed more than a tithe of what her gude man trusted to her keeping, in rewarding the zeal of these self-chosen apostles. These sable ministers walk from house to house, or if the distance be considerable, ride on a comfortable ambling nag. They are not only as empty as wind, but resemble it in other particulars; for they blow where they list, and no man knoweth whence they come, nor whither they go. When they see a house that promises comfortable lodging and entertainment, they enter there, and say to the good woman of the house, "Sister, shall I pray with you?: If the answer be favourable, and it is seldom otherwise, he instals himself and his horse till after breakfast the next morning. The best meat, drink, and lodging are his, while he stays, and he seldom departs without some little contribution in money for the support of the crucified and suffering church. Is it not strange that "the most intelligent people in the world" should prefer such a religion as this, to a form established by the wisdom and piety of the ablest and best among the erring sons of men, solemnly sanctioned by the nation's law, and rendered sacred by the use of their fathers?

It would be well for all reasoners on the social system to observe steadily, and with an eye obscured by no beam of prejudice, the result of the experiment that is making on the other side of the Atlantic. If I mistake not, they might learn there, better than by any abstract speculation, what are the points on which the magistrates of a great people should dictate to them, and on what points they should be left freely to their own guidance. I sincerely believe, that if a fire worshipper, or an Indian Brahmin, were to come to the United States, prepared to preach and pray in English, he would not be long without a "very respectable congregation."

The influence of a religion, sanctioned by the government, could in no country, in the nineteenth century, interfere with the speculations of a philosopher in his closet, but it might, and must, steady the wake and wavering opinions of the multitude. There is something really pitiable in the effect produced by the want of this rudder oar. I knew a family where one was a Methodist, one a Presbyterian, and a third a Baptist; and another, where one was a Quaker, one a declared Atheist, and another an Universalist. These are all females, and all moving in the best society that America affords; but one and all of them as incapable of reasoning on things past, present, and to come, as the infants they nourish, yet one and all of them perfectly fit to move steadily and usefully in a path marked out for them. But I shall be called an itinerant preacher myself if I pursue this theme.

*   *   *   *   *

CHAPTER XIII

Theatre . . . Delicacy . . .
Visit of the President . . .

The theatre at Cincinnati is small, and not very brilliant in decoration, but in the absence of every other amusement our young men frequently attended it, and in the bright clear nights of autumn and winter, the mile and a half of distance was not enough to prevent the less enterprising members of the family from sometimes accompanying them. The great inducement to this was the excellent acting of Mr. and Mrs. Alexander Drake, the managers. Nothing could be more distinct than their line of acting, but the great versatility of their powers enabled them often to appear together. Her cast was the highest walk of tragedy, and his the broadest comedy; but yet, as Goldsmith says of his sister heroines, I have known them change characters for a whole evening together, and have wept with him and laughed with her, as it was their will and pleasure to ordain.

*   *   *   *   *

It was painful to see these excellent performers playing to a miserable house, not a third full, and the audience probably not including half a dozen persons who would prefer their playing to that of the vilest strollers. In proof of this, I saw them, as managers, give place to paltry third-rate actors from London, who would immediately draw crowded houses, and be overwhelmed with applause.

Poor Drake died just before we left Ohio, and his wife, who, besides her merit as an actress, is a most estimable and amiable woman, is left with a large family. I have little, or rather no doubt, of her being able to obtain an excellent engagement in London, but her having property in several of the Western theatres will, I fear, detain her in a neighbourhood, where she is neither understood nor appreciated.

*   *   *   *   *

The theatre was really not a bad one, though the very poor receipts rendered it impossible to keep it in high order; but an annoyance infinitely greater than decorations indifferently clean, was the style and manner of the audience. Men came into the lower tier of boxes without their coats; and I have seen shirt sleeves tucked up to the shoulder; the spitting was incessant, and the mixed smell of onions and whiskey was enough to make one feel even the Drakes' acting dearly bought by the obligation of enduring its accompaniments.

The bearing and attitudes of the men are perfectly indescribable; the heels thrown higher than the head, the entire rear of the person presented to the audience, the whole length supported on the benches, are among the varieties that these exquisite posture-masters exhibit. The noises, too, were perpetual, and of the most unpleasant kind; the applause is expressed by cries and thumping with the feet, instead of clapping; and when a patriotic fit seized them, and "Yankee Doodle" was called for, every man seemed to think his reputation as a citizen depended on the noise he made.

Two very indifferent figurantes [dancers] ... made their appearance at Cincinnati while we were there; and had Mercury stepped down, and danced a *pas seul* upon earth, his godship could not have produced a more violent sensation. But wonder and admiration were by no means the only feelings excited; horror and dismay were produced in at least an equal degree. No one, I believe, doubted their being admirable dancers, but every one agreed that the morals of the Western world would never recover the shock. When I was asked if I had ever seen any thing so dreadful before, I was embarrassed how to answer; for the young women had been exceedingly careful, both in their dress and in their dancing, to meet the taste of the people; but had it been Virginie in her most transparent attire, or Taglioni in her most remarkable pirouette, they could not have been more reprobated. The ladies altogether forsook the theatre; the gentlemen muttered under their breath, and turned their heads aside when the subject was mentioned; the clergy denounced them from the pulpit; and if they were named at the meetings of the saints, it was to show how deep the horror such a theme could produce. I could not but ask myself if virtue were a plant, thriving under one form in one country, and flourishing under a different one in another? If these Western Americans are right, then how dreadfully wrong are we! It is really a very puzzling subject.

But this was not the only point on which I found my notions of right and wrong utterly confounded; hardly a day passed in which I did not discover that something or other that I had been taught to consider lawful as eating, was held in abhorrence by those around me; many words to which I had never heard an objectionable meaning attached, were totally interdicted, and the strangest paraphrastic sentences substituted. I confess it struck me, that notwithstanding a general stiffness of manner, which I think must exceed that of the Scribes and Pharisees, the Americans have imaginations that kindle with alarming facility. I could give many anecdotes to prove this, but will content myself with a few.

A young German gentleman of perfectly good manners, once came to me greatly chagrined at having offended one of the principal families in the neighbourhood, by having pronounced the word *corset* before the ladies of it. An old female friend had kindly overcome her own feelings so far as to mention to him the cause of the coolness he had remarked, and strongly advised his making an apology. He told me that he was perfectly well disposed to do so, but felt himself greatly at a loss how to word it.

An English lady who had long kept a fashionable boarding-school in one of the Atlantic cities, told me that one of her earliest cares with every new comer, was the endeavour to substitute real delicacy for this affected precision of manner; among many anecdotes, she told me one of a young lady about fourteen, who on entering the receiving room, where she only expected to see a lady who had enquired for her, and finding a young man with her, put her hands before her eyes, and ran out of the room again, screaming "A man! a man! a man!"

On another occasion, one of the young ladies in going up

stairs to the drawing-room, unfortunately met a boy of fourteen coming down, and her feelings were so violently agitated, that she stopped panting and sobbing, nor would pass on till the boy had swung himself up on the upper banisters, to leave the passage free.

At Cincinnati there is a garden where the people go to eat ices, and to look at roses. For the preservation of the flowers, there is placed at the end of one of the walks a signpost sort of daub, representing a Swiss peasant girl, holding in her hand a scroll, requesting that the roses might not be gathered. Unhappily for the artist, or for the proprietor, or for both, the petticoat of this figure was so short as to shew her ancles. The ladies saw, and shuddered; and it was formally intimated to the proprietor, that if he wished for the patronage of the ladies of Cincinnati, he must have the petticoat of this figure lengthened. The affrighted purveyor of ices sent off an express for the artist and his paint pot. He came, but unluckily not provided with any colour that would match the petticoat; the necessity, however, was too urgent for delay, and a flounce of blue was added to the petticoat of red, giving bright and shining evidence before all men of the immaculate delicacy of the Cincinnati ladies.

I confess I was sometimes tempted to suspect that this ultra refinement was not very deep seated. It often appeared to me like the consciousness of grossness, that wanted a veil; but the veil was never gracefully adjusted. Occasionally, indeed, the very same persons who appeared ready to faint at the idea of a statue, would utter some unaccountable sally that was quite startling, and which made me feel that the indelicacy of which we were accused had its limits. The following anecdote is hardly fit to tell, but it explains what I mean too well to be omitted.

A young married lady, of *high standing* and most fastidious delicacy, who had been brought up at one of the Atlantic seminaries of highest reputation, told me that her house, at the distance of half a mile from a populous city, was unfortunately opposite a mansion of worse than doubtful reputation. "It is abominable," she said, "to see the people that go there; they ought to be exposed. I and another lady, an intimate friend of mine, did make one of them look foolish enough last summer: she was passing the day with me, and, while we were sitting at the window, we saw a young man we both knew ride up there, we went into the garden and watched at the gate for him to come back, and when he did, we both stepped out, and I said to him, 'Are you not ashamed, Mr. William D., to ride by my house and back again in that manner?" I never saw a man look so foolish!"

In conversing with ladies on the customs and manners of Europe, I remarked a strong propensity to consider every thing as wrong to which they were not accustomed. I once mentioned to a young lady that I thought a pic-nic party would be very agreeable, and that I would propose it to some of our friends. She agreed that it would be delightful, but she added, "I fear you will not succeed; we are not used to such sort of things here, and I know it is considered very indelicate for ladies and gentlemen to sit down together on the grass."

I could multiply anecdotes of this nature; but I think these sufficient to give an accurate idea of the tone of manners in this particular, and I trust to justify the observations I have made.

*   *   *   *   *

And now the time arrived that our domestic circle was again to be broken up. Our eldest son was to be entered at Oxford, and it was necessary that his father should accompany him; and, after considerable indecision, it was at length determined that I and my daughters should remain another year, with our second son. It was early in February, and our travellers prepared themselves to encounter some sharp gales upon the mountains, though the great severity of the cold appeared to be past. We got buffalo robes and double shoes prepared for them, and they were on the eve of departure when we heard that General Jackson, the newly-elected President, was expected to arrive immediately at Cincinnati, from his residence in the West, and to proceed by steam-boat to Pittsburgh, on his way to Washington. This determined them not to fix the day of their departure till they heard of his arrival, and then, if possible, to start in the same boat with him; the decent dignity of a private conveyance not being deemed necessary for the President of the United States.

The day of his arrival was however quite uncertain, and we could only determine to have every thing very perfectly in readiness, let it come when it would. This resolution was hardly acted upon when the news reached us that the General had arrived at Louisville, and was expected at Cincinnati in a few hours. All was bustle and hurry at Mohawk-cottage; we quickly dispatched our packing business, and this being the first opportunity we had had of witnessing such a demonstration of popular feeling, we all determined to be present at the debarkation of the great man. We accordingly walked to Cincinnati, and secured a favourable station at the landing-place, both for the purpose of seeing the first magistrate and of observing his reception by the people. We had waited but a few moments when the heavy panting of the steam-engines and then a discharge of cannon told that we were just in time; another moment brought his vessel in sight.

Nothing could be better of its kind than his approach to the shore: the noble steam-boat which conveyed him was flanked on each side by one of nearly equal size and splendour; the roofs of all three were covered by a crowd of men; cannon saluted them from the shore as they passed by, to the distance of a quarter of a mile above the town; there they turned about, and came down the river with a rapid but stately motion, the three vessels so close together as to appear one mighty mass upon the water.

When they arrived opposite the principal landing they swept gracefully round, and the side vessels, separating themselves from the centre, fell a few feet back, permitting her to approach before them with her honoured freight. All this manœuvring was extremely well executed, and really beautiful.

The crowd on the shore awaited her arrival in perfect stillness. When she touched the bank the people on board gave a faint huzza, but it was answered by no note of welcome from the land: this cold silence was certainly not produced by any want of friendly feeling towards the new President, during the whole of the canvassing he had been decidedly the popular candidate at Cincinnati, and, for months past, we had been accustomed to the cry of "Jackson for ever" from an overwhelming majority; but enthusiasm is not either the virtue or the vice of America.

More than one private carriage was stationed at the water's edge to await the General's orders, but they were dismissed with the information that he would walk to the hotel. Upon receiving this intimation the silent crowd divided itself in a very orderly manner, leaving a space for him to walk through them. He did so, uncovered, though the distance was considerable, and the weather very cold; but he alone (with the exception of a few European gentlemen who were present) was without a hat. He wore his grey hair, carelessly, but not ungracefully arranged, and, spite of his harsh gaunt features, he looks like a gentleman and a soldier. He was in deep mourning, having very recently lost his wife; they were said to have been very happy together, and I was pained by hearing a voice near me exclaim, as he approached the spot where I stood, "There goes Jackson, where is his wife?" Another sharp voice, at a little distance, cried, "Adams for ever!" And these sounds were all I heard to break the silence.

"They manage these matters better" in the East, I have no doubt, but as yet I was still in the West, and still inclined to think, that however meritorious the American character may be, it is not amiable.

Mr. T. and his sons joined the group of citizens who waited upon him to the hotel, and were presented to the President in form; that is, they shook hands with him. Learning that he intended to remain a few hours there, or more properly, that it would be a few hours before the steam-boat would be ready to proceed, Mr. T. secured berths on board, and returned, to take a hasty dinner with us. At the hour appointed by the captain, Mr. T. and his son accompanied the General on board; and by subsequent letters I learnt that they had conversed a good deal with him, and were pleased by his conversation and manners, but deeply disgusted by the brutal familiarity to which they saw him exposed at every place on their progress at which they stopped; I am tempted to quote one passage, as sufficiently descriptive of the manner which so painfully grated against their European feelings.

"There was not a hulking boy from a keel-boat who was not introduced to the President, unless, indeed, as was the case with some, they introduced themselves: for instance, I was at his elbow when a greasy fellow accosted him thus:—

"General Jackson, I guess?'

"The General bowed assent.

"Why they told me you was dead.'

"No! Providence has hitherto preserved my life.'

" 'And is your wife alive too?'

"The General, apparently much hurt, signified the contrary, upon which the courtier concluded his harangue, by saying 'Aye, I thought it was the one or the t'other of ye.' "

CHAPTER XIV

American Spring . . . Public ball . . .
Separation of the sexes . . .

The American spring is by no means so agreeable as the American autumn; both move with faultering step, and slow; but this lingering pace, which is delicious in autumn, is most tormenting in the spring. In the one case you are about to part with a friend, who is becoming more gentle and agreeable at every step, and such steps can hardly be made too slowly; but in the other you are making your escape from a dreary cavern, where you have been shut up with black frost and biting blasts, and where your best consolation was being smoke-dried.

But, upon second thoughts, I believe it would be more correct, instead of complaining of the slow pace of the American spring, to declare that they have no spring at all. The beautiful autumn often lingers on till Christmas, after which winter can be trifled with no longer, and generally keeps stubborn hold through the months which we call spring, when he suddenly turns his back, and summer takes his place.

The inconceivable uncertainty of the climate is, however, such, that I will not venture to state about what time this change takes place, for it is certain, that let me name what time I would, it would be easy for any weather journaliser to prove me wrong, by quoting that the thermometer was at 100 at a period which my statement included in the winter; or 50 long after I made the summer commence.

The climate of England is called uncertain, but it can never, I think, be so described by any who have experienced that

84

of the United States. A gentleman, on whose accuracy I could depend, told me he had repeatedly known the thermometer vary above 40 degrees in the space of twelve hours. This most unpleasant caprice of the temperature is, I conceive, one cause of the unhealthiness of the climate.

At length, however, after shivering and shaking till we were tired of it, and having been half ruined in fire-wood (which, by the way, is nearly as dear as at Paris, and dearer in many parts of the Union), the summer burst upon us full blown, and the ice-house, the piazza, and the jalousies were again in full requisition.

*   *   *   *   *

In noting the various brilliant events which diversified our residence in the western metropolis, I have omitted to mention the Birth-day Ball, as it is called, a festivity which, I believe, has place on the 22nd of February, in every town and city throughout the Union. It is the anniversary of the birth of General Washington, and well deserves to be marked by the Americans as a day of jubilee.

I was really astonished at the *coup d'oeil* on entering, for I saw a large room filled with extremely well-dressed company, among whom were many very beautiful girls. The gentlemen also were exceedingly smart, but I had not yet been long enough in Western America not to feel startled at recognising in almost every full-dressed *beau* that passed me, the master or shopman that I had been used to see behind the counter, or lolling at the door of every shop in the city. The fairest and finest *belles* smiled and smirked on them with as much zeal and satisfaction as I ever saw bestowed on an eldest son, and I therefore could feel no doubt of their being considered as of the highest rank. Yet it must not be supposed that there is no distinction of classes: at this same ball I was looking among the many very beautiful girls I saw there for one more beautiful still, with whose lovely face I had been particularly struck. . . . I could not find her, and asked a gentleman why the beautiful Miss C. was not there.

"You do not yet understand our aristocracy," he replied, "the family of Miss C. are mechanics."

"But the young lady has been educated at the same school as these, whom I see here, and I know her brother has a shop in

85

the town, quite as large, and apparently as prosperous, as those belonging to any of these young men. What is the difference?"

"He is a mechanic; he assists in making the articles he sells; the others call themselves merchants."

The dancing was not quite like, yet not very unlike, what we see at an assize or race-ball in a country town. They call their dances cotillions instead of quadrilles, and the figures are called from the orchestra in English, which has a very ludicrous effect on European ears.

The arrangements for the supper were very singular, but eminently characteristic of the country. The gentlemen had a splendid entertainment spread for them in another large room of the hotel, while the poor ladies had each a plate put into their hands, as they pensively promenaded the ballroom during their absence; and shortly afterwards servants appeared, bearing trays of sweetmeats, cakes, and creams. The fair creatures then sat down on a row of chairs placed round the walls, and each making a table of her knees, began eating her sweet, but sad and sulky repast. The effect was extremely comic; their gala dresses and the decorated room forming a contrast the most unaccountable with their uncomfortable and forlorn condition.

This arrangement was owing neither to economy nor want of a room large enough to accommodate the whole party, but purely because the gentlemen liked it better. This was the answer given me, when my curiosity tempted me to ask why the ladies and gentlemen did not sup together; and this was the answer repeated to me afterwards by a variety of people to whom I put the same question.

I am led to mention this feature of American manners very frequently, not only because it constantly recurs, but because I consider it as being in a great degree the cause of that universal deficiency in good manners and graceful demeanour, both in men and women, which is so remarkable.

*　　*　　*　　*　　*

In America, with the exception of dancing, which is almost wholly confined to the unmarried of both sexes, all the enjoyments of the men are found in the absence of the women. They dine, they play cards, they have musical meetings, they have suppers, all in large parties, but all without women. Were it not that such is the custom, it is impossible but that they would have ingenuity enough to find some expedient for sparing the wives and daughters of the opulent the sordid offices of household drudgery which they almost all perform in their families. Even in the slave states, though they may not clear-starch and iron, mix puddings and cakes one half of the day, and watch them baking the other half, still the very highest occupy themselves in their household concerns, in a manner that precludes the possibility of their becoming elegant and enlightened companions. In Baltimore, Philadelphia, and New York, I met with some exceptions to this; but speaking of the country generally, it is unquestionably true.

*　　*　　*　　*　　*

CHAPTER XV

Camp-Meeting . . .

It was in the course of this summer that I found the opportunity I had long wished for, of attending a camp-meeting, and I gladly accepted the invitation of an English lady and gentleman to accompany them in their carriage to the spot where it is held; this was in a wild district on the confines of Indiana.

The prospect of passing a night in the back woods of Indiana was by no means agreeable, but I screwed my courage to the proper pitch, and set forth determined to see with my own eyes, and hear with my own ears, what a camp-meeting really was. I had heard it said that being at a camp-meeting was like standing at the gate of heaven, and seeing it opening before you; I had heard said that being at a camp-meeting was like finding yourself within the gates of hell; in either case there must be something to gratify curiosity, and compensate one for the fatigue of a long rumbling ride and a sleepless night.

We reached the ground about an hour before midnight, and the approach to it was highly picturesque. The spot chosen was the verge of an unbroken forest, where a space of about twenty acres appeared to have been partially cleared for the purpose. Tents of different sizes were pitched very near together in a circle round the cleared space; behind them were ranged an exterior circle of carriages of every description, and at the back of each were fastened the horses which had drawn them thither. Through this triple circle of defence we distinguished numerous fires burning brightly within it; and still more numerous lights flickering from the trees that were left in the enclosure. The moon was in meridian splendour above our heads.

We left the carriage to the care of a servant, who was to prepare a bed in it for Mrs. B. and me, and entered the inner circle. The first glance reminded me of Vauxhall, from the effect of the lights among the trees, and the moving crowd below them; but the second shewed a scene totally unlike any thing I had ever witnessed. Four high frames, constructed in the form of altars, were placed at the four corners of the enclosure; on these were supported layers of earth and sod, on which burned immense fires of blazing pine-wood. On one side a rude platform was erected to accommodate the preachers, fifteen of whom attended this meeting, and with very short intervals for necessary refreshment and private devotion, preached in rotation, day and night, from Tuesday to Saturday.

When we arrived, the preachers were silent; but we heard issuing from nearly every tent mingled sounds of praying, preaching, singing, and lamentation. The curtains in front of each tent were dropped, and the faint light that gleamed through the white drapery, backed as it was by the dark forest, had a beautiful and mysterious effect, that set the imagination at work; and had the sounds which vibrated around us been less discordant, harsh, and unnatural, I should have enjoyed it; but listening at the corner of a tent, which poured forth more than its proportion of clamour, in a few moments chased every feeling derived from imagination, and furnished realities that could neither be mistaken or forgotten.

Great numbers of persons were walking about the ground, who appeared like ourselves to be present only as spectators; some of these very unceremoniously contrived to raise the drapery of this tent, at one corner, so as to afford us a perfect view of the interior.

The floor was covered with straw, which round the sides was heaped in masses, that might serve as seats, but which at that moment were used to support the heads and the arms of the close-packed circle of men and women who kneeled on the floor.

Out of about thirty persons thus placed, perhaps half a dozen were men. One of these, a handsome looking youth of eighteen or twenty, kneeled just below the opening through which I looked. His arm was encircling the neck of a young girl

89

who knelt beside him. with her hair hanging dishevelled upon her shoulders, and her features working with the most violent agitation; soon after they both fell forward on the straw, as if unable to endure in any other attitude the burning eloquence of a tall grim figure in black, who, standing erect in the centre, was uttering with incredible vehemence an oration that seemed to hover between praying and preaching; his arms hung stiff and immoveable by his side, and he looked like an ill-constructed machine, set in action by a movement so violent, as to threaten its own destruction, so jerkingly, painfully, yet rapidly, did his words tumble out; the kneeling circle ceasing not to call in every variety of tone, on the name of Jesus; accompanied with sobs, groans, and a sort of low howling inexpressibly painful to listen to. But my attention was speedily withdrawn from the preacher, and the circle round him, by a figure which knelt alone at some distance; it was a living image of Scott's Macbriar, as young, as wild, and as terrible. His thin arms tossed above his head, had forced themselves so far out of the sleeves, that they were bare to the elbow; his large eyes glared frightfully, and he continued to scream without an instant's intermission the word "Glory!" with a violence that seemed to swell every vein to bursting. It was too dreadful to look upon long, and we turned away shuddering.

We made the circuit of the tents, pausing where attention was particularly excited by sounds more vehement than ordinary. We contrived to look into many; all were strewed with straw, and the distorted figures that we saw kneeling, sitting, and lying amongst it, joined to the woeful and convulsive cries, gave to each, the air of a cell in Bedlam.

One tent was occupied exclusively by Negroes. They were all full-dressed, and looked exactly as if they were performing a scene on the stage. One woman wore a dress of pink gauze trimmed with silver lace; another was dressed in pale yellow silk; one or two had splendid turbans; and all wore a profusion of ornaments. The men were in snow white pantaloons, with gay coloured linen jackets. One of these, a youth of coal-black comeliness, was preaching with the most violent gesticulations, frequently springing high from the ground, and clapping his hands over his head. Could our missionary societies have heard the trash he uttered, by way of an address to the Deity, they might perhaps have doubted whether his conversion had much enlightened his mind.

At midnight a horn sounded through the camp, which, we were told, was to call the people from private to public worship; and we presently saw them flocking from all sides to the front of the preachers' stand. Mrs. B. and I contrived to place ourselves with our backs supported against the lower part of this structure, and we where thus enabled to witness the scene which followed without personal danger. There were about two thousand persons assembled.

One of the preachers began in a low nasal tone, and, like all other Methodist preachers, assured us of the enormous depravity of man as he comes from the hands of his Maker, and of his perfect sanctification after he had wrestled sufficiently with the Lord to get hold of him, *et caetera*. The admiration of the crowd was evinced by almost constant cries of "Amen! Amen!" "Jesus! Jesus!" "Glory! Glory!" and the like. But this comparative tranquility did not last long: the preacher told them that "this night was the time fixed upon for anxious sinners to wrestle with the Lord;" that he and his brethren "were at hand to help them," and that such as needed their help were to come forward into "the pen." The phrase forcibly recalled Milton's lines—

> *"Blind mouths! that scarce themselves know how to hold*
> *A sheep-hook, or have learned aught else, the least*
> *That to the faithful herdsman's art belongs!*
> *— But when they list their lean and flashy songs,*
> *Grate on their scrannel pipes of wretched straw;—*
> *The hungry sheep look up, and are not fed!*
> *But swoln with wind, and the rank mist they draw,*
> *Rot inwardly—and foul contagion spread."*

"The pen" was the space immediately below the preachers' stand; we were therefore placed on the edge of it, and were enabled to see and hear all that took place in the very centre of this extraordinary exhibition.

The crowd fell back at the mention of the *pen*, and for some minutes there was a vacant space before us. The preachers came down from their stand and placed themselves in the midst of it, beginning to sing a hymn, calling upon the penitents to come forth. As they sung they kept turning themselves round to every part of the crowd, and, by degrees, the voices of the whole multitude joined in chorus. This was the only moment at which I perceived any thing like the solemn and beautiful effect, which I had heard ascribed to this woodland worship. It is certain that the combined voices of such a multitude, heard at dead of night, from the depths of their eternal forests, the many fair young faces turned upward, and looking paler and lovelier as they met the moon-beams, the dark figures of the officials in the middle of the circle, the lurid glare thrown by the altar-fires on the woods beyond, did altogether produce a fine and solemn effect, that I shall not easily forget; but ere I had well enjoyed it, the scene changed, and sublimity gave place to horror and disgust.

The exhortation nearly resembled that which I had heard at "the Revival," but the result was very different; for, instead of the few hysterical women who had distinguished themselves on that occasion, above a hundred persons, nearly all females, came forward, uttering howlings and groans, so terrible that I shall never cease to shudder when I recall them. They appeared to drag each other forward, and on the word being given, "let us pray," they all fell on their knees; but this posture was soon changed for others that permitted greater scope for the convulsive movements of their limbs; and they were soon all lying on the ground in an indescribable confusion of heads and legs. They threw about their limbs with such incessant and violent motion, that I was every instant expecting some serious accident to occur.

But how am I to describe the sound that proceeded from this strange mass of human beings? I know no words which can convey an idea of it. Hysterical sobbings, convulsive groans, shrieks and screams the most appalling, burst forth on all sides. I felt sick with horror. As if their hoarse and over-strained voices failed to make noise enough, they soon began to clap their hands violently. . . .

        *   *   *   *   *

Many of these wretched creatures were beautiful young females. The preachers moved about among them, at once exciting and soothing their agonies. I heard the muttered "Sister!

dear sister!" I saw the insidious lips approach the cheeks of the unhappy girls; I heard the murmured confessions of the poor victims, and I watched their tormentors, breathing into their ears consolations that tinged the pale cheek with red. Had I been a man, I am sure I should have been guilty of some rash act of interference; nor do I believe that such a scene could have been acted in the presence of Englishmen without instant punishment being inflicted; not to mention the salutary discipline of the tread-mill, which, beyond all question, would, in England, have been applied to check so turbulent and so vicious a scene.

After the first wild burst that followed their prostration, the moanings, in many instances, became loudly articulate; and I then experienced a strange vibration between tragic and comic feeling.

A very pretty girl, who was kneeling in the attitude of Canova's Magdalene immediately before us, amongst an immense quantity of jargon, broke out thus: "Woe! woe to the backsliders! hear it, hear it Jesus! when I was fifteen my mother died, and I backslided, oh Jesus, I backslided! take me home to my mother, Jesus! take me home to her, for I am weary! Oh John Mitchel! John Mitchel!" and after sobbing piteously behind her raised hands, she lifted her sweet face again, which was as pale as death, and said, "Shall I sit on the sunny bank of salvation with my mother? my own dear mother? oh Jesus, take me home, take me home!"

Who could refuse a tear to this earnest wish for death in one so young and so lovely? But I saw her, ere I left the ground, with her hand fast locked, and her head supported by a man who looked very much as Don Juan might, when sent back to earth as too bad for the regions below.

One woman near us continued to "call on the Lord," as it is termed, in the loudest possible tone, and without a moment's interval, for the two hours that we kept our dreadful station. She became frightfully hoarse, and her face so red as to make me expect she would burst a blood-vessel. Among the rest of her rant, she said, "I will hold fast to Jesus, I never will let him go; if they take me to hell, I will still hold him fast, fast, fast!"

The stunning noise was sometimes varied by the preachers beginning to sing; but the convulsive movements of the poor maniacs only became more violent. At length the atrocious wickedness of this horrible scene increased to a degree of grossness, that drove us from our station; we returned to the carriage at about three o'clock in the morning, and passed the remainder of the night in listening to the ever increasing tumult at the pen. To sleep was impossible. At day-break the horn again sounded, to send them to private devotion; and it about an hour afterwards I saw the whole camp as joyously and eagerly employed in preparing and devouring their most substantial breakfasts as if the night had been passed in dancing; and I marked many a fair but pale face, that I recognised as a demoniac of the night, simpering beside a swain, to whom she carefully administered hot coffee and eggs. The preaching saint and the howling sinner seemed alike to relish this mode of recruiting their strength.

After enjoying abundance of strong tea, which proved a delightful restorative after a night so strangely spent, I wandered alone into the forest, and I never remember to have found perfect quiet more delightful.

We soon after left the ground; but before our departure we learnt that a very *satisfactory* collection had been made by the preachers, for Bibles, Tracts, and *all other religious purposes*.

* * * * *

CHAPTER XVI

(omitted)

CHAPTER XVII

Departure from Cincinnati . . .
Society on board the Steam-boat . . .
Arrival at Wheeling . . .

We quitted Cincinnati the beginning of March, 1830, and I believe there was not one of our party who did not experience a sensation of pleasure in leaving it. We had seen again and again all the queer varieties of it's little world; had amused ourselves with it's consequence, it's taste, and it's ton [tone], till they had ceased to be amusing. Not a hill was left unclimbed, nor a forest path unexplored; and, with the exception of two or three individuals, who bore heads and hearts peculiar to no clime, but which are found scattered through the world, as if to keep us every where in good humour with it, we left nought to regret at Cincinnati. The only regret was, that we had ever entered it; for we had wasted health, time, and money there.

We got on board the steam-boat which was to convey us to Wheeling at three o'clock. She was a noble boat, by far the finest we had seen. The cabins were above, and the deck passengers, as they are called, were accommodated below. In front of the ladies' cabin was an ample balcony, sheltered by an awning; chairs and sofas were placed here, and even at that early season, nearly all the female passengers passed the whole day there. The name of this splendid vessel was the Lady Franklin. By the way, I was often amused by the evident fondness which the Americans shew for titles. The wives of their eminent men constantly receive that of "Lady." We heard of Lady Washington, Lady Jackson, and many other "ladies." The eternal recurrence of their militia titles is particularly ludicrous, met with, as they are, among the tavern-keepers, market-gardeners, &c. But I think the most remarkable instance which we noticed of this sort of aristocratical longing occurred at Cincinnati. Mr. T——in speaking of a gentleman of the neighbourhood, called him Mr. M——. "General M——, sir," observed his companion. "I beg his pardon," rejoined Mr. T——, "but I was not aware of his being in the army." "No, sir, not in the army," was the reply, "but he was surveyor-general of the district."

The weather was delightful; all trace of winter had disappeared, and we again found ourselves moving rapidly up the stream, and enjoying all the beauty of the Ohio.

Of the male part of the passengers we saw nothing, excepting at the short silent periods allotted for breakfast, dinner, and supper, at which we were permitted to enter their cabin, and place ourselves at their table.

In the Lady Franklin we had decidedly the best of it, for we had our beautiful balcony to sit in. In all respects, indeed, our accommodations were very superior to what we had found in the boat which brought us from New Orleans to Memphis, where we were stowed away in a miserable little chamber close aft, under the cabin, and given to understand by the steward, that it was our duty there to remain "till such time as the bell should ring for meals."

The separation of the sexes, so often mentioned, is no where more remarkable than on board the steam-boats. Among the passengers on this occasion we had a gentleman and his wife, who really appeared to suffer from the arrangement. She was an invalid, and he was extremely attentive to her, as far, at least, as the regulations permitted. When the steward opened the door of communication between the cabins, to permit our approaching the table, her husband was always stationed close to it, to hand her to her place; and when he accompanied her again to the door, he always lingered for a moment or two on the forbidden threshold, nor left his station, till the last female had passed through. Once or twice he ventured, when all but his wife were on the balcony, to sit down beside her for a moment in our cabin, but the instant either of us entered, he started like a guilty thing and vanished.

While mentioning the peculiar arrangements which are thought necessary to the delicacy of the American ladies, or to the comfort of the American gentlemen, I am tempted to allude to a story which I saw in the papers respecting the visits which it was stated Captain Basil Hall persisted in making to his wife and child on board a Mississippi steam-boat, after being informed that doing so was contrary to law. Now I happen to know that neither himself or Mrs. Hall ever entered the ladies' cabin during the whole voyage, as they occupied a state-room which Captain Hall had secured for his party. The veracity of newspaper statements is, perhaps, nowhere quite unimpeachable, but if I am not greatly mistaken, there are more direct falsehoods circulated by the American newspapers than by all the others in the world, and the one great and never-failing source of these voluminous works of imagination is England and the English. How differently would such a voyage be managed on the other side the Alantic, were such a mode of travelling possible there. Such long calm river excursions would be perfectly delightful, and parties would be perpetually formed to enjoy them. Even were all the parties strangers to each other, the knowledge that they were to eat, drink, and steam away together for a week or fortnight, would induce something like a social feeling in any other country.

It is true that the men became sufficiently acquainted to game together, and we were told that the opportunity was considered as so favourable, that no boat left New Orleans without having as cabin passengers one or two gentlemen from that city whose profession it was to drill the fifty-two elements of a pack of cards to profitable duty. This doubtless is an additional reason for the strict exclusion of the ladies from their society. The constant drinking of spirits is another, for though they do not scruple to chew tobacco and to spit incessantly in the presence of women, they generally prefer drinking and gaming in their absence.

I often used to amuse myself with fancying the different scene which such a vessel would display in Europe. The noble length of the gentlemen's cabin would be put into requisition for a dance, while that of the ladies, with their delicious balcony, would be employed for refreshments, instead of sitting down in two long silent melancholy rows, to swallow as much coffee and beef-steak as could be achieved in ten minutes. The song and music would be heard borne along by the midnight breeze; but on the Ohio, when light failed to shew us the bluffs, and the trees, with their images inverted in the stream, we crept into our little cots, listening to the ceaseless churning of the engine, in hope it would prove a lullaby till morning.

We were three days in reaching Wheeling, where we arrived at last, at two o'clock in the morning, an uncomfortable hour to disembark with a good deal of luggage, as the steamboat was obliged to go on immediately; but we were instantly supplied with a dray, and in a few moments found ourselves comfortably seated before a good fire, at an hotel near the landing-place; our rooms, with fires in them, were immediately ready for us, and refreshments brought, with all that sedulous attention which in this country distinguishes a slave state. In making this observation I am very far from intending to advocate the system of slavery; I conceive it to be essentially wrong; but so far as my observation has extended, I think its influence is far less injurious to the manners and morals of the people than the fallacious ideas of equality, which are so fondly cherished by the working classes of the white population in America. That these ideas are fallacious is obvious, for in point of fact the man possessed of dollars does command the services of the man possessed of no dollars; but these services are given grudgingly, and of necessity, with no appearance of cheerful good-will on the one side, or of kindly interest on the other. I never failed to mark the difference on entering a slave state. I was immediately comfortable, and at my ease, and felt that the intercourse between me and those who served me, was profitable to both parties and painful to neither.

It was not till I had leisure for more minute observation that I felt aware of the influence of slavery upon the owners of slaves; when I did, I confess I could not but think that the citizens of the United States had contrived, by their political alchymy, to extract all that was most noxious both in democracy and in slavery, and had poured the strange mixture through every vein of the moral organization of their country.

Wheeling is in the state of Virginia, and appears to be a flourishing town. It is the point at which most travellers from the West leave the Ohio, to take the stages which travel the mountain road to the Atlantic cities.

It has many manufactories, among others, one for blowing

and cutting glass, which we visited. We were told by the work-men that the articles finished there were equal to any in the world; but my eyes refused their assent. The cutting was very good, though by no means equal to what we see in daily use in London; but the chief inferiority is in the material, which is never altogether free from colour. I had observed this also in the glass of the Pittsburgh manufactory, the labour bestowed on it always appearing greater than the glass deserved. They told us also, that they were rapidly improving in the art, and I have no doubt that this was true.

Wheeling has little of beauty to distinguish it, except the ever lovely Ohio, to which we here bade adieu, and a fine bold hill, which rises immediately behind the town. This hill, as well as every other in the neighbourhood, is bored for coal. Their mines are all horizontal. The coal burns well, but with a very black and dirty cinder.

We found the coach, by which we meant to proceed to Little Washington, full, and learnt that we must wait two days before it would again leave the town. Posting was never heard of in the country, and the mail travelled all night, which I did not approve of; we therefore found ourselves compelled to pass two days at the Wheeling hotel.

*   *   *   *   *

100

CHAPTER XVIII

Departure for the Mountains in the Stage . . .
Scenery of the Alleghany . . .
Haggerstown . . .

The weather was bleak and disagreeable during the two days we were obliged to remain at Wheeling. . . . I set off on my journey towards the mountains with more pleasure than is generally felt in quitting a pillow before day-light, for a cold corner in a rumbling stage-coach.

This was the first time we had got into an American stage, though we had traversed above two thousand miles of the country, and we had all the satisfaction in it, which could be derived from the conviction that we were travelling in a foreign land. This vehicle had no step, and we climbed into it by a ladder; when that was removed I remembered, with some dismay, that the females at least were much in the predicament of sailors, who "in danger have no door to creep out:" but when a misfortune is absolutely inevitable, we are apt to bear it remarkably well; who would utter that constant petition of ladies on rough roads, "let me get out," when compliance would oblige the pleader to make a step of five feet before she could touch the ground?

The coach had three rows of seats, each calculated to hold three persons, and as we were only six, we had, in the phrase of Milton, to "inhabit lax" this exalted abode, and, accordingly, we were for some miles tossed about like a few potatoes in a wheelbarrow. Our knees, elbows, and heads required too much care for their protection to allow us leisure to look out of the windows; but at length the road became smoother, and we became

101

more skilful in the art of balancing ourselves, so as to meet the concussion with less danger of dislocation.

We then found that we were travelling through a very beautiful country, essentially different in its features from what we had been accustomed to round Cincinnati: it is true we had left *"la belle rivire"* behind us, but the many limpid and rapid little streams that danced through the landscape to join it, more than atoned for its loss.

The country already wore an air of more careful husbandry, and the very circumstance of a wide and costly road (though not a very smooth one), which in theory might be supposed to injure picturesque effect, was beautiful to us, who, since we had entered the muddy mouth of the Mississippi, had never seen any thing except a steam-boat and the *levée* professing to have so noble an object as public accommodation. Through the whole of the vast region we had passed, excepting at New Orleans itself, every trace of the art of man appeared to be confined to the individual effort of "getting along," which, in western phrase, means contriving to live with as small a portion of the incumbrances of civilized society as possible.

This road was made at the expense of the government as far as Cumberland, a town situated among the Alleghany mountains, and, from the nature of the ground, must have been a work of great cost. I regretted not having counted the number of bridges between Wheeling and Little Washington, a distance of thirty-four miles; over one stream only there are twenty-five, all passed by the road. They frequently occurred within a hundred yards of each other, so serpentine is its course; they are built of stone, and sometimes very neatly finished.

Little Washington is in Pennsylvania, across a corner of which the road runs. This is a free state, but we were still waited upon by Negroes, hired from the neighbouring state of Virginia. We arrived at night, and set off again at four in the morning; all, therefore, that we saw of Little Washington was its hotel, which was clean and comfortable. The first part of the next day's journey was through a country much less interesting: its character was unvaried for nearly thirty miles, consisting of an uninterrupted succession of forest-covered hills. As soon as we had wearily dragged to the top of one of these, we began to rumble down the other side as rapidly as our four horses could trot; and no sooner arrived at the bottom than we began to crawl up again; the trees constantly so thick and so high as to preclude the possibility of seeing fifty yards in any direction.

The latter part of the day, however, amply repaid us. At four o'clock we began to ascent the Alleghany mountains: the first ridge on the western side is called Laurel Hill, and takes its name from the profuse quantity of evergreens with which it is covered; not any among them, however, being the shrub to which we give the name of laurel.

The whole of this mountain region, through ninety miles of which the road passes, is a garden. The almost incredible variety of plants, and the lavish profusion of their growth, produce an effect perfectly enchanting. I really can hardly conceive a higher enjoyment than a botanical tour among the Alleghany mountains, to anyone who had science enough to profit by it.

*   *   *   *   *

The first night we passed among the mountains recalled us painfully from the enjoyment of nature to all the petty miseries of personal discomfort. Arrived at our inn, a forlorn parlour, filled with the blended fumes of tobacco and whiskey, received us; and chilled, as we began to feel our selves with the mountain air, we preferred going to our cold bed-rooms rather that sup in such an atmosphere. We found linen on the beds which they assured us had only been used a *few nights;* every kind of refreshment we asked for we were answered, "We do not happen to have that article."

We were still in Pennsylvania, and no longer waited upon by slaves; it was, therefore, with great difficulty that we procured a fire in our bed-rooms from the surly-looking *young lady* who condescended to officiate as chamber-maid, and with much more, that we extorted clean linen for our beds; that done, we patiently crept into them supperless, while she made her exit muttering about the difficulty of "fixing English folks."

The next morning cheered our spirits again; we now enjoyed a new kind of alpine witchery; the clouds were floating around, and below us, and the distant peaks were indistinctly visible as through a white gauze veil, which was gradually lifted up, till the sun arose, and again let in upon us the full glory of these interminable heights.

We were told before we began the ascent, that we should find snow four inches deep on the road; but as yet we had seen none, and indeed it was with difficulty we persuaded ourselves that we were not travelling in the midst of summer. As we proceeded, however, we found the northern declivities still covered with it, and at length, towards the summit, the road itself had the promised four inches. The extreme mildness of the air, and the brilliant hue of the evergreens, contrasted strangely with this appearance of winter; it was difficult to understand how the snow could help melting in such an atmosphere.

*   *   *   *   *

We dined, on the second day, at a beautiful spot, which we were told was the highest point on the road, being 2,846 feet above the level of the sea. We were regaled luxuriously on wild turkey and mountain venison; which latter is infinitely superior to any furnished by the forests of the Mississippi, or the Ohio. The vegetables also were extremely fine, and we were told by a pretty girl, who superintended the slaves that waited on us, (for we were again in Virginia), that the vegetables of the Alleghany were reckoned the finest in America. She told us also, that wild strawberries were profusely abundant, and very fine; that their cows found for themselves, during the summer, plenty of flowery food, which produced a copious supply of milk; that their spring gave them the purest water, of icy coldness in the warmest seasons; and that the climate was the most delicious in the world, for through the thermometer sometimes stood at ninety, their cool breeze never failed them. What a spot to turn hermit in for a summer! My eloquent mountaineer gave me some specimens of ground plants, far unlike any thing I had ever seen. One particularly, which she called the ground pine, is peculiar, as she told me, to the Alleghany, and in some places runs over whole acres of ground; it is extremely beautiful. The rooms were very prettily decorated with this elegant plant, hung round it in festoons.

*   *   *   *   *

Our second night in the mountains was past at a solitary house of rather forlorn appearance; but we fared much better than the night before, for they gave us clean sheets, a good fire, and no scolding. We again started at four o'clock in the morning, and eagerly watched for the first gleam of light that should show the same lovely spectacle we had seen the day before; nor were we disappointed, though the show was somewhat different. The vapours caught the morning ray, as it first darted over the mountain top, and passing it to the scene below, we seemed enveloped in a rainbow.

*   *   *   *   *

After descending the last ridge we reached Haggerstown, a small neat place, between a town and a village; and here by the piety of the Presbyterian coach-masters, we were doomed to pass an entire day, and two nights, "as the accommodation line must not run on the sabbath."

I must, however, mention that this day of enforced rest was *not* Sunday. Saturday evening we had taken in at Cumberland a portly passenger, whom we soon discovered to be one of the proprietors of the coach. He asked us, with great politeness, if we should wish to travel on the sabbath, or to delay our journey. We answered that we would rather proceed; "The coach, then, shall go on to-morrow," replied the liberal coach-master, with the greatest courtesy; and accordingly we travelled all Sunday, and arrived at Haggerstown on Sunday night. At the door of the inn our civil proprietor left us; but when we enquired of the waiter at what hour we were to start on the morrow, he told us that we should be obliged to pass the whole of Monday there, as the coach which was to convey us forward would not arrive from the east, till Tuesday morning.

Thus we discovered that the waiving the sabbath-keeping by the proprietor, was for his own convenience, and not for ours, and that we were to be tied by the leg for four-and-twenty hours notwithstanding. This was quite a Yankee trick.

Luckily for us, the inn at Haggerstown was one of the most comfortable I ever entered. It was there that we became fully aware that we had left Western America behind us. Instead of being scolded, as we literally were at Cincinnati, for asking for a private sitting-room, we here had two, without asking at all. A waiter, quite *comme il faut*, summoned us to breakfast, dinner, and tea, which we found prepared with abundance, and even elegance. The master of the house met us at the door of the

105

eating-room, and, after asking if we wished for any thing not on the table, retired. The charges were in no respect higher than at Cincinnati.

*   *   *   *   *

On leaving Haggerstown we found, to our mortification, that we were not to be the sole occupants of the bulky accommodation, two ladies and two gentlemen appearing at the door ready to share it with us. We again started, at four o'clock, by the light of a bright moon, and rumbled and nodded through roads considerable worse than those over the mountains.

As the light began to dawn we discovered our ladies to be an old woman and her pretty daughter.

Soon after day-light we found that our pace became much slower than usual, and that from time to time our driver addressed to his companion on the box many and vehement exclamations. The gentlemen put their heads out, to ask what was the matter, but could get no intelligence, till the mail over-took us, when both vehicles stopped, and an animated colloquy of imprecations took place between the coachmen. At length we learnt that one of our wheels was broken in such a manner as to render it impossible for us to proceed. Upon this the old lady immediately became a principal actor in the scene. She sprung to the window, and addressing the set of gentlemen who completely filled the mail, exclaimed "Gentlemen! can't you make room for two? Only me and my daughter?" The *naïve* simplicity of this request set both the coaches into an uproar of laughter. . . . Our laugh, however, never daunted the old woman, or caused her for a moment to cease the reiteration of her request, "only for two of us, gentlemen! can't you find room for two?"

Our situation was really very embarrassing, but not to laugh was impossible. After it was ascertained that our own vehicle could not convey us, and that the mail had not even room for two, we decided upon walking to the next village, a distance, fortunately, of only two miles, and awaiting there the repair of the wheel. We immediately set off, at the brisk pace that six o'clock and a frosty morning in March were likely to inspire, leaving our old lady and her pretty daughter considerably in the rear; our hearts having been rather hardened by the exclusive nature of her prayer for aid.

When we had again started upon our new wheel, the driver, to recover the time he had lost, drove rapidly over a very rough road, in consequence of which, our self-seeking old lady fell into a perfect agony of terror, and her cries of "we shall be over! oh, Lord! we shall be over! we must be over! we shall be over!" lasted to the end of the stage, which with laughing, walking, and shaking, was a most fatiguing one.

CHAPTER XIX

Baltimore . . . Catholic Cathedral . . .
St. Mary's College . . .

As we advanced towards Baltimore the look of cultivation increased, the fences wore an air of greater neatness, the houses began to look like the abodes of competence and comfort, and we were consoled for the loss of the beautiful mountains by knowing that we were approaching the Atlantic.

*   *   *   *   *

Baltimore, is, I think, one of the handsomest cities to approach in the Union. The noble column erected to the memory of Washington, and Catholic Cathedral, with its beautiful dome, being built on a commanding eminence, are seen at a great distance. As you draw nearer, many other domes and towers become visible, and as you enter Baltimore-street, you feel that you are arrived in a handsome and populous city.

We took up our quarters at an excellent hotel, where the coach stopped, and the next day were fortunate enough to find accommodation in the house of a lady, well known to many of my European friends. With her and her amiable daughter, we spent a fortnight very agreeably, and felt quite aware that if we had not arrived in London or Paris, we had, at least, left far behind the "half-horse, half-alligator" tribes of the West, as the Kentuckians call themselves.

Baltimore is in many respects a beautiful city; it has several handsome buildings, and even the private dwelling-houses have a look of magnificence, from the abundance of white marble with which many of them are adorned. The ample flights of steps, and the lofty door frames, are in most of the best houses formed of this beautiful material.

This has been called the city of monuments, from its having the stately column erected to the memory of General Washington, and which bears a colossal statue of him at the top; and another pillar of less dimensions, recording some victory; I forget which. Both these are of brilliant white marble. There are also several pretty marble fountains in different parts of the city which greatly add to its beauty. These are not, it is true, quite so splendid as that of the Innocents, or many others at Paris, but they are fountains of clear water, and they are built of white marble. There is one which is sheltered from the sun by a roof supported by light columns; it looks like a temple dedicated to the genius of the spring. The water flows into a marble cistern, to which you descend by a flight of steps of delicate whiteness, and return by another. These steps are never without groups of negro girls, some carrying the water on their heads, with that graceful steadiness of step, which requires no aid from the hand; some tripping gaily with their yet unfilled pitchers; many of them singing in the soft rich voice, peculiar to their race; and all dressed with that strict attention to taste and smartness, which seems the distinguishing characteristic of the Baltimore females of all ranks.

The Catholic Cathedral is considered by all Americans as a magnificent church, but it can hardly be so classed by any one who has seen the churches of Europe; its interior, however, has an air of neatness that amounts to elegance. The form is a Greek cross, having a dome in the centre; but the proportions are ill-preserved; the dome is too low, and the arches which support it are flattened, and too wide for their height. On each side of the high altar are chapels to the Saviour and the Virgin. The altars in these, as well as the high altar, are of native marble of different colours, and some of the specimens are very beautiful. The decorations of the altar are elegant and costly. The prelate is a cardinal, and bears, moreover, the title of "Archbishop of Baltimore."

*   *   *   *   *

We attended mass in this church the Sunday after our

109

arrival, and I was perfectly astonished at the beauty and splendid appearance of the ladies who filled it. Excepting on a very brilliant Sunday at the Tuilleries, I never saw so shewy a display of morning costume, and I think I never saw any where so many beautiful women at one glance. They all appeared to be in full dress, and were really all beautiful.

*   *   *   *   *

There are a vast number of churches and chapels in the city, in proportion to its extent, and several that are large and well-built; the Unitarian church is the handsomest I have ever seen dedicated to that mode of worship. But the prettiest among them is a little *bijou* of a thing belonging to the Catholic college. The institution is dedicated to St. Mary, but this little chapel looks, though in the midst of a city, as if it should have been sacred to St. John of the wilderness. There is a sequestered little garden behind it, hardly large enough to plant cabbages in, which yet contains a Mount Calvary, bearing a lofty cross. The time path which leads up to this sacred spot, is not much wider than a sheep-track, and its cedars are but shrubs, but all is in proportion; and notwithstanding its fairy dimensions, there is something of holiness, and quiet beauty about it, that excites the imagination strangely. The little chapel itself has the same touching and impressive character. A solitary lamp, whose glare is tempered by delicately painted glass, hangs before the altar. The light of day enters dimly, yet richly, through crimson curtains, and the silence with which the well-lined doors opened from time to time, admitting a youth of the establishment, who, with noiseless tread, approached the altar, and kneeling, offered a whispered prayer, and retired, had something in it more calculated, perhaps, to generate holy thoughts, than even the swelling anthem heard beneath the resounding dome of St. Peter's.

Baltimore has a handsome museum, superintended by one of the Peale family, well known for their devotion to natural science, and to works of art. It is not their fault if the specimens which they are enabled to display in the latter department are very inferior to their splendid exhibitions in the former.

The theatre was closed when we were in Baltimore, but we were told that it was very far from being a popular or fashionable amusement. We were, indeed, told this every where

110

throughout the country, and the information was generally accompanied by the observation, that the opposition of the clergy was the cause of it. But I suspect that this is not the principal cause, especially among the men, who, if they were so implicit in their obedience to the clergy, would certainly be more constant in their attendance at the churches; nor would they, moreover, deem the theatre more righteous because an English actor, or a French dancer, performed there; yet on such occasions the theatres overflow. The cause, I think, is in the character of the people. I never saw a population so totally divested of gaiety; there is no trace of this feeling from one end of the Union to the other. They have no fêtes, no fairs, no merry-makings, no music in the streets, no Punch, no puppet-shows. If they see a comedy or a farce, they may laugh at it; but they can do very well without it; and the consciousness of the number of cents that must be paid to enter a theatre, I am very sure turns more steps from its door than any religious feeling. A distinguished publisher of Philadelphia told me that no comic publication had ever yet been found to answer in America.

*   *   *   *   *

CHAPTER XX

Voyage to Washington . . .
Capitol . . . City of Washington . . .
Congress . . . Indians . . .
Funeral of a Member of Congress . . .

By far the shortest route to Washington, both as to distance and time, is by land; but I much wished to see the celebrated Chesapeak bay, and it was therefore decided that we should take our passage in the steam-boat. It is indeed a beautiful little voyage, and well worth the time it costs; but as to the beauty of the bay, it must, I think, be felt only by sailors. It is, I doubt not, a fine shelter for ships, from the storms of the Atlantic, but its very vastness prevents its striking the eye as beautiful: it is, in fact, only a fine sea view. But the entrance from it into the Potomac river is very noble, and is one of the points at which one feels conscious of the gigantic proportions of the country, without having recourse to a graduated pencil-case.

The passage up this river to Washington is interesting, from many objects that it passed, but beyond all else, by the view it affords of Mount Vernon, the seat of General Washington. It is there that this truly great man passed the last years of his virtuous life, and it is there that he lies buried: it was easy to distinguish, as we passed, the cypress that waves over his grave.

The latter part of the voyage shews some fine river scenery; but I did not discover this till some months afterwards, for we now arrived late at night.

Our first object the next morning was to get a sight of the capitol, and our impatience sent us forth before breakfast. The mists of morning still hung around this magnificent building when first it broke upon our view, and I am not sure that the

112

effect produced was not the greater for this circumstance. At all events, we were struck with admiration and surprise. None of us, I believe, expected to see so imposing a structure on that side the Atlantic. I am ill at describing buildings, but the beauty and majesty of the American capitol might defy an abler pen than mine to do it justice. It stands so finely too, high, and alone.

The magnificent western facade is approached from the city by terraces and steps of bolder proportions than I ever before saw. The elegant eastern front, to which many persons give the preference, is on level with a newly-planted but exceedingly handsome inclosure, which, in a few years, will offer the shade of all the most splendid trees which flourish in the Union, to cool the brows and refresh the spirits of the members. The view from the capitol commands the city and many miles around, and it is itself n object of imposing beauty to the whole country adjoining.

We were again fortunate enough to find a very agreeable family to board with; and soon after breakfast left our comfortless hotel near the water, for very pleasant apartments in F. street.

I was delighted with the whole aspect of Washington; light, cheerful, and airy, it reminded me of our fashionable watering-places. It has been laughed at by foreigners, and even by natives, because the original plan of the city was upon an enormous scale, and but a very small part of it has been as yet executed. But I confess I see nothing in the least degree ridiculous about it; the original design, which was as beautiful as it was extensive, has been in no way departed from, and all that has been done has been done well. From the base of the hill on which the capitol stands extends a street of most magnificent width, planted on each side with trees, and ornamented by many splendid shops. This street, which is called Pennsylvania Avenue, is above a mile in length, and at the end of it is the handsome mansion of the President; conveniently near to his residence are the various public offices, all handsome, simple, and commodious; ample areas are left round each, where grass and shrubs refresh the eye. In another of the principal streets is the general post-office, and not far from it a very noble town-hall. Towards the quarter of the President's house are several handsome dwellings, which are chiefly occupied by the foreign ministers. The houses in the other parts of the city are scattered, but without ever losing sight of the regularity of the original plan; and to a person who has been travelling much through the country, and marked the immense quantity of new manufactories, new canals, new rail-roads, new towns, and new cities, which are springing, as it were, from the earth in every part of it, the appearance of the metropolis rising gradually into life and splendour, is a spectacle of high historic interest.

Commerce had already produced large and handsome cities in America before she had attained to an individual political existence, and Washington may be scorned as a metropolis, where such cities as Philadelphia and New York exist; but I considered it as the growing metropolis of the growing population of the Union, and it already possesses features noble enough to sustain its dignity as such.

The residence of the foreign legations and their families gives a tone to the society of this city which distinguishes it greatly from all others. It is also, for a great part of the year, the residence of the senators and representatives, who must be presumed to be the *élite* of the entire body of citizens, both in respect to talent and education. This cannot fail to make Washington a more agreeable abode than any other city in the Union.

The total absence of all sights, sounds, or smells of commerce, adds greatly to the charm. Instead of drays you see handsome carriages; and instead of the busy bustling hustle of men, shuffling on to a sale of "dry goods" or "prime broad stuffs," you see very well-dressed personages lounging leisurely up and down Pennsylvania Avenue.

Mr. Pishey Thompson, the English bookseller, with his pretty collection of all sorts of pretty literature, fresh from London, and Mr. Somebody, the jeweller, with his brilliant shop full of trinkets, are the principal points of attraction and business. What a contrast to all other American cities! The members, who pass several months every year in this lounging easy way, with no labour but a little talking, and with the *douceur* of eight dollars a day to pay them for it, must feel the change sadly when their term of public service is over.

There is another circumstance which renders the evening parties at Washington extremely unlike those of other places in the Union; this is the great majority of gentlemen. The expense, the trouble, or the necessity of a ruling eye at home, one or all of these reasons, prevents the members' ladies from accompanying them to Washington; at least, I heard of very few who had their wives with them. The female society is chiefly to be found among the families of the foreign ministers, those of the officers of state, and of the few members, the wealthiest and most aristocratic of the land, who bring their families with them. Some few independent persons reside in or near the city, but this is a class so thinly scattered that they can hardly be accounted a part of the population.

But, strange to say, even here a theatre cannot be supported for more than a few weeks at a time. I was told that gambling is the favourite recreation of the gentlemen, and that it is carried to a very considerable extent; but here, as elsewhere within the country, it is kept extremely well out of sight. I do not think I was present with a pack of cards a dozen times during more than three years that I remained in the country. Billiards are much played, though in most places the amusement is illegal. It often appeared to me that the old women of a state made the laws, and the young men broke them.

Notwithstanding the diminutive size of the city, we found much to see, and to amuse us.

The patent office is a curious record of the fertility of the mind of man when left to its own resources; but it gives ample proof also that it is not under such circumstances it is most usefully employed. This patent office contains models of all the mechanical inventions that have been produced in the Union, and the number is enormous. I asked the man who shewed these, what proportion of them had been brought into use, he said about one in a thousand; he told me also, that they chiefly proceeded from mechanics and agriculturists settled in remote parts of the country, who had began by endeavouring to hit upon some contrivance to enable them to *get along* without sending some thousand and odd miles for the thing they wanted. If the contrivance succeeded, they generally became so fond of this offspring of their ingenuity, that they brought it to Washington for a patent.

At the secretary of state's office we were shewn autographs of all the potentates with whom the Union were in alliance; which, I believe, pretty well includes all. To the parchments bearing these royal signs manual were appended, of course, the official seals of each, enclosed in gold or silver boxes of handsome workmanship: I was amused by the manner in which one of their own, just prepared for the court of Russia, was displayed to us, and the superiority of their decorations pointed out. They were superior, and in much better taste than the rest; and I only wish that the feeling that induced this display would spread to every corner of the Union, and mix itself with every act and with every sentiment. Let America give a fair portion of her attention to the arts and the graces that embellish life, and I will make her another visit, and write another book as unlike this as possible.

*　　*　　*　　*　　*

The bureau for Indian affairs contains a room of great interest: the walls are entirely covered with original portraits of all the chiefs who, from time to time, have come to negotiate with their great father, as they call the President. These portraits are by Mr. King, and, it cannot be doubted, are excellent likenesses, as are all the portraits I have ever seen from the hands of that gentleman. The countenances are full of expression, but the expression in most of them is extremely similar; or rather, I should say that they have but two sorts of expressions; the one is that of very noble and warlike daring, the other of a gentle and naïve simplicity, that has no mixture of folly in it, but which is inexpressibly engaging, and the more touching, perhaps, because at the moment we were looking at them, those very hearts which lent the eyes such meek and friendly softness, were wrung by a base, cruel, and most oppressive act of their *great father*.

We were at Washington at the time that the measure for chasing the last of several tribes of Indians from their forest homes, was canvassed in congress, and finally decided upon by the *fiat* of the President. If the American character may be judged by their conduct in this matter, they are most lamentably deficient in every feeling of honour and integrity. It is among themselves, and from themselves, that I have heard the statements which represent them as treacherous and false almost beyond belief in their intercourse with the unhappy Indians. Had I, during my residence in the United States, observed any

116

single feature in their national character that could justify their eternal boast of liberality and the love of freedom, I might have respected them, however much my taste might have been offended by what was peculiar in their manners and customs. But it is impossible for any mind of common honesty not to be revolted by the contradictions in their principles and practice. They inveigh against the governments of Europe, because, as they say, they favour the powerful and oppress the weak. You may hear this declaimed upon in Congress, roared out in taverns, discussed in every drawing-room, satirized upon the stage, nay, even anathematized from the pulpit: listen to it, and then look at them at home; you will see them with one hand hoisting the cap of liberty, and with the other flogging their slaves. You will see them one hour lecturing their mob on the indefeasible rights of man, and the next driving from their homes the children of the soil, whom they have bound themselves to protect by the most solemn treaties.

*   *   *   *   *

There were many objects of much interest shewn us at this Indian bureau; but, from the peculiar circumstances of this most unhappy and ill-used people, it was a very painful interest.

The dresses worn by the chiefs when their portraits were taken, are many of them splendid, from the embroidery of beads and other ornaments; and the room contains many specimens of their ingenuity, and even of their taste. There is a glass case in the room, wherein are arranged specimens of worked muslin, and other needle-work, some very excellent hand-writing, and many other little productions of male and female Indians, all proving clearly that they are perfectly capable of civilization. Indeed, the circumstance which renders their expulsion from their own, their native lands, so peculiarly lamentable, is, that they were yielding rapidly to the force of example; their lives were no longer those of wandering hunters, but they were becoming agriculturists, and the tyrannical arm of brutal power has not now driven them, as formerly, only from their hunting grounds, their favourite springs, and the sacred bones of their fathers, but it has chased them from the dwellings their advancing knowledge had taught them to make comfortable; from the newly-ploughed fields of their pride; and from the crops their

117

sweat had watered. And for what? To add some thousand acres of territory to the half-peopled wilderness which borders them.*

+   +   +   +   +

The Potomac, on arriving at Washington, makes a beautiful sweep, which forms a sort of bay, round which the city is built. Just where it makes the turn, a wooden bridge is thrown across, connecting the shores of Maryland and Virginia. This bridge is a mile and a quarter in length, and is ugly enough. The navy-yard, and arsenal, are just above it, on the Maryland side, and make a handsome appearance on the edge of the river, following the sweep above mentioned. Near the arsenal (much too near) is the penitentiary, which, as it was just finished, and not inhabited, we examined in every part. It is built for the purpose of solitary confinement for life. A gallows is a much less nerve-shaking spectacle than one of these awful cells, and assuredly, when imprisonment therein for life is substituted for death, it is no mercy to the criminal; but if it be a greater terror to the citizen, it may answer the purpose better. I do not conceive, that out of a hundred human beings who had been thus confined for a year, one would be found at the end of it who would continue to linger on there, *certain it was for ever*, if the alternative of being hanged were offered to them. . . .

Still following the sweep of the river, at the distance of two miles from Washington, is George Town, formerly a place of considerable commercial importance, and likely, I think, to become so again, when the Ohio and Chesapeak canal, which there mouths into the Potomac shall be in full action. It is a very pretty town, commanding a lovely view, of which the noble Potomac and the almost nobler capitol, are the great features. The country rises into a beautiful line of hills behind Washington, which form a sort of undulating terrace on to George Town; this terrace is almost entirely occupied by a succession of gentlemen's seats. At George Town the Potomac suddenly contracts itself, and begins to assume that rapid, rocky, and irregular character which marks it afterwards, and renders its course, till

*The reference here is to the forced removal of the Cherokees from Georgia.

118

it meets the Shenandoah at Harper's Ferry, a series of the most wild and romantic views that are to be found in America.

Attending the debates in Congress was, of course, one of our great objects; and, as an English woman, I was perhaps the more eager to avail myself of the privilege allowed. It was repeatedly observed to me that, at least in this instance, I must acknowledge the superior gallantry of the Americans, and that they herein give a decided proof of surpassing the English in a wish to honour the ladies, as they have a gallery in the House of Representatives erected expressly for them, while in England they are rigorously excluded from every part of the House of Commons.

But the inference I draw from this is precisely the reverse of that suggested. It is well known that the reason why the House of Commons was closed against ladies was, that their presence was found too attractive, and that so many members were tempted to neglect the business before the House, that they might enjoy the pleasure of conversing with the fair critics in the galleries, that it became a matter of national importance to banish them—and they were banished. It will be long ere the American legislature will find it necessary to pass the same law for the same reason.

*   *   *   *   *

The privilege of attending these debates would be more valuable could the speakers be better heard from the gallery; but, with the most earnest attention, I could only follow one or two of the orators, whose voices were peculiarly loud and clear. This made it really a labour to listen; but the extreme beauty of the chamber was of itself a reason for going again and again. It was, however, really mortifying to see this splendid hall, fitted up in so stately and sumptuous a manner, filled with men, sitting in the most unseemly attitudes, a large majority with their hats on, and nearly all, spitting to an excess that decency forbids me to describe.

Among the crowd, who must be included in this description, a few were distinguished by not wearing their hats, and by sitting on their chairs like other human beings, without throwing their legs above their heads. Whenever I enquired the name

119

of one of these exceptions, I was told that it was Mr. This, or Mr. That, *of Virginia.*

One day we were fortunate enough to get placed on the sofas between the pillars, on the floor of the House; the galleries being shut up, for the purpose of making some alterations, which it was hoped might improve the hearing in that part of the House occupied by the members, and which is universally complained of, as being very defective. But in our places on the sofas we found we heard very much better than up stairs, and well enough to be extremely amused by the rude eloquence of a thorough horse and alligator orator from Kentucky, who entreated the house repeatedly to "go the whole hog."

If I mistake not, every debate I listened to in the American Congress was upon one and the same subject, namely, the entire independence of each individual state, with regard to the federal government. The jealousy on this point appeared to me to be the very strangest political feeling that ever got possession of the mind of man. I do not pretend to judge the merits of this question. I speak solely of the very singular effect of seeing man after man start eagerly to his feet, to declare that the greatest injury, the basest injustice, the most obnoxious tyranny that could be practised against the state of which he was a member, would be a vote of a few million dollars for the purpose of making their roads or canals; or for drainage; or, in short, for the purpose of improvement whatsoever.

*   *   *   *   *

The Senate-chamber is, like the Hall of Congress, a semicircle, but of very much smaller dimensions. It is most elegantly fitted up, and what is better still, the senators, generally speaking, look like gentlemen. They do not wear their hats, and the activity of youth being happily past, they do not toss their heels above their heads. I would I could add they do not spit; but, alas! "I have an oath in heaven," and may not write an untruth.

A very handsome room, opening on a noble stone balcony is fitted up as a library for the members. The collection, as far as a very cursory view could enable me to judge, was very like that of a private English gentleman, but with less Latin, Greek, and Italian. This room also is elegantly furnished; rich Brussels carpet; library tables, with portfolios of engravings; abundance of sofas, and so on. The view from it is glorious, and it looks like the abode of luxury and taste.

I can by no means attempt to describe all the apartments of this immense building, but the magnificent rotunda in the centre must not be left unnoticed. It is, indeed, a noble hall, a hundred feet in diameter, and of an imposing loftiness, lighted by an ample dome.

Almost any pictures (excepting the cartoons) would look paltry in this room, from the immense height of the walls; but the subjects of the four pictures which are placed there, are of such high historic interest that they should certainly have a place somewhere, as national records. One represents the signing of the declaration of independence; another the resignation of the presidency the great Washington; another the celebrated victory of General Gates at Saratoga; and the fourth. . . . I do not well remember, but I think it is some other martial scene, commemorating a victory; I rather think that of York Town.

*　　*　　*　　*　　*

The theatre was not open while we were in Washington but we afterwards took advantage of our vicinity to the city, to visit it. The house is very small, and most astonishingly dirty and void of decoration, considering that it is the only place of public amusement that the city affords. I have before mentioned the want of decorum at the Cincinnati theatre, but certainly that of the capital at least rivalled it in the freedom of action and attitude; a freedom which seems to disdain the restraints of civilized manners. One man in the pit was seized with a violent fit of vomiting, which appeared not in the least to annoy or surprise his neighbours; and the happy coincidence of a physician being at that moment personated on the stage, was hailed by many of the audience as an excellent joke, of which the actor took advantage, and elicited shouts of applause by saying, "I expect my services are wanted elsewhere."

The spitting was incessant; and not one in ten of the male part of the illustrious legislative audience sat according to the usual custom of human beings; the legs were thrown sometimes over the front of the box, sometimes over the side of it; here and there a senator stretched his entire length along a bench, and in many instances the front rail was preferred as a seat.

121

I remarked one young man, whose handsome person, and most elaborate toilet, led me to conclude he was a first-rate personage, and so I doubt not he was; nevertheless, I saw him take from the pocket of his silk waistcoat a lump of tobacco, and daintily deposit it within his cheek.

* * * * *

A member of Congress died while we were at Washington, and I was surprised by the ceremony and dignity of his funeral. It seems that whenever a senator or member of Congress dies during the session, he is buried at the expense of the government, (this ceremony not coming under the head of internal improvement), and the arrangements for the funeral are not interfered with by his friends, but become matters of State. I transcribed the order of the procession as being rather grand and stately.

Chaplains of both Houses.
Physicians who attended the deceased.
Committee of arrangement.
THE BODY,
(Pall borne by six members.)
The Relations of the deceased, with the Senators and Representatives of the State to which he belonged, as
Mourners.
Sergeant at arms of the House of Representatives.
The House of Representatives,
Their Speaker and Clerk preceding.
The Senate of the United States,
The Vice-president and Secretary preceding.
THE PRESIDENT

The procession was of considerable extent, but not on foot, and the majority of the carriages were hired for the occasion. The body was interred in an open "grave yard" near the city. I did not see the monument erected on this occasion, but I presume it was in the same style as several others I had remarked in the same burying-ground, inscribed to the memory of members who had died at Washington. These were square blocks of masonry without any pretension to splendour.

* * * * *

122

CHAPTER XXI

(omitted)

CHAPTER XXII

Small Landed Proprietors . . . Slavery . . .

I now, for the first time since I crossed the mountains, found myself sufficiently at leisure to look deliberately round, and mark the different aspects of men and things in a region which, though bearing the same name, and calling itself the same land, was, in many respects, as different from the one I had left, as Amsterdam from St. Petersburgh. There every man was straining, and struggling, and striving for himself (heaven knows!). Here every white man was waited upon, more or less, by a slave. There, the newly-cleared lands, rich with the vegetable manure accumulated for ages, demanded the slightest labour to return the richest produce; where the plough entered, crops the most abundant followed; but where it came not, no spot of native verdure, no native fruits, no native flowers cheered the eye; all was close, dark, stiffling forest. Here the soil had long ago yielded its first fruits; much that had been cleared and cultivated for tobacco (the most exhausting of crops) by the English, required careful and laborious husbandry to produce any return; and much was left as sheep-walks. It was in these spots that the natural bounty of the soil and climate was displayed by the innumerable wild fruits and flowers which made every dingle and bushy dell seem a garden.

On entering the cottages I found also a great difference in the manner of living. Here, indeed, there were few cottages without a slave, but there were fewer still that had their beefsteak and onions for breakfast, dinner, and supper. The herrings of the bountiful Potomac supply their place. These are excellent "relish," as they call it, when salted, and, if I mistake not, are sold at a dollar and a half per thousand. Whiskey, however, flows every where at the same fatally cheap rate of twenty cents (about one shilling) the gallon, and its hideous effects are visible on the countenance of every man you meet.

The class of people the most completely unlike any existing in England, are those who, farming their own freehold estates, and often possessing several slaves, yet live with as few of the refinements, and I think I may say, with as few of the comforts of life, as the very poorest English peasant. When in Maryland, I went into the houses of several of these small proprietors, and remained long enough, and looked and listened sufficiently, to obtain a tolerably correct idea of their manner of living.

One of these families consisted of a young man, his wife, two children, a female slave, and two young lads, slaves also. The farm belonged to the wife, and, I was told, consisted of about three hundred acres of indifferent land, but all cleared. The house was built of wood, and looked as if the three slaves might have overturned it, had they pushed hard against the gable end. It contained one room, of about twelve feet square, and another adjoining it, hardly larger than a closet; this second chamber was the lodging-room of the white part of the family. Above these rooms was a loft, without windows, where I was told the "staying company" who visited them, were lodged. Near this mansion was a "shanty," a black hole, without any window, which served as kitchen and all other offices, and also as the lodging of the blacks.

We were invited to take tea with this family, and readily consented to do so. The furniture of the room was one heavy huge table, and about six wooden chairs. When we arrived the lady was in rather a dusky dishabille, but she vehemently urged us to be seated, and then retired into the closet-chamber above mentioned, whence she continued to address to us from behind the door, all kinds of "genteel country visiting talk," and at length emerged upon us in a smart new dress.

Her female slave set out the great table, and placed upon it cups of the very coarsest blue ware, a little brown sugar in one, and a tiny drop of milk in another, no butter, though the lady assured us she had a *"deary"* and two cows. Instead of butter, she "hoped we would fix a little relish with our crackers," in ancient English, eat salt meat and dry biscuits. Such was the fare, and for guests that certainly were intended to be honoured. I could not help recalling the delicious repasts which I remembered to have enjoyed at little dairy farms in England, not *possessed*, but rented, and at high rents too; where the clean, fresh-coloured, bustling mistress herself skimmed the delicious cream, herself spread the yellow butter on the delightful brown loaf, and placed her curds, and her junket, and all the delicate treasures of her dairy before us, and then, with hospitable pride, placed herself at her board, and added the more delicate "relish" of good tea and good cream. I remembered all this, and did not think the difference atoned for, by the dignity of having my cup handed to me by a slave. The lady I now visited, however, greatly surpassed my quondam friends in the refinement of her conversation. She ambled through the whole time the visit lasted, in a sort of elegantly mincing familiar style of gossip, which, I think, she was imitating from some novel, for I was told she was a great novel reader, and left all household occupations to be performed by her slaves. To say she addressed us in a tone of equality, will give no adequate idea of her manner; I am persuaded that no misgiving on the subject ever entered her head. She told us that their estate was her divi-*dend* of her father's property. She had married a first cousin, who was as fine a gentleman as she was a lady, and as idle, preferring hunting (as they call shooting) to any other occupation. The consequence was, that but a very small portion of the divi-*dend* was cultivated, and their poverty was extreme. The slaves, particularly the lads, were considerably more than half naked, but the air of dignity with which, in the midst of all this misery, the lanky lady said to one of the young negroes, "Attend to your young master, Lycurgus," must have been heard to be conceived in the full extent of its mock heroic.

Another dwelling of one of these landed proprietors was a hovel as wretched as the one above described, but there was more industry within it. The gentleman, indeed was himself one of the numerous tribe of regular whiskey drinkers, and was rarely capable of any work; but he had a family of twelve children, who, with their skeleton mother, worked much harder than I ever saw negroes do. They were, accordingly, much less elegant and much less poor than the heiress; yet they lived with no appearance of comfort, and with, I believe, nothing beyond the necessaries of life. One proof of this was, that the worthless father would not suffer them to raise, even by their own labour, any garden vegetables, and they lived upon their fat pork, salt fish, and corn bread, summer and winter, without variation. This, I found, was frequently the case among the farmers. The luxury of whiskey is more appreciated by the men than all the green delicacies from the garden, and if all the ready money goes for that and their darling chewing tobacco, none can be spent by the wife for garden seeds; and as far as my observation extended, I never saw any American *ménage* where the toast and no toast question would have been decided in favour of the lady.

There are some small farmers who hold their lands as tenants, but these are by no means numerous: they do not pay their rent in money, but by making over a third of the produce to the owner; a mode of paying rent, considerably more advantageous to the tenant, than the landlord; but the difficulty of obtaining *money* in payment, excepting for mere retail articles, is very great in all American transactions. "I can pay in pro-*duce*," is the offer which I was assured is constantly made on all occasions, and if rejected, "Then I guess we can't deal," is the usual rejoinder. This statement does not, of course, include the great merchants of great cities, but refers to the mass of the people scattered over the country; it has, indeed, been my object, in speaking of the customs of the people, to give an idea of what they are *generally*.

The effect produced upon English people by the sight of slavery in every direction is very new, and not very agreeable, and it is not the less painfully felt from hearing upon every breeze the mocking words, "All men are born free and equal."

*   *   *   *   *

The condition of domestic slaves, however, does not generally appear to be bad; but the ugly feature is, that should it be so, they have no power to change it. I have seen much kind attention bestowed upon the health of slaves; but it is on these occasions impossible to forget, that did this attention fail, a valuable piece of property would be endangered. Unhappily the slaves, too, know this, and the consequence is, that real kindly feeling very rarely can exist between the parties. It is said that slaves born in a family are attached to the children of it, who have grown up with them. This may be the case where the petty acts of infant tyranny have not been sufficient to conquer the kindly feeling naturally produced by long and early association; and this sort of attachment may last as long as the slave can be kept in that state of profound ignorance which precludes reflection. The law of Virginia has taken care of this. The State legislators may truly be said to be "wiser in their generation than the children of light," and they ensure their safety by forbidding light to enter among them. By the law of Virginia it is penal to teach any slave to read, and it is penal to be aiding and abetting in the act of instructing them. This law speaks volumes. Domestic slaves are, generally speaking, tolerably well fed, and decently clothed; and the mode in which they are lodged seems a matter of great indifference to them. They are rarely exposed to the lash, and they are carefully nursed in sickness. These are the favourable features of their situation. The sad one is, that they *may* be sent to *the south* and sold. This is the dread of all the slaves north of Louisiana. The sugar plantations, and more than all, the rice grounds of Georgia and the Carolinas, are the terror of American negroes; and well they may be, for they open an early grave to thousands; and to *avoid loss* it is needful to make their previous labour pay their value.

There is something in the system of breeding and rearing negroes in the Northern States,* for the express purpose of sending them to be sold in the South, that strikes painfully against every feeling of justice, mercy, or common humanity. During my residence in America I became perfectly persuaded that the state of a domestic slave in a gentleman's family was preferable to that of a hired American "help," both because they are more cared for and valued, and because their condition being born with them, their spirits do not struggle against it with that pining discontent which seems the lot of all free servants in America. But the case is widely different with such as, in their own persons, or those of their children, "loved in vain," are exposed to the dreadful traffic above mentioned. In what is their condition better than that of the kidnapped negroes on the coast of

*She means here the upper South.

128

Africa? Of the horror in which this enforced migration is held I had a strong proof during our stay in Virginia. The father of a young slave, who belonged to the lady with whom we boarded, was destined to this fate, and within an hour after it was made known to him, he sharpened the hatchet with which he had been felling timber, and with his right hand severed his left from the wrist.

But this is a subject on which I do not mean to dilate. . . . Its effects on the moral feelings and external manners of the people are all I wish to observe upon, and these are unquestionably most injurious. The same man who beards his wealthier and more educated neighbour with the bullying boast, "I'm as good as you," turns to his slave, and knocks him down, if the furrow he has ploughed, or the log he has felled, please not this stickler for equality. There is a glaring falsehood on the very surface of such a man's principles that is revolting. It is not among the higher classes that the possession of slaves produces the worst effects. Among the poorer class of landholders, who are often as profoundly ignorant as the negroes they own, the effect of this plenary power over males and females is most demoralising; and the kind of coarse, not to say brutal, authority which is exercised, furnishes the most disgusting moral spectacle I ever witnessed. In all ranks, however, it appeared to me that the greatest and best feelings of the human heart were paralyzed by the relative positions of slave and owner. The characters, the hearts of children, are irretrievably injured by it. In Virginia we boarded for some time in a family consisting of a widow and her four daughters, and I there witnessed a scene strongly indicative of the effect I have mentioned. A young female slave, about eight years of age, had found on the shelf of a cupboard a biscuit, temptingly buttered, of which she had eaten a considerable portion before she was observed. The butter had been copiously sprinkled with arsenic for the destruction of rats, and had been thus most incautiously placed by one of the young ladies of the family. As soon as the circumstance was known, the lady of the house came to consult me as to what had best be done for the poor child; I immediately mixed a large cup of mustard and water (the most rapid of all emetics) and got the little girl to swallow it. The desired effect was instantly produced, but the poor child, party from nausea, and partly from the terror of hearing her death proclaimed by half a dozen voices round her, trembled so violently that I thought she would fall. I sat down in the court where we were standing, and, as a matter of course, took the little sufferer in my lap. I observed a general titter among the white members of the family, while the black stood aloof, and looked stupified. The youngest of the family, a little girl about the age of the young slave, after gazing at me for a few moments in utter astonishment, exclaimed, "My! If Mrs. Trollope has not taken her in her lap, and wiped her nasty mouth! Why I would not have touched her mouth for two hundred dollars!"

The little slave was laid on a bed, and I returned to my own apartments; some time afterwards I sent to enquire for her, and learnt that she was in great pain. I immediately went myself to enquire farther, when another young lady of the family, the one by whose imprudence the accident had occurred, met my anxious enquiries with ill-suppressed mirth—told me they had sent for the doctor—and then burst into uncontrollable laughter. The idea of really sympathising in the sufferings of a slave, appeared to them as absurd as weeping over a calf that had been slaughtered by the butcher. The daughters of my hostess were as lovely as features and complexion could make them; but the neutralizing effect of this total want of feeling upon youth and beauty, must be witnessed, to be conceived.

There seems in general a strong feeling throughout America, that none of the negro race can be trusted, and as fear, according to their notions, is the only principle by which a slave can be actuated, it is not wonderful if the imputation be just. But I am persuaded that were a different mode of moral treatment pursued, most important and beneficial consequences would result from it. Negroes are very sensible to kindness, and might, I think, be rendered more profitably obedient by the practice of it towards them, than by any other mode of discipline whatever. To emancipate them entirely throughout the Union cannot, I conceive, be thought of, consistently with the safety of the country; but were the possibility of amelioration taken into the consideration of the legislature, with all the wisdom, justice, and mercy, that could be brought to bear upon it, the negro population of the Union might cease to be a terror, and their situation no longer be a subject either of indignation or of pity.

I observed every where throughout the slave states that all articles which can be taken and consumed are constantly locked up, and in large families where the extent of the establishment multiplies the number of keys, these are deposited in a basket, and consigned to the care of a little negress, who is constantly seen following her mistress's steps with this basket on her arm, and this, not only that the keys may be always at hand, but because should they be out of sight one moment, that moment would infallibly be employed for purposes of plunder. It seemed to me in this instance, as in many others, that the close personal attendance of these sable shadows, must be very annoying; but whenever I mentioned it, I was assured that no such feeling existed, and that use rendered them almost unconscious of their presence.

I had, indeed, frequent opportunities of observing this habitual indifference to the presence of their slaves. They talk of them, of their condition, of their faculties, of their conduct, exactly as if they were incapable of hearing. I once saw a young lady, who, when seated at table between a male and a female, was induced by her modesty to intrude on the chair of her female neighbour to avoid the indelicacy of touching the elbow of *a man*. I once saw this very young lady lacing her stays with the most perfect composure before a negro footman. A Virginian gentleman told me that ever since he had married, he had been accustomed to have a negro girl sleep in the same chamber with himself and his wife. I asked for what purpose this nocturnal attendance was necessary? "Good heaven!" was the reply, "if I wanted a glass of water during the night, what would become of me?"

CHAPTER XXIII

Fruits and Flowers of Maryland and
Virginia . . . Elections . . .

Our summer in Maryland, (1830,) was delightful. The thermometer stood at 94, but the heat was by no means so oppressive as what we had felt in the West. In no part of North America are the natural productions of the soil more various, or more beautiful. Strawberries of the richest flavour sprung beneath our feet; and when these past away, every grove, every lane, every field looked like a cherry orchard, offering an inexhaustible profusion of fruit to all who would take the trouble to gather it. Then followed the peaches; every hedge-row was planted with them, and though the fruit did not equal in size or flavour those ripened on our garden walls, we often found them good enough to afford a delicious refreshment on our long rambles. But it was the flowers, and the flowering shrubs that, beyond all else, rendered this region the most beautiful I had ever seen, (the Alleghany always excepted.) No description can give an idea of the variety, the profusion, the luxuriance of them.

 *   *   *   *   *

There is another charm that haunts the summer wanderer in America, and it is perhaps the only one found in greatest perfection in the West: but it is beautiful every where. In a bright day, during any of the summer months, your walk is through an atmosphere of butterflies, so gaudy in hue, and so varied in form, that I often thought they looked like flowers on the wing.

132

Some of them are very large, measuring three or four inches across the wings; but many, and I think the most beautiful, are smaller than ours. Some have wings of the most dainty lavender colour, and bodies of black; others are fawn and rose colour; and others again are orange and bright blue. But pretty as they are, it is their number, even more than their beauty, that delights the eye. Their gay and noiseless movement as they glance through the air, crossing each other in chequered maze, is very beautiful. The humming-bird is another pretty summer toy; but they are not sufficiently numerous, nor do they live enough on the wing to render them so important a feature in the trans-atlantic show, as the rainbow-tinted butterflies. The fire-fly was a far more brilliant novelty. In moist situations, or before a storm, they are very numerous, and in the dark sultry evening of a burning day, when all employment was impossible, I have often found it a pastime to watch their glancing light, now here, now there; now seen, now gone; shooting past with the rapidity of lightning, and looking like a shower of falling stars, blown about in the breeze of evening.

*   *   *   *   *

Even in the retirement in which we passed this summer, we were not beyond reach of the election fever which is constantly raging through the land. Had America every attraction under heaven that nature and social enjoyment can offer, this electioneering madness would make me fly it in disgust. It engrosses every conversation, it irritates every temper, it substitutes party spirit for personal esteem; and, in fact, vitiates the whole system of society.

When a candidate for any office starts, his party endow him with every virtue, and with all the talents. They are all ready to peck out the eyes of those who oppose him, and in the warm and mettlesome south-western states, do literally often perform this operation: but as soon as he succeeds, his virtues and his talents vanish, and, excepting those holding office under his appointment, every man Jonathan of them sets off again full gallop to elect his successor. When I first arrived in America Mr. John Quincy Adams was President, and it was impossible to doubt, even from the statement of his enemies, that he was every way calculated to do honour to the office. All I ever heard

133

against him was, that "he was too much of a gentleman;" but a new candidate must be set up, and Mr. Adams was out-voted for no other reason, that I could learn, but because it was "best to change." "Jackson for ever!" was, therefore, screamed from the majority of mouths, both drunk and sober, till he was elected; not no sooner in his place, than the same ceaseless operation went on again, with "Clay for ever" for its war-whoop.

I was one morning paying a visit, when a party of gentlemen arrived at the same house on horseback. The one whose air proclaimed him the chief of his party, left us not long in doubt as to his business, for he said, almost in entering,

"Mr. P——, I come to ask for your vote."

"Who are you for, sir?" was the reply.

"Clay for ever!" the rejoinder; and the vote was promised.

This gentleman was candidate for a place in the state representation, whose members have a vote in the presidential election.

I was introduced to him as an English woman: he addressed me with, "Well, madam, you see we do these things openly and above-board here; you mince such matters more, I expect."

After his departure, his history and standing were discussed. "Mr. M. is highly respectable, and of very good standing; there can be no doubt of his election if he is a thorough-going Clay-man," said my host.

I asked what his station was.

The lady of the house told me that his father had been a merchant, and when this future legislator was a young man, he had been sent by him to some port in the Mediterranean as his supercargo. The youth, being a free-born high-spirited youth, appropriated the proceeds to his own uses, traded with great success upon the fund thus obtained, and returned, after an absence of twelve years, a gentleman of fortune and excellent standing. I expressed some little disapprobation of this proceeding, but was assured that Mr. M. was considered by every one as a very "honourable man."

Were I to relate one-tenth part of the dishonest transactions recounted to me by Americans, of their fellow-citizens and friends, I am confident that no English reader would give me

134

credit for veracity; it would, therefore, be very unwise to repeat them, but I cannot refrain from expressing the opinion that nearly four years of attentive observation impressed on me, namely, that the moral sense is on every point blunter than with us.

*   *   *   *   *

CHAPTER XXIV

Journey to Philadelphia . . .
Chesapeak and Delaware Canal . . .
City of Philadelphia . . .

In the latter part of August, 1830,* we paid a visit to Philadelphia, and, notwithstanding the season, we were so fortunate as to have both bright and temperate weather for the expedition. The road from Washington to Baltimore, which was our first day's journey, is interesting in summer from the variety and luxuriance of the foliage which borders great part of it.

We passed the night at Baltimore, and embarked next morning on board a steam-boat for Philadelphia. The scenery of the Elk river, upon which you enter soon after leaving the port of Baltimore, is not beautiful. We embarked at six in the morning, and at twelve reached the Chesapeak and Delaware canal; we then quitted the steam-boat, and walked two or three hundred yards to the canal, where we got on board a pretty little decked boat, sheltered by a neat awning, and drawn by four horses. This canal cuts across the state of Delaware, and connects the Chesapeak and Delaware rivers: it has been a work of great expense, though the distance is not more than thirteen miles; for a considerable part of this distance the cutting has been very deep, and the banks are in many parts thatched, to prevent their crumbling. At the point where the cutting is deepest, a light bridge is thrown across, which, from its great height, forms a striking object to the travellers passing below it. Every boat that passes this canal pays a toll of twenty dollars.

*Smalley found this date to be in error; the trip in question took place in June. See Smalley, ed., *Domestic Manners*, p 258n.

Nothing can be less interesting than that part of the state of Delaware through which this cut passes, the Mississippi hardly excepted. At one, we reached the Delaware river, at a point nearly opposite Delaware Fort, which looks recently built, and is very handsome. Here we again changed our vessel, and got on board another of their noble steam-boats; both these changes were made with the greatest regularity and dispatch.

There is nothing remarkable in the scenery of the Delaware. The stream is wide and the banks are flat; a short distance before you reach Philadelphia two large buildings of singular appearance strike the eye. On enquiry I learnt that they were erected for the purpose of sheltering two ships of war. They are handsomely finished, with very neat roofs, and are ventilated by many windows. The expense of these buildings must have been considerable, but, as the construction of the vast machines they shelter was more so, it may be good economy.

We reached Philadelphia at four o'clock in the afternoon. The approach to this city is not so striking as that to Baltimore; though much larger, it does not now shew itself so well: it wants domes and columns: it is, nevertheless, a beautiful city. Nothing can exceed its neatness; the streets are well paved, the foot-way, as in all the Old American cities, is of brick, like the old pantile walk at Tunbridge Wells. This is almost entirely sheltered from the sun by the awnings, which, in all the principal streets, are spread from the shop windows to the edge of the pavement.

The city is built with extreme and almost wearisome regularity; the streets, which run north and south, are distinguished by numbers, from one to—I know not how many, but I paid a visit in Twelfth Street; these are intersected at right angles by others, which are known by the names of various trees; Mulberry (more commonly called Archstreet), Chesnut, and Walnut, appear the most fashionable: in each of these there is a theatre. This mode of distinguishing the streets is commodious to strangers, from the facility it gives of finding our whereabouts you are; if you ask for the United States Bank, you are told it is in Chesnut, between Third and Fourth, and as the streets are all divided from each other by equal distances, of about three hundred feet, you are sure of not missing your mark. There are many handsome houses, but none that are very splendid; they are generally of brick, and those of the better order have white marble steps, and some few, door frames of the same beautiful material; but, on the whole, there is less display of it in the private dwellings than at Baltimore.

The Americans all seem greatly to admire this city, and to give it the preference in point of beauty, to all others in the Union, but I do not agree with them. There are some very handsome buildings, but none of them so placed as to produce a striking effect, as is the case both with the Capitol and the President's house, at Washington. Notwithstanding these fine buildings, one or more of which are to be found in all the principal streets, the *coup d'oeil* is every where the same. There is no Place de Louis Quinze or Carrousel, no Regent Street, or Green Park, to make one exclaim "how beautiful" all is even, straight, uniform, and uninteresting.

* * * * *

CHAPTER XXV

Washington Square . . . American Beauty . . .

Our mornings were spent, as all travellers' mornings must be, in asking questions, and in seeing all that the answers told us it was necessary to see. Perhaps this can be done in no city with more facility than in Philadelphia; you have nothing to do but to walk up one straight street, and down another, till all the parallelograms have been threaded. In doing this you will see many things worth looking at. The United States, and Pennsylvania banks, are the most striking buildings, and are both extremely handsome, being of white marble, and built after Grecian models. The State House has nothing externally to recommend it, but the room shewn as that in which the declaration of independence was signed, and in which the estimable Lafayette was received half a century after he had shed his noble blood in aiding to obtain it, is an interesting spot. At one end of this room is a statue in wood of General Washington; on its base is the following inscription:—

FIRST IN PEACE,
FIRST IN WAR,
AND
FIRST IN THE HEARTS OF HIS COUNTRYMEN.

There is a very pretty enclosure before the Walnut Street entrance to the State House, with good well-kept gravel walks, and many of their beautiful flowering trees. It is laid down in grass, not in turf; that, indeed, is a luxury I never saw in America. Near this enclosure is another of much the same description, called Washington Square. Here there was an excellent crop of clover; but as the trees are numerous, and highly beautiful, and several commodious seats are placed beneath their shade, it is, spite of the long grass, a very agreeable retreat from heat and dust. It was rarely, however, that I saw any of these seats occupied; the Americans have either no leisure, or no inclination for these moments of *delassement* that all other people, I believe, indulge in. Even their drams, so universally taken by rich and poor, are swallowed standing, and, excepting at church, they never have the air of leisure or repose. This pretty Washington Square is surrounded by houses on three sides, but (lasso!) has a prison on the fourth; it is nevertheless the nearest approach to a London square that is to be found in Philadelphia.

One evening, while the rest of my party went to visit some object which I had before seen, I agreed to await their return in this square, and sat down under a magnificent catalpa, which threw its fragrant blossoms in all directions; the other end of the bench was occupied by a young lady, who was employed in watching the gambols of a little boy. There was something in her manner of looking at me, and exchanging a smile when her young charge performed some extraordinary feat of activity on the grass, that persuaded me she was not an American. I do not remember who spoke first, but we were presently in a full flow of conversation. She spoke English with elegant correctness, but she was a German, and with an ardour of feeling which gave her a decidedly foreign air in Philadelphia, she talked to me of her country, of all she had left, and of all she had found, or rather of all she had not found, for thus ran her lament: —

"They do not love music, Oh no! and they never amuse themselves—no; and their hearts are not warm, at least they seem not so to strangers; and they have no ease, no forgetfulness of business and of care—no, not for a moment. But I will not stay long, I think, for I should not live."

She told me that she had a brother settled there as a merchant, and that she had passed a year with him; but she was hoping soon to return to her father land.

I never so strongly felt the truth of the remark, that expression is the soul of beauty, as in looking at, and listening to this young German. She was any thing but handsome; it is true she had large eyes full of gentle expression, but every feature was irregular; but, oh! the charm of that smile, of that look of deep feeling which animated every feature when she spoke of her own Germany! The tone of her voice, the slight and graceful action which accompanied her words, all struck me as so attractive, that the half hour I passed with her was continually recurring to my memory. I had often taxed myself with feeling something like prejudice against the beautiful American women; but this half hour set my conscience at rest; it is not prejudice which causes one to feel that regularity of features is insufficient to interest, or even to please, beyond the first glance. I certainly believe the women of America to be the handsomest in the world, but as surely do I believe that they are the least attractive.

*   *   *   *   *

CHAPTER XXVI

Quakers . . . Presbyterians . . .
Itinerant Methodist Preacher . . . Market . . .
Influence of females in society . . .

I had never chanced, among all my wanderings, to enter a Quaker Meeting-house; and as I thought I could no where make my first visit better than at Philadelphia, I went under the protection of a Quaker lady to the principal *orthodox* meeting of the city. The building is large, but perfectly without ornament; the men and women are separated by a rail which divides it into two equal parts; the meeting was very full on both sides, and the atmosphere almost intolerably hot.

*   *   *   *   *

The little bonnets and the large hats were ranged in long rows, and their stillness was for a long time so unbroken, that I could hardly persuade myself the figures they surmounted were alive. At length a grave square man arose, laid aside his ample beaver, and after another solemn interval of silence, he gave a deep groan, and as it were by the same effort uttered, "Keep thy foot." Again he was silent for many minutes, and then he continued for more than an hour to put forth one word at a time, but as such an interval from each other that I found it quite impossible to follow his meaning, if, indeed, he had any. My Quaker friend told me she knew not who he was, and that she much regretted I had heard so poor a preacher. After he had concluded, a gentleman-like old man (a physician by profession) arose, and delivered a few moral sentences in an agreeable manner; soon after he had sat down, the whole congregation rose, I know not at what signal, and made their exit. It is a singular kind of worship, if worship it may be called, where all prayer is forbidden; yet it appeared to me, in its decent quietness, infinitely preferable to what I had witnessed at the Presbyterian and Methodist meeting-houses. A great schism had lately taken place among the Quakers of Philadelphia; many objecting to the over-strict discipline of the orthodox. Among the seceders there are again various shades of difference; I met many who called themselves Unitarian Quakers, others were Hicksites, and others again, though still wearing the Quaker habit, were said to be Deists.

We visited many churches and chapels in the city, but none that would elsewhere be called handsome, either internally or externally.

I went one evening, not a Sunday, with a party of ladies to see a Presbyterian minister inducted. The ceremony was woefully long, and the charge to the young man awfully impossible to obey, at least if he were a man, like unto other men. It was matter of astonishment to me to observe the deep attention, and the unwearied patience with which some hundreds of beautiful young girls who were assembled there, (not to mention the old ladies,) listened to the whole of this tedious ceremony; surely there is no country in the world where religion makes so large a part of the amusement and occupation of the ladies. Spain, in its most catholic days, could not exceed it: besides, in spite of the gloomy horrors of the Inquisition, gaiety and amusement were not there offered as a sacrifice by the young and lovely.

The religious severity of Philadelphian manners is in nothing more conspicuous than in the number of chains thrown across the streets on a Sunday to prevent horses and carriages from passing. Surely the Jews could not exceed this country in their external observances. What the gentlemen of Philadelphia do with themselves on a Sunday, I will not pretend to guess, but the prodigious majority of females in the churches is very remarkable. Although a large proportion of the population of this city are Quakers, the same extraordinary variety of faith exists here, as every where else in the Union, and the priests have, in some circles, the same unbounded influence which has been mentioned elsewhere.

One history reached me, which gave a terrible picture of

the effect this power may produce; it was related to me by my mantua-maker; a young woman highly estimable as a wife and mother, and on whose veracity I perfectly rely. She told me that her father was a widower, and lived with his family of three daughters, at Philadelphia. A short time before she married, an itinerant preacher came to the city, who contrived to obtain an intimate footing in many respectable families. Her father's was one of these, and his influence and authority were great with all the sisters, but particularly with the youngest. The young girl's feelings for him seem to have been a curious mixture of spiritual awe and earthly affection. When she received a hint from her sisters that she ought not to give him too much encouragement till he spoke out, she shewed as much holy resentment as if they had told her not to say her prayers too devoutly. At length the father remarked the sort of covert passion that gleamed through the eyes of his godly visitor, and he saw too, the pallid anxious look which had settled on the young brow of his daughter; either this, or some rumours he had heard abroad, or both together, led him to forbid this man his house. The three girls were present when he did so, and all uttered a deprecating "Oh father!" but the old man added stoutly, "If you shew yourself here again, reverend sir, I will not only teach you the way out of my house, but out of the city also." The preacher withdrew, and was never heard of in Philadelphia afterwards; but when a few months had passed, strange whispers began to creep through the circle which had received and honoured him, and, in due course of time, no less than seven unfortunate girls produced living proofs of the wisdom of my informant's worthy father. In defence of this dreadful story I can only make the often repeated quotation, "I tell the tale as 'twas told to me;" but, in all sincerity I must add, that I have no doubt of its truth.

+ + + + +

I was particularly requested to visit the market of Philadelphia, at the hour when it presented the busiest scene; I did so, and thought few cities had anything to shew better worth looking at; it is, indeed, the very perfection of a market, the *beau ideal* of a notable housewife, who would confide to no deputy the important office of caterer. The neatness, freshness, and entire absence of every thing disagreeable to sight or smell, must be witnessed to be believed. The stalls were spread with snow-white napkins; flowers and fruit, if not quite of Paris or London perfection, yet bright, fresh, and fragrant; with excellent vegetables in the greatest variety and abundance, were all so delightfully exhibited, that objects less pleasing were overlooked and forgotten. The dairy, the poultry-yard, the forest, the river and the ocean, all contributed their spoil; in short, for the first time in my life, I thought a market a beautiful object. The prices of most articles were, as nearly as I could calculate between dollars and francs, about the same as at Paris; certainly much cheaper than in London, but much dearer than at Exeter.

My letters of introduction brought me acquainted with several amiable and interesting people. There is something in the tone of manners at Philadelphia that I liked; it appeared to me that there was less affectation of ton [tone] there than elsewhere. There is a quietness, a composure in a Philadelphia drawing-room, that is quite characteristic of a city founded by William Penn. The dress of the ladies, even those who are not Quakers, partakes of this; they are most elegantly neat, and there was a delicacy and good taste in the dress of the young ladies that might serve as a model to the whole Union. There can hardly be a stronger contrast in the style of dress between any two cities than may be remarked between Baltimore and Philadelphia; both are costly, but the former is distinguished by gaudy splendour, the latter by elegant simplicity.

It is said that this city has many gentlemen distinguished by their scientific pursuits; I conversed with several well-informed and intelligent men, but there is a cold dryness of manner and an apparent want of interest in the subjects they discuss, that, to my mind, robs conversation of all its charm. On one occasion I heard the character and situation of an illustrious officer discussed, who had served with renown under Napoleon, and whose high character might have obtained him favour under the Bourbons, could he have abandoned the principles which led him to dislike their government. This distinguished man had retreated to America after the death of his master, and was endeavoring to establish a sort of Polytechnic academy at New York: in speaking of him, I observed, that his devotion to the cause of freedom must prove a strong recommendation in the United States. "Not the least in the world, madam,"

145

answered a gentleman who ranked deservedly high among the *literati* of the city, "it might avail him much in England, perhaps, but here we are perfectly indifferent as to what people's principles may be."

This I believe to be exactly true, though I never before heard it avowed as a national feature.

The want of warmth, of interest, of feeling, upon all subjects which do not immediately touch their own concerns, is universal, and has a most paralysing effect upon conversation. All the enthusiasm of America is concentrated to the one point of her own emancipation and independence; on this point nothing can exceed the warmth of her feelings. She may, I think, be compared to a young bride, a sort of Mrs. Major Waddle; her independence is to her as a newly-won bridegroom; for him alone she has eyes, ears, or heart;—the honeymoon is not over yet;—when it is, America will, perhaps, learn more coquetry, and know better how to *fair l'aimable* to other nations.

I conceive that no place in the known world can furnish so striking a proof of the immense value of literary habits as the United States, not only in enlarging the mind, but what is of infinitely more importance, in purifying the manners. During my abode in the country I not only never met a literary man who was a tobacco chewer or a whiskey drinker, but I never met any who were not, that had escaped these degrading habits. On the women, the influence is, if possible, still more important; unfortunately, the instances are rare, but they are to be found. One admirable example occurs in the person of a young lady of Cincinnati: surrounded by a society totally incapable of appreciating, or even of comprehending her, she holds a place among it, as simply and unaffectedly as if of the same species; young, beautiful, and gifted by nature with a mind singularly acute and discriminating, she has happily found such opportunities of cultivation as might distinguish her in any country; it is, indeed, that best of all cultivation which is only to be found in domestic habits of literature, and in that hourly education which the daughter of a man of letters receives when she is made the companion and friend of her father. This young lady is the more admirable as she contrives to unite all the multifarious duties which usually devolve upon American ladies, with her intellectual pursuits. The companion and efficient assistant of her father's literary labours, the active aid in all the household cares of her mother, the tender nurse of a delicate infant sister, the skilful artificer of her own always elegant wardrobe, ever at leisure, and ever prepared to receive with the sweetest cheerfulness her numerous acquaintance, the most animated in conversation, the most indefatigable in occupation, it was impossible to know her, and study her character without feeling that such women were "the glory of all lands," and, could the race be multiplied, would speedily become the reformers of all the grossness and ignorance that now degrade her own. Is it to be imagined, that if fifty modifications of this charming young woman were to be met at a party, the men would dare to enter it reeking with whiskey, their lips blackened with tobacco, and convinced, to the very centre of their hearts and souls, that women were made for no other purpose than to fabricate sweetmeats and gingerbread, construct shirts, darn stockings, and become mothers of possible presidents? Assuredly not. Should the women of America ever discover what their power might be, and compare it with what it is, much improvement might be hoped for. While, at Philadelphia, among the handsomest, the wealthiest, and the most distinguished of the land, their comparative influence in society, with that possessed in Europe by females holding the same station, occurred forcibly to my mind.

Let me be permitted to describe the day of a Philadelphian lady of the first class, and the inference I would draw from it will be better understood.

It may be said that the most important feature in a woman's history is her maternity. It is so; but the object of the present observation is the social, and not the domestic influence of woman.

This lady shall be the wife of a senator and a lawyer in the highest repute and practice. She has a very handsome house, with white marble steps and door-posts, and a delicate silver knocker and door-handle; she has very handsome drawing-rooms, very handsomely furnished, (there is a sideboard in one of them, but it is very handsome, and has very handsome decanters and cut glass water-jugs upon it); she has a very handsome carriage, and a very handsome free black coachman; she is always very handsomely dressed; and, moreover, she is very handsome herself.

She rises, and her first hour is spent in the scrupulously nice arrangement of her dress; she decends to her parlour neat, stiff, and silent; her breakfast is brought in by her free black footman; she eats her fried ham and her salt fish, and drinks her coffee in silence, while her husband reads one newspaper, and puts another under his elbow; and then, perhaps, she washes the cups and saucers. Her carriage is ordered at eleven; till that hour she is employed in the pastry-room, her snow-white apron protecting her mouse-coloured silk. Twenty minutes before her carriage should appear, she retires to her chamber, as she calls it, shakes, and folds up her still snow-white apron, smooths her rich dress, and with nice care, sets on her elegant bonnet, and all the handsome *et cætera;* then walks down stairs, just at the moment that her free black coachman announces to her free black footman that the carriage waits. She steps into it, and gives the word, "Drive to the Dorcas society." Her footman stays at home to clean the knives, but her coachman can trust his horses while he opens the carriage door, and his lady not being accustomed to a hand or an arm, gets out very safely without, though one of her own is occupied by a work-basket, and the other by a large roll of all those indescribable matters which ladies take as offerings to Dorcas societies. She enters the parlour appropriated for the meeting, and finds seven other ladies, very like herself, and takes her place among them; she presents her contribution, which is accepted with a gentle circular smile, and her parings of broad cloth, her ends of ribbon, her gilt paper, and her minikin pins, are added to the parings of broad cloth, the ends of ribbon, the gilt paper, and the minikin pins with which the table is already covered; she also produces from her basket three ready-made pincushions, four ink-wipers, seven paper-matches, and a paste-board watch-case; these are welcomed with acclamations, and the youngest lady present deposits them carefully on shelves, amid a prodigious quantity of similar articles. She then produces her thimble, and asks for work; it is presented to her, and the eight ladies all stitch together for some hours. Their talk is of priests and of missions; of the profits of their last sale, of their hopes from the next; of the doubt whether young Mr. This, or young Mr. That should receive the fruits of it to fit him out for Liberia; of the very ugly bonnet seen at church on Sabbath morning, of the very hand-

148

some preacher who performed on Sabbath afternoon, and of the very large collection made on Sabbath evening. This lasts till three, when the carriage again appears, and the lady and her basket return home; she mounts to her chamber, carefully sets aside her bonnet and its appurtenances, puts on her scolloped black silk apron, walks into the kitchen to see that all is right, then into the parlour, where, having cast a careful glance over the table prepared for dinner, she sits down, work in hand, to await her spouse. He comes, shakes hands with her, spits, and dines. The conversation is not much, and ten minutes suffices for the dinner; fruit and toddy, the newspaper and the work-bag succeed. In the evening the gentleman, being a savant, goes to the Wister society, and afterwards plays a snug rubber at a neighbour's. The lady receives at tea a young missionary and three members of the Dorcas society. —And so ends her day.

For some reason or other, which English people are not very likely to understand, a great number of young married persons board by the year, instead of "going to house-keeping." as they call having an establishment of their own. Of course this statement does not include persons of large fortune, but it does include very many whose rank in society would make such a mode of life quite impossible with us. I can hardly imagine a contrivance more effectual for ensuring the insignificance of a woman, than marrying her at seventeen, and placing her in a boarding-house. Nor can I easily imagine a life of more uniform dulness for the lady herself; but this certainly is a matter of taste. I have heard many ladies declare that it is "just quite the perfection of comfort to have nothing to fix for oneself." Yet despite these assurances I always experienced a feeling which hovered between pity and contempt, when I contemplated their mode of existence.

How would a newly-married Englishwoman endure it, her head and her heart full of the one dear scheme—
"Well ordered home, *his* dear delight to make?"
She must rise exactly in time to reach the boarding table at the hour appointed for breakfast, or she will get a stiff bow from the lady president, cold coffee, and no egg. I have been sometimes greatly amused upon these occasions by watching a little scene in which the bye-play had much more meaning than the words uttered. The fasting, but tardy lady, looks round the table, and

having ascertained that there was no egg left, says distinctly, "I will take an egg if you please." But as this is addressed to no one in particular, no one in particular answers it, unless it happen that her husband is at table before her, and then he says, "There are no eggs, my dear." Whereupon the lady president evidently cannot hear, and the greedy culprit who has swallowed two eggs (for there are always as many eggs as noses) looks pretty considerably afraid of being found out. The breakfast proceeds in sombre silence, save that sometimes a parrot, and sometimes a canary bird, ventures to utter a timid note. When it is finished, the gentlemen hurry to their occupations, and the quiet ladies mount the stairs, some to the first, some to the second, and some to the third stories, in an inverse proportion to the number of dollars paid, and ensconce themselves in their respective chambers. As to what they do there it is not very easy to say; but I believe they clear-starch a little, and iron a little, and sit in a rocking-chair, and sew a great deal. I always observed that the ladies who boarded wore more elaborately worked collars and petticoats than any one else. The plough is hardly a more blessed instrument in America than the needle. How could they live without it? But time and the needle wear through the longest morning, and happily the American morning is not very long, even though they breakfast at eight.

It is generally about two o'clock that the boarding gentlemen meet the boarding ladies at dinner. Little is spoken, except a whisper between the married pairs. Sometimes a sulky bottle of wine flanks the plate of one or two individuals, but it adds nothing to the mirth of the meeting, and seldom more than one glass to the good cheer of the owners. It is not then, and it is not there, that the gentlemen of the Union drink. Soon, very soon, the silent meal is done, and then, if you mount the stairs after them, you will find from the doors of the more affectionate and indulgent wives, a smell of cigars steam forth, which plainly indicates the felicity of the couple within. If the gentleman be a very polite husband, he will, as soon as he has done smoking and drinking this toddy, offer his arm to his wife, as far as the corner of the street, where his store, or his office is situated, and there he will leave her to turn which way she likes. As this is the hour for being full dressed, of course she turns the way she can be most seen. Perhaps she pays a few visits; perhaps she goes to chapel; or, perhaps, she enters some store where her husband deals, and ventures to order a few notions; and then she goes home again—no, not home—I will not give that name to a boarding-house, but she re-enters the cold heartless atmosphere in which she dwells, where hospitality can never enter, and where interest takes the management instead of affection. At tea they all meet again, and a little trickery is perceptible to a nice observer in the manner of partaking the pound-cake, &c. After this, those who are happy enough to have engagements, hasten to keep them; those who have not, either mount again to the solitude of their chamber, or, what appeared to me much worse, remain in the common sitting-room, in a society cemented by no tie, endeared by no connection, which choice did not bring together, and which the slightest motive would break asunder. I remarked that the gentlemen were generally obliged to go out every evening on business, and, I confess, the arrangement did not surprise me.

It is not thus that the women can obtain that influence in society which is allowed to them in Europe, and to which, both sages and men of the world have agreed in ascribing such salutary effects. It is in vain that "collegiate institutes" are formed for young ladies, or that "academic degrees" are conferred upon them. It is after marriage, and when these young attempts upon all the sciences are forgotten, that the lamentable insignificance of the American women appears, and till this be remedied, I venture to prophesy that the tone of their drawing-rooms will not improve.

Whilst I was at Philadelphia a great deal of attention was excited by the situation of two criminals, who had been convicted of robbing the Baltimore mail, and were lying under sentence of death. The rare occurrence of capital punishment in America makes it always an event of great interest; and the approaching execution was repeatedly the subject of conversation at the boarding table. One day a gentleman told us he had that morning been assured that one of the criminals had declared to the visiting clergyman that he was certain of being reprieved, and that nothing the clergyman could say to the contrary made any impression upon him. Day after day this same story was repeated, and commented upon at table, and it appeared that the report had been heard in so many quarters,

151

that not only was the statement received as true, but it began to be conjectured that the criminal had some ground for his hope. I learnt from these daily conversations that one of the prisoners was an American, and the other an Irishman, and it was the former who was so strongly persuaded he should not be hanged. Several of the gentlemen at table, in canvassing the subject, declared, that if the one were hanged and the other spared, this hanging would be a murder, and not a legal execution. In discussing this point, it was stated that very nearly all the white men who had suffered death since the Declaration of Independence had been Irishmen. What truth there may be in this general statement I have no means of ascertaining; all I know is, that I heard it made. On this occasion, however, the Irish-man was hanged, and the American was not.

CHAPTER XXVII

Return to Stonington . . . Thunder-storm . . .
Emigrants . . . Illness . . . Alexandria . . .

A fortnight passed rapidly away in this great city, and, doubtless, there was still much left unseen when we quitted it, according to previous arrangement, to return to our friends in Maryland. We came back by a different route, going by land from Newcastle to French Town, instead of passing by the canal. We reached Baltimore in the middle of the night, but finished our repose on board the steam-boat, and started for Washington at five o'clock the next morning.

Our short abode amid the heat and closeness of a city made us enjoy more than ever the beautiful scenery around Stonington. The autumn, which soon advanced upon us, again clothed the woods in colours too varied and gaudy to be conceived by those who have never quitted Europe; and the stately maize, waving its flowing tassels, as the long drooping blossoms are called, made every field look like a little forest. A rainy spring had been followed by a summer of unusual heat; and towards the autumn frequent thunderstorms of terrific violence cleared the air, but at the same time frightened us almost out of our wits. On one occasion I was exposed, with my children, to the full fury of one of these awful visitations. We suffered considerable terror during this storm, but when we were all again safe, and comfortably sheltered, we rejoiced that the accident had occurred, as it gave us the best possible opportunity of witnessing, in all its glory, a transatlantic thunder-storm. It was, however, great imprudence that exposed us to it, for we quitted the

153

house, and mounted a hill at a considerable distance from it, for the express purpose of watching to advantage the extraordinary aspect of the clouds. When we reached the top of the hill half the heavens appeared hung with a heavy curtain; a sort of deep blue black seemed to colour the very air; the buzzards screamed, as with heavy wing they sought the earth. We ought, in common prudence, to have immediately retreated to the house, but the scene was too beautiful to be left. For several minutes after we reached our station, the air appeared perfectly without movement, no flash broke through the seven-fold cloud, but a flickering light was visible, darting to and fro behind it; and by degrees the thunder rolled onward, nearer and nearer, till the inky cloud burst asunder, and cataracts of light came pouring from behind it. From that moment there was no interval, no pause, the lightning did not flash, there were no claps of thunder, but the heavens blazed and bellowed above and around us, till stupor took the place of terror, and we stood utterly confounded. But we were speedily aroused, for suddenly, as if from beneath our feet, a gust arose which threatened to mix all the elements in one. Torrents of water seemed to bruise the earth by their violence; eddies of thick dust rose up to meet them; the fierce fires of heaven only blazed the brighter for the falling flood; while the blast almost out-roared the thunder. But the wind was left at last the lord of all, for after striking with wild force, now here, now there, and bringing worlds of clouds together in most hostile contact, it finished by clearing the wide heavens of all but a few soft straggling masses, whence sprung a glorious rainbow, and then retired, leaving the earth to raise her half crushed forests; and we, poor pigmies, to call back our frighted senses, and recover breath as we might.

During this gust, it would have been impossible for us to have kept our feet; we crouched down under the shelter of a heap of stones, and, as we informed each other, looked most dismally pale.

Many trees were brought to the earth before our eyes; some torn up by the roots, and some mighty stems snapt off several feet from the ground. If the West Indian hurricanes exceed this, they must be terrible indeed.

The situation of Mrs. S****'s house was considered as remarkably healthy, and I believe justly so, for on more than one occasion, persons who were suffering from fever and ague at the distance of a mile or two, were perfectly restored by passing a week or fortnight at Stonington; but the neighbourhood of it, particularly on the side bordering the Potomac, was much otherwise, and the mortality among the labourers on the canal was frightful.

I have elsewhere stated my doubts if the labouring poor of our country mend their condition by emigrating to the United States, but it was not till the opportunity which a vicinity to the Chesapeake and Ohio canal gave me, of knowing what their situation was after making the change, that I became fully aware how little it was to be desired for them.

Of the white labourers on this canal, the great majority are Irishmen; their wages are from ten to fifteen dollars a month, with a miserable lodging, and a large allowance of whiskey. It is by means of this hateful poison that they are tempted, and indeed enabled for a time, to stand the broiling heat of the sun in a most noxious climate: for through such, close to the romantic but unwholesome Potomac, the line of the canal has hitherto run. The situation of these poor strangers, when they sink at last in *"the fever,"* which sooner or later is sure to overtake them, is dreadful. There is a strong feeling against the Irish in every part of the Union, but they will do twice as much work as a negro, and therefore they are employed. When they fall sick, they may, and must, look with envy on the slaves around them; for they are cared for; they are watched and physicked, as a valuable horse is watched and physicked: not so the Irishman; he is literally thrown on one side, and a new comer takes his place. Details of their sufferings, and unheeded death, too painful to dwell upon, often reached us; on one occasion a farmer calling at the house, told the family that a poor man, apparently in a dying condition, was lying beside a little brook at the distance of a quarter of a mile. The spot was immediately visited by some of the family, and there in truth lay a poor creature, who was already past the power of speaking; he was conveyed to the house, and expired during the night. By enquiring at the canal, it was found that he was an Irish labourer, who having fallen sick, and spent his last cent, had left the stiffing shantee where he lay, in the desperate attempt of finding his way to Washington, with what hope I know not. He did not appear above

155

twenty, and as I looked on his pale young face, which even in death expressed suffering, I thought that perhaps he had left a mother and a home to seek wealth in America. I saw him buried under a group of locust trees, his very name unknown to those who laid him there, but the attendance of the whole family at the grave, gave a sort of decency to his funeral which rarely, in that country, honours the poor relics of British dust: but no clergyman attended, no prayer was said, no bell was tolled; these, indeed, are ceremonies unthought of, and in fact unattainable without much expence, at such a distance from a town; had the poor youth been an American, he would have been laid in the earth in the same unceremonious manner. But had this poor Irish lad fallen sick in equal poverty and destitution among his own people, he would have found a blanket to wrap his shivering limbs, and a kindred hand to close his eyes.

* * * * *

I never saw so many autumn flowers as grow in the woods and sheep-walks of Maryland; a second spring seemed to clothe the fields, but with grief and shame I confess, that of these precious blossoms I scarcely knew a single name. I think the Michaelmas daisy, in wonderful variety of form and colour, and the prickly pear, were almost my only acquaintance: let no one visit America without having first studied botany; it is an amusement, as a clever friend of mine once told me, that helps one wonderfully up and down hill, and must be superlatively valuable in America, both from the plentiful lack of other amusements, and the plentiful material for enjoyment in this; besides, if one is dying to know the name of any of these lovely strangers, it is a thousand to one against his finding any one who can tell it.

The prettiest eclipse of the moon I ever saw was that of September, of this year, (1830.) We had been passing some hours amid the solemn scenery of the Potomac falls, and just as we were preparing to quit it, the full moon arose above the black pines, with half our shadow thrown across her. The effect of her rising thus eclipsed was more strange, more striking by far, than watching the gradual obscuration; and as I turned to look at the black chasm behind me, and saw the deadly alder, and the poison-vine waving darkly on the rocks around, I thought the scene wanted nothing but the figure of a palsied crone, plucking the fatal branches to concoct some charm of mischief.

Whether some such maga dogged my steps, I know not, but many hours had not elapsed ere I again felt the noxious influence of an American autumn. This fever, "built in th' eclipse," speedily brought me very low, and though it lasted not so long as that of the preceding year, I felt persuaded I should never recover from it. Though my forebodings were not verified by the event, it was declared that change of air was necessary, and it was arranged for me, (for I was perfectly incapable of settling any thing for myself,) that I should go to Alexandria, a pretty town at the distance of about fifteen miles, which had the reputation of possessing a skilful physician.

It was not without regret that we quitted our friends at Stonington; but the prescription proved in a great degree efficacious; a few weeks' residence in Alexandria restored my strength sufficiently to enable me to walk to a beautiful little grassy terrace, perfectly out of the town, but very near it, from whence we could watch the various craft that peopled the Potomac between Alexandria and Washington. But though gradually regaining strength, I was still far from well; all plans for winter gaiety were abandoned, and finding ourselves very well accommodated, we decided upon passing the winter where we were. It proved unusually severe; the Potomac was so completely frozen as to permit considerable traffic to be carried on by carts, crossing on the ice, from Maryland. This had not occurred before for thirty years. The distance was a mile and a quarter, and we ventured to brave the cold, and walk across this bright and slippery mirror, to make a visit on the opposite shore; the fatigue of keeping our feet was by no means inconsiderable, but we were rewarded by seeing as noble a winter landscape around us as the eye could look upon.

When at length the frost gave way, the melting snow produced freshes so violent as to carry away the long bridge at Washington; large fragments of it, with the railing still erect came floating down amidst vast blocks of ice, during many successive days, and it was curious to see the intrepidity with which the young sailors of Alexandria periled their lives to make spoil of the timber.

The solar eclipse on the 12th of February, 1831, was nearer

157

total than any I ever saw, or ever shall see. It was completely annular at Alexandria, and the bright ring which surrounded the moon's shadow, though only 81° in breadth, gave light sufficient to read the smallest print; the darkness was considerable lessened by the snow, which, as the day was perfectly unclouded, reflected brightly all the light that was left us.

Notwithstanding the extreme cold we passed the whole time in the open air, on a rising ground near the river; in this position many beautiful effects were perceptible; the rapid approach and change of shadows, the dusky hue of the broad Potomac, that seemed to drink in the feeble light, which its snow-coloured banks gave back to the air, the gradual change of every object from the coloring of bright sunshine to one sad universal tint of dingy purple, the melancholy lowing of the cattle, and the short, but remarkable suspension of all labour, gave something of mystery and awe to the scene that we shall long remember.

During the following months I occupied myself partly in revising my notes, and arranging these pages; and partly in making myself acquainted, as much as possible, with the literature of the country.

While reading and transcribing my notes, I underwent a strict self-examination. I passed in review all I had seen, all I had felt, and scrupulously challenged every expression of disapprobation; the result was, that I omitted in transcription much that I had written, as containing unnecessary details of things which had displeased me; yet, as I did so, I felt strongly that there was no exaggeration in them; but such details, though true, might be ill-natured, and I retained no more than were necessary to convey the general impressions I received. While thus reviewing my notes, I discovered that many points, which all scribbling travellers are expected to notice, had been omitted; but a few pages of miscellaneous observations will, I think, supply all that can be expected from so idle a pen.

CHAPTER XXVIII

American Cooking... Evening Parties...
Dress... Sleighing...
Money-getting Habits...
Tax-Gatherer's Notice...
Indian Summer...

In relating all I know of America, I surely must not omit so important a feature as the cooking. There are sundry anomalies in the mode of serving even a first-rate table; but as these are altogether matters of custom, they by no means indicate either indifference or neglect in this important business; and whether castors are placed on the table or on the side-board; whether soup, fish, patties, and salad be eaten in orthodox order or not, signifies but little. I am hardly capable, I fear, of giving a very erudite critique on the subject; general observations therefore must suffice. The ordinary mode of living is abundant, but not delicate. They consume an extraordinary quantity of bacon. Ham and beef-steaks appear morning, noon, and night. In eating, they mix things together with the strangest incongruity imaginable. I have seen eggs and oysters eaten together; the sempiternal ham with apple-sauce; beef-steak with stewed peaches; and salt fish with onions. The bread is everywhere excellent, but they rarely enjoy it themselves, as they insist upon eating horrible half-baked hot rolls both morning and evening. The butter is tolerable; but they have seldom such cream as every little dairy produces in England; in fact, the cows are very roughly kept, compared with our's. Common vegetables are abundant and very fine. I never saw sea-cale, or cauliflowers, and either from the want of summer rain, or the want of care, the harvest of green vegetables is much sooner over than with us. They eat the Indian corn in a great variety of forms; some-

159

times it is dressed green, and eaten like peas; sometimes it is broken to pieces when dry, boiled plain, and brought to table like rice; this dish is called hominy. The flour of it is made into a least a dozen different sorts of cakes; but in my opinion all bad. This flour, mixed in the proportion of one-third, with fine wheat, makes by far the best bread I every tasted.

I never saw turbot, salmon, or fresh cod; but the rock and shad are excellent. There is a great want of skill in the composition of sauces; not only with fish, but with every thing. They use very few made dishes, and I never saw any that would be approved by our savants. They have an excellent wild duck, called the Canvass Back, which, if delicately served, would surpass the black cock; but the game is very inferior to our's; they have no hares, and I never saw a pheasant. They seldom indulge in second courses, with all their ingenious temptations to the eating a second dinner; but almost every table has its dessert, (invariably pronounced desart) which is placed on the table before the cloth is removed, and consists of pastry, preserved fruits, and creams. They are "extravagantly fond," to use their own phrase, of puddings, pies, and all kinds of "sweets," particularly the ladies; but are by no means such connoisseurs in soups and ragoûts as the gastronomes of Europe. Almost every one drinks water at table, and by a strange contradiction, in the country where hard drinking is more prevalent than in any other, there is less wine taken at dinner; ladies rarely exceed one glass, and the great majority of females never take any. In fact, the hard drinking, so universally acknowledged, does not take place in jovial dinners, but to speak plain English, in solitary dram-drinking. Coffee is not served immediately after dinner, but makes part of the serious matter of tea drinking, which comes some hours later. Mixed dinner parties of ladies and gentlemen are very rare, and unless several foreigners are present, but little conversation passes at table. It certainly does not, in my opinion, add to the well ordering a dinner table, to set the gentlemen at one end of it, and the ladies at the other; but it is very rarely that you find it otherwise.

Their large evening parties are supremely dull; the men sometimes play cards by themselves, but if a lady plays, it must not be for money; no ecarté, no chess; very little music, and that little lamentably bad. Among the blacks, I heard some good voices, singing in tune; but I scarcely every heard a white American, male or female, go through an air without being out of tune before the end of it; nor did I ever meet any trace of science in the singing I heard in society. To eat inconceivable quantities of cake, ice, and pickled oysters—and to shew half their revenue in silks and satins, seem to be the chief object they have in these parties.

The most agreeable meetings, I was assured by all the young people, were those to which no married women are admitted; of the truth of this statement I have not the least doubt. These exclusive meetings occur frequently, and often last to a late hour; on these occasions, I believe, they generally dance. At regular balls, married ladies are admitted, but seldom take much part in the amusement. The refreshments are always profuse and costly, but taken in a most uncomfortable manner. I have known many private balls, where every thing was on the most liberal scale of expense, where the gentlemen sat down to supper in one room, while the ladies took theirs, standing, in another.

What we call pic-nics are very rare, and when attempted, do not often succeed well. The two sexes can hardly mix for the greater part of a day without great restraint and ennui; it is quite contrary to their general habits; the favourite indulgences of the gentlemen (smoking cigars and drinking spirits), can neither be indulged in with decency, not resigned with complacency.

The ladies have strange ways of adding to their charms. They powder themselves immoderately, face, neck, and arms, with pulverised starch; the effect is indescribably disagreeable by day-light, and not very favourable at any time. They are also most unhappily partial to false hair, which they wear in surprising quantities; this is the more to be lamented, as they generally have very fine hair of their own. I suspect this fashion to arise from an indolent mode of making their toilet, and from accomplished ladies' maids not being very abundant; it is less trouble to append a bunch of waving curls here, there, and every where, than to keep their native tresses in perfect order.

Though the expense of the ladies' dress greatly exceeds, in proportion to their general style of living, that of the ladies of Europe, it is very far (excepting in Philadelphia) from being in

161

good taste. They do not consult the seasons in the colours or in the style of their costume; I have often shivered at seeing a young beauty picking her way through the snow with a pale rose-coloured bonnet, set on the very top of her head: I knew one young lady whose pretty little ear was actually frost-bitten from being thus exposed. They never wear muffs or boots, and appear extremely shocked at the sight of comfortable walking shoes and cotton stockings, even when they have to step to their sleigh over ice and snow. They walk in the middle of winter with their poor little toes pinched into a miniature slipper, incapable of excluding as much moisture as might bedew a primrose. I must say in their excuse, however, that they have, almost universally, extremely pretty feet. They do not walk well, nor, in fact, do they ever appear to advantage when in movement. I know not why this should be, for they have abundance of French dancing-masters among them, but somehow or other it is the fact. I fancied I could often trace a mixture of affectation and of shyness in their little mincing unsteady step, and the ever changing position of the hands. They do not dance well; perhaps I should rather say they do not look well when dancing; lovely as their faces are, they cannot, in a position that exhibits the whole person, atone for the want of *tournure,* and for the universal defect in the formation of the bust, which is rarely full, or gracefully formed.

I never saw an American man walk or stand well; notwithstanding their frequent militia drillings, they are nearly all hollow chested and round shouldered: perhaps this is occasioned by no officer daring to say to a brother free-born "hold up your head;" whatever the cause, the effect is very remarkable to a stranger. In stature, and in physiognomy, a great majority of the population, both male and female, are strikingly handsome, but they know not how to do their own honours; half as much comeliness elsewhere would produce ten times as much effect.

Nothing can exceed their activity and perseverance in all kinds of speculation, handicraft, and enterprise, which promises a profitable pecuniary result. I heard an Englishman, who had been long resident in America, declare that in following, in meeting, or in overtaking, in the street, on the road, or in the field, at the theatre, the coffee-house, or an home, he had never overheard Americans conversing without the word DOLLAR being pronounced between them. Such unity of purpose, such sympathy of feeling, can, I believe, be found nowhere else, except, perhaps, in an ants' nest. The result is exactly what might be anticipated. This sordid object, for ever before their eyes, must inevitably produce a sordid tone of mind, and, worse still, it produces a seared and blunted conscience on all questions of probity. I know not a more striking evidence of the low tone of morality which is generated by this universal pursuit of money, than the manner in which the New England States are described by Americans. All agree in saying that they present a spectacle of industry and prosperity delightful to behold, and this is the district and the population most constantly quoted as the finest specimen of their admirable country; yet I never met a single individual in any part of the Union who did not paint these New Englanders as sly, grinding, selfish, and tricking. The Yankees (as the New Englanders are called) will avow these qualities themselves with a complacent smile, and boast that no people on the earth can match them at over-reaching in a bargain. I have heard them unblushingly relate stories of their cronies and friends, which, if believed among us, would banish the heroes from the fellowship of honest men for ever; and all this is uttered with a simplicity which sometimes led me to doubt if the speakers knew what honour and honesty meant. Yet the Americans declare that "they are the most moral people upon earth." Again and again I have heard this asserted, not only in conversation, and by their writings, but even from the pulpit. Such broad assumption of superior virtue demands examination, and after four years of attentive and earnest observation and enquiry, my honest conviction is, that the standard of moral character in the United States is very greatly lower than in Europe. Of their religion, as it appears outwardly, I have had occasion to speak frequently; I pretend not to judge the heart, but, without any uncharitable presumption, I must take permission to say, that both Protestant England and Catholic France shew an infinitely superior religious and moral aspect to mortal observation, both as to reverend decency of external observance, and as to the inward fruit of honest dealing between man and man.

In other respects I think no one will be disappointed who visits the country, expecting to find no more than common sense might teach him to look for, namely, a vast continent, by far the greater part of which is still in the state in which nature left it, and a busy, bustling, industrious population, hacking and hewing their way through it. What greatly increases the interest of this spectacle, is the wonderful facility for internal commerce, furnished by the rivers, lakes, and canals, which thread the country in every direction, producing a rapidity of progress in all commercial and agricultural speculation altogether unequalled. This remarkable feature is perceptible in every part of the Union into which the fast spreading population has hitherto found its way, and forms, I think, the most remarkable and interesting peculiarity of the country. I hardly remember a single town where vessels of some description or other may not constantly be seen in full activity.

Their carriages of every kind are very unlike ours; those belonging to private individuals seem all constructed with a view to summer use, for which they are extremely well calculated, but they are by no means comfortable in winter. The waggons and carts are built with great strength, which is indeed necessary, from the roads they often have to encounter. The stage-coaches are heavier and much less comfortable than those of France; to those of England they can bear no comparison. I never saw any harness that I could call handsome, nor any equipage which, as to horses, carriage, harness, and servants, could be considered as complete. The sleighs are delightful, and constructed at so little expense that I wonder we have not all got them in England, lying by, in waiting for the snow, which often remains with us long enough to permit their use. Sleighing is much more generally enjoyed by night than by day, for what reason I could never discover, unless it be, that no gentlemen are to be found disengaged from business in the mornings. Nothing, certainly, can be more agreeable than the gliding smoothly and rapidly along, deep sunk in soft furs, the moon shining with almost mid-day splendour, the air of crystal brightness, and the snow sparkling on every side, as if it were sprinkled with diamonds. And then the noiseless movement of the horses, so mysterious and unwonted, and the gentle tinkling of the bells you meet and carry, all help at once to soothe and excite the spirits: in short, I had not the least objection to sleighing by night, I only wished to sleigh by day also.

*   *   *   *   *

Their steam-boats, were the social arrangements somewhat improved, would be delightful, as a mode of travelling; but they are very seldom employed for excursions of mere amusement: nor do I remember seeing pleasure-boats, properly so called, at any of the numerous places where they might be used with so much safety and enjoyment.

How often did our homely adage recur to me, "All work and no play would make Jack a dull boy;" Jonathan is a very dull boy. We are by no means so gay as our lively neighbours on the other side of the channel, but, compared with Americans, we are whirligigs and tetotums; every day is a holyday, and every night a festival.

Perhaps if the ladies had quite their own way, a little more relaxation would be permitted; but there is one remarkable peculiarity in their manners which precludes the possibility of any dangerous out-breaking of the kind; few ladies have any command of ready money entrusted to them. I have been a hundred times present when bills for a few dollars, perhaps for one, have been brought for payment to ladies living in perfectly easy circumstances, who have declared themselves without money, and referred the claimant to their husbands for payment. On every occasion where immediate disbursement is required it is the same; even in shopping for ready cash they say, "send a bill home with the things, and my husband will give you a draft."

I think that it was during my stay at Washington, that I was informed of a government regulation, which appeared to me curious; I therefore record it here.

Every Deputy Post-Master is required to insert in his return the title of every newspaper received at his office for distribution. This return is laid before the Secretary of State, who, perfectly knowing the political character of each newspaper, is thus enabled to feel the pulse of every limb of the monster mob. This is a well imagined device for getting a peep at the politics of a country where newspapers make part of the daily food, but is it quite consistent with their entire freedom? I do not believe

165

we have any such tricks to regulate the deposal of offices and appointments.

I believe it was in Indiana that Mr. T. met with a printed notice relative to the payment of taxes, which I preserved as a curious sample of the manner in which the free citizens are coaxed and reasoned into obeying the laws.

"LOOK OUT DELINQUENTS

"Those indebted to me for taxes, fees, notes, and accounts, are specially requested to call and pay the same on or before the 1st day of December, 1828, as no longer indulgence will be given. I have called time and again, by advertisement and otherwise, to little effect; but now the time has come when my situation requires immediate payment from all indebted to me. It is impossible for me to pay off the amount of the duplicates of taxes and my other debts without recovering the same of those from whom it is due. I am at a loss to know the reason why those charged with taxes neglect to pay; from the negligence of many it would seem that they think the money is mine, or that I have funds to discharge the taxes due to the State, and that I can wait with them until it suits their convenience to pay. The money is not mine; neither have I the funds to settle amount of the duplicate. My only resort is to collect; in doing so I should be sorry to have to resort to the authority given me by law for the recovery of the same. It should be the first object of every good citizen to pay his taxes, for it is in that way government is supported. Why are taxes assessed unless they are collected? Depend upon it I shall proceed to collect agreeably to law, so govern yourselves accordingly.

> "John Spencer
> "Sh'ff and Collector, D. C.

"Nov. 20, 1828.

"N.B. on Thursday, the 27th inst. A. St. Clair and Geo. H. Dunn, Esqrs. depart for Indianapolis; I wish as many as can pay to do so, to enable me to forward as much as possible, to save the twenty-one per cent. that will be charged against me after the 8th of December next.

"J.S."

The first autumn I passed in America, I was surprised to find a great and very oppressive return of heat, accompanied with a heavy mistiness in the air, long after the summer heats were over; when this state of the atmosphere comes on, they say, "we have got to the Indian summer." On desiring to have this phrase explained, I was told that the phenomenon described as the *Indian summer* was occasioned by the Indians setting fire to the woods, which spread heat and smoke to a great distance; but I afterwards met with the following explanation, which appears to me much more reasonable. "The Indian summer is so called because, at the particular period of the year in which it obtains, the Indians break up their village communities, and go to the interior to prepare for their winter hunting. This season seems to mark a dividing line, between the heat of summer, and the cold of winter, and is from its mildness, suited to these migrations. The cause of this heat is the slow combustion of the leaves and other vegetable matter of the boundless and interminable forests. Those who at this season of the year have penetrated these forests, know all about it. To the feet the heat is quite sensible, whilst the ascending vapour warms every thing it embraces, and spreading out into the wide atmosphere, fills the circuit of the heavens with its peculiar heat and smokiness."

This unnatural heat sufficiently accounts for the sickliness of the American autumn. The effect of it is extremely distressing to the nerves, even when the general health continues good; to me, it was infinitely more disagreeable than the glowing heat of the dog-days.

*   *   *   *   *

CHAPTER XXIX

Education . . .

* * * * *

Much is said about the universal diffusion of education in America, and a vast deal of genuine admiration is felt and expressed at the progress of mind throughout the Union. They believe themselves in all sincerity to have surpassed, to be surpassing, and to be about to surpass, the whole earth in the intellectual race. I am aware that not a single word can be said, hinting a different opinion, which will not bring down a transatlantic anathema on my head; yet the subject is too interesting to be omitted. Before I left England I remember listening, with much admiration, to an eloquent friend, who deprecated our system of public education, as confining the various and excursive faculties of our children to one beaten path, paying little or no attention to the peculiar powers of the individual.

This objection is extremely plausible, but doubts of its intrinsic value must, I think, occur to every one who has marked the result of a different system throughout the United States.

From every enquiry, I could make, and I took much pains to obtain accurate information, it appeared that much is attempted, but very little beyond reading, writing, and bookkeeping, is thoroughly acquired. Were we to read a prospectus of the system pursued in any of our public schools, and that of a first-rate seminary in America, we should be struck by the confined scholastic routine of the former, when compared to the varied and expansive scope of the latter; but let the examination go a little farther, and I believe it will be found that the old fashioned school discipline of England has produced something higher, and deeper too, than that which roars so loud, and thunders in the index.

They will not afford to let their young men study till two or three and twenty, and it is therefore declared, ex *cathedrâ Americanâ*, to be unnecessary. At sixteen, often much earlier, education ends, and money-making begins; the idea that more learning is necessary than can be acquired by that time, is generally ridiculed as obsolete monkish bigotry; added to which, if the seniors willed a more prolonged discipline, the juniors would refuse submission. When the money-getting begins, leisure ceases, and all of lore which can be acquired afterwards, is picked up from novels, magazines, and newspapers.

At what time can the taste be formed? How can a correct and polished style, even of speaking, be acquired? or when can the fruit of the two thousand years of past thinking be added to the native growth of American intellect? These are the tools, if I may so express myself, which our elaborate system of school discipline puts into the hands of our scholars; possessed of these, they may use them in whatever direction they please afterwards, they can never be an incumbrance.

No people appear more anxious to excite admiration and receive applause than the Americans, yet none take so little trouble, or make so few sacrifices to obtain it. This may answer among themselves, but it will not, with the rest of the world; individual sacrifices must be made, and national economy enlarged, before America can compete with the old world in taste, learning, and liberality.

The reception of General Lafayette is the one single instance in which the national pride has overcome the national thrift;* and this was clearly referable to the one single feeling of enthusiasm of which they appear capable, namely, the triumph of their successful struggle for national independence. But though this feeling will be universally acknowledged as a worthy and lawful source of triumph and of pride, it will not serve to trade upon for ever, as a fund of glory and high station among the nations. Their fathers were colonists; they fought stoutly,

*In 1824, Lafayette returned to the United States for a triumphal tour. His visit was celebrated extravagantly everywhere he went.

169

and became an independent people. Success and admiration, even the admiration of those whose yoke they had broken, cheered them while living, still sheds a glory round their remote and untitled sepulchres, and will illumine the page of their history for ever.

Their children inherit the independence; they inherit too the honour of being the sons of brave fathers; but this will not give them the reputation at which they aim, of being scholars and gentlemen, nor will it enable them to sit down for evermore to talk of their glory, while they drink mint julap and chew tobacco, swearing by the beard of Jupiter (or some other oath) that they are very graceful and agreeable, and, moreover, abusing every body who does not cry out Amen!

To doubt that talent and mental power of every kind, exist in America would be absurd; why should it not? But in taste and learning they are woefully deficient; and it is this which renders them incapable of graduating a scale by which to measure themselves. Hence arises that overweening complacency and self-esteem, both national and individual, which at once renders them so extremely obnoxious to ridicule, and so peculiarly restive under it.

If they will scorn the process by which other nations have become what they avowedly intend to be, they must rest satisfied with the praise and admiration they receive from each other; and turning a deaf ear to the criticisms of the old world, consent to be their "own prodigious great reward."

*   *   *   *   *

170

CHAPTER XXX

Journey to New York . . .
Delaware River . . . Stage-coach . . .
City of New York . . .
Collegiate Institute for Young Ladies . . .
Public Garden . . . Churches . . .
Morris Canal . . . Carriages . . .

At length, spite of the lingering pace necessarily attending consultations, and arrangements across the Atlantic, our plans were finally settled; the coming spring was to shew us New York, and Niagara, and the early summer was to convey us home.

No sooner did the letter arrive which decided this, than we began our preparations for departure. We took our last voyage on the Potomac, we bade a last farewell to Virginia, and gave a last day to some of our kind friends near Washington.

The spring, though slow and backward, was sufficiently advanced to render the journey pleasant; and though the road from Washington to Baltimore was less brilliant in foliage than when I had seen it before, it still had much of beauty. The azaleas were in full bloom, and the delicate yellow blossom of the sassafras almost rivalled its fruit in beauty.

At Baltimore we again embarked on a gigantic steam-boat, and reached Philadelphia in the middle of the night. Here we changed our boat, and found time, before starting in the morning, to take a last look at the Doric and Corinthian porticos of the two celebrated temples dedicated to Mammon.

The Delaware river, above Philadelphia, still flows through a landscape too level for beauty, but it is rendered interesting by a succession of gentlemen's seats, which, if less elaborately fin-

171

ished in architecture, and garden grounds, than the lovely villas on the Thames, are still beautiful objects to gaze upon as you float rapidly past on the broad silvery stream that washes their lawns. They present a picture of wealth and enjoyment that accords well with the noble city to which they are an appendage. One mansion arrested our attention, not only from its being more than usually large and splendid, but from its having the monument which marked the family resting-place, rearing itself in all the gloomy grandeur of black and white marble, exactly opposite the door of entrance.

*   *   *   *   *

At Trenton, the capital of New Jersey, we left our smoothly-gliding comfortable boat for the most detestable stage-coach that ever Christian built to dislocate the joints of his fellow men. Ten of these torturing machines were crammed full of the passengers who left the boat with us. The change in our movement was not more remarkable than that which took place in the tempers and countenances of our fellow-travellers. Gentlemen who had lounged on sofas, and balanced themselves in chairs, all the way from Philadelphia, with all the conscious fascinations of stiff stays and neck-cloths, which, while doing to death the rash beauties who ventured to gaze, seemed but a whalebone panoply to guard the wearer, these pretty youths so guarded from without, so sweetly at peace within, now crushed beneath their armour, looked more like victims on the wheel, than dandies armed for conquest; their whalebones seemed to enter into their souls, and every face grew grim and scowling. The pretty ladies too, with their expansive bonnets, any one of which might handsomely have filled the space allotted to three,—how sad the change! I almost fancied they must have been of the race of Undine, and that it was only when they heard the splashing of water that they could smile. As, I looked into the altered eyes of my companions, I was tempted to ask, "Look I as cross as you?" Indeed, I believe that, if possible, I looked crosser still, for the roads and the vehicle together were quite too much for my philosophy.

At length, however, we found ourselves alive on board the boat which was to convey us down the Raraton River to New York.

We fully intended to have gone to bed, to heal our bones, on entering the steam-boat, but the sight of a table neatly spread, determined us to go to dinner instead. Sin and shame would it have been, indeed, to have closed our eyes upon the scene which soon opened before us. I have never seen the bay of Naples, I can therefore make no comparison, but my imagination is incapable of conceiving any thing of the kind more beautiful than the harbour of New York. Various and lovely are the objects which meet the eye on every side, but the naming them would only be to give a list of words, without conveying the faintest idea of the scene.

* * * * *

We seemed to enter the harbour of New York upon waves of liquid gold, and as we darted past the green isles which rise from its bosom, like guardian centinels of the fair city, the setting sun stretched his horizontal beams farther and farther at each moment, as if to point out to us some new glory in the landscape.

New York, indeed, appeared to us, even when we saw it by a soberer light, a lovely and noble city. To us who had been so long travelling through half-cleared forests, and sojourning among an "I'm-as-good-as-you" population, it seemed, perhaps, more beautiful, more splendid, and more refined than it might have done, had we arrived there directly from London; but making every allowance for this, I must still declare that I think New York one of the finest cities I ever saw, and as much superior to every other in the Union, (Philadelphia not excepted,) as London to Liverpool, or Paris to Rouen. Its advantages of position are, perhaps, unequalled any where. Situated on an island, which I think it will one day cover, it rises, like Venice, from the sea, and like that fairest of cities in the days of her glory, receives into its lap tribute of all the riches of the earth.

The southern point of Manhatten Island divides the waters of the harbour into the north and east rivers; on this point stands the city of New York, extending from river to river, and running northward to the extent of three or four miles. I think it covers nearly as much ground as Paris, but is much less thickly peopled. The extreme point is fortified towards the sea by a battery, and forms an admirable point of defence; but in

173

these piping days of peace, it is converted into a public prome-
nade, and one more beautiful, I should suppose, no city could
boast. From hence commences the splendid Broadway, as the
fine avenue is called, which runs through the whole city. This
noble street may vie with any I ever saw, for its length and
breadth, its handsome shops, neat awnings, excellent *trottoir*,
and well-dressed pedestrians. It has not the crowded glitter of
Bond street equipages, nor the gorgeous fronted palaces of
Regent-street; but it is magnificent in its extent, and ornamented by several handsome buildings, some of them surrounded by grass and trees. The Park, in which stands the noble
city-hall, is a very fine area. I never found that the most graphic
description of a city could give me any feeling of being there;
and even if others have the power, I am very sure I have not, of
setting churches and squares, and long drawn streets, before
the mind's eye. I will not, therefore, attempt a detailed description of this great metropolis of the new world, but will only say
that during the seven weeks we stayed there, we always found
something new to see and to admire; and were it not so very far
from all the old-world things which cling about the heart of an
European, I should say that I never saw a city more desirable as
a residence.

The dwelling houses of the higher classes are extremely
handsome, and very richly furnished. Silk or satin furniture is
as often, or oftener, seen than chintz; the mirrors are as handsome as in London; the cheffoniers, slabs, and marble tables as
elegant; and in addition, they have all the pretty tasteful decoration of French porcelaine, and or-molu in much greater abundance, because at a much cheaper rate. Every part of their
houses is well carpeted, and the exterior finishing, such as steps,
railings, and door-frames, are very superior. Almost every house
has handsome green blinds on the outside; balconies are not
very general, nor do the houses display, externally, so many
flowers as those of Paris and London; but I saw many rooms decorated within, exactly like those of an European *petite maîtresse*.
Little tables, looking and smelling like flower beds, portfolios,
nick-nacks, bronzes, busts, cameos, and alabaster vases, illus-
trated copies of lady-like rhymes bound in silk, and, in short, all
the pretty coxcomalities of the drawing-room scattered about
with the same profuse and studied negligence as with us.

174

Hudson Square and its neighbourhood is, I believe, the most fashionable part of the town; the square is beautiful, excellently well planted with a great variety of trees, and only wanting our frequent and careful mowing to make it equal to any square in London. The iron railing which surrounds this enclosure is as high and as handsome as that of the Tuilleries, and it will give some idea of the care bestowed on its decoration, to know that the gravel for the walks was conveyed by barges from Boston, not as ballast, but as freight.

The great defect in the houses is their extreme uniformity—when you have seen one, you have seen all. Neither do I quite like the arrangement of the rooms. In nearly all the houses the dining and drawing-rooms are on the same floor, with ample folding doors between them; when thrown together they certainly make a very noble apartment; but no doors can be barrier sufficient between dining and drawing-rooms. Mixed dinner parties of ladies and gentlemen, however, are very rare, which is a great defect in the society; not only as depriving them of the most social and hospitable manner of meeting, but as leading to frequent dinner parties of gentlemen without ladies, which certainly does not conduce to refinement.

The evening parties, excepting such as are expressly for young people, are chiefly conversational; we were too late in the season for large parties, but we saw enough to convince us that there is society to be met with in New York, which would be deemed delightful any where. Cards are very seldom used; and music, from their having very little professional aid at their parties, is seldom, I believe, as good as what is heard at private concerts in London.

*   *   *   *   *

Whilst at New York, the prospectus of a fashionable boarding-school was presented to me. I made some extracts from it, as a specimen of the enlarged scale of instruction proposed for young females.

Brooklyn Collegiate Institute
for Young Ladies,
Brooklyn Heights, opposite the City of
New York.

175

JUNIOR DEPARTMENT.

Sixth Class.

Latin Grammar, Liber Primus; Jacob's Latin Reader, (first part); Modern Geography; Intellectual and Practical Arithmetic finished; Dr. Barber's Grammar of Elocution; Writing, Spelling, Composition, and Vocal Music.

Fifth Class.

Jacob's Latin Reader, (second part); Roman Antiquities, Sallust; Clark's Introduction to the Making of Latin; Ancient and Sacred Geography; Studies of Poetry; Short Treatise on Rhetoric; Map Drawing, Composition, Spelling, and Vocal Music.

Fourth Class.

Cæsar's Commentaries; first five books of Virgil's Æneid; Mythology; Watts on the Mind; Political Geography, (Woodbridge's large work); Natural History; Treatise on the Globes; Ancient History; Studies of Poetry concluded; English Grammar, Composition, Spelling, and Vocal Music.

SENIOR DEPARTMENT

Third Class.

Virgil, (finished); Cicero's Select Orations; Modern History; Plane Geometry; Moral Philosophy; Critical Reading of Young's Poems; Perspective Drawing; Rhetoric; Logic, Composition, and Vocal Music.

Second Class.

Livy; Horace, (Odes); Natural Theology; small Compend of Ecclesiastical History; Female Biography; Algebra; Natural Philosophy, (Mechanics, Hydrostatics, Pneumatics, and Acoustics); Intellectual Philosophy; Evidences of Christianity; Composition, and Vocal Music.

First Class.

Horace, (finished); Tacitus; Natural Philosophy, (Electricity, Optics, Magnetism, Galvanism); Astronomy, Chemistry, Mineralogy, and Geology; Compend of Political Economy; Composition, and Vocal Music.

The French, Spanish, Italian, or Greek languages may be attended to, if required, at any time.

The Exchange is very handsome, and ranks about midway between the heavy gloom that hangs over our London merchants, and the light and lofty elegance which decorates the Bourse at Paris. The churches are plain, but very neat, and kept in perfect repair within and without; but I saw none which had the least pretension to splendour; the Catholic cathedral at Baltimore is the only church in America which has.

At New York, as every where else, they shew within, during the time of service, like beds of tulips, so gay, so bright, so beautiful, are the long rows of French bonnets and pretty faces; rows but rarely broken by the unripened heads of the male population; the proportion is about the same as I have remarked elsewhere. Excepting at New York, I never saw the other side of the picture, but there I did. On the opposite side of the North River, about three miles higher up, is a place called Hoboken. A gentleman who possessed a handsome mansion and grounds there, also possessed the right of ferry, and to render this productive, he has restricted his pleasure grounds to a few beautiful acres, laying out the remainder simply and tastefully as a public walk. It is hardly possible to imagine one of greater attraction; a broad belt of light underwood and flowering shrubs, studded at intervals with lofty forest trees, runs for two miles along a cliff which overhangs the matchless Hudson; sometimes it feathers the rocks down to its very margin, and at others leaves a pebbly shore, just rude enough to break the gentle waves, and make a music which mimics softly the loud chorus of the ocean.— Through this beautiful little wood, a broad well-gravelled terrace is led by every point which can exhibit the scenery to advantage; narrower and wilder paths diverge at intervals, some into the deeper shadow of the woods, and some shelving gradually to the pretty coves below.

The price of entrance to this little Eden, is the six cents you pay at the ferry. We went there on a bright Sunday afternoon, expressly to see the humours of the place. Many thousand persons were scattered through the grounds; of these we ascertained, by repeatedly counting, that nineteen-twentieths were men. The ladies were at church. Often as the subject has pressed

177

upon my mind, I think I never so strongly felt the conviction that the Sabbath-day, the holy day, the day on which alone the great majority of the Christian world can spend their hours as they please, is ill passed (if passed entirely) within brick walls, listening to an earth-born preacher, charm he never so wisely.

> *"Oh! how can they renounce the boundless store*
> *of charms, which Nature to her vot'ries yields!*
> *The warbling woodland, the resounding shore,*
> *The pomp of groves, and garniture of fields,*
> *All that the genial ray of morning gilds,*
> *And all that echoes to the song of even,*
> *All that the mountain's sheltering bosom yields,*
> *And all the dread magnificence of heaven;*
> *Oh! how can they renounce, and hope to be forgiven!"*

How is it that the men of America, who are reckoned good husbands and good fathers, while they themselves enjoy sufficient freedom of spirit to permit their walking forth into the temple of the living God, can leave those they love best on earth, bound in the iron chains of a most tyrannical fanaticism? How can they breathe the balmy air, and not think of the tainted atmosphere so heavily weighing upon breasts still dearer than their own? How can they gaze upon the blossoms of the spring, and not remember the fairer cheeks of their young daughters, waxing pale, as they sit for long sultry hours, immured with hundreds of fellow victims, listening to the roaring vanities of a preacher canonized by a college of old women? They cannot think it needful to salvation, or they would not withdraw themselves. Wherefore is it? Do they fear these self-elected, self-ordained priests, and offer up their wives and daughters to propitiate them? Or do they deem their hebdomadal freedom more complete, because their wives and daughters are shut up four or five times in the day at church or chapel? It is true, that at Hoboken, as every where else, there are *reposoires*, which, as you pass them, blast the sense for a moment, by reeking forth the fumes of whiskey and tobacco, and it may be that these cannot be entered with a wife or daughter. The proprietor of the grounds, however, has contrived with great taste to render these abominations not unpleasing to the eye; there is one in particular, which has quite the air of a Grecian temple, and did they drink wine instead of whiskey, it might be inscribed to Bacchus; but in this particular, as in many others, the ancient and modern Republics differ.

It is impossible not to feel, after passing one Sunday in the churches and chapels of New York, and the next in the gardens of Hoboken, that the thousands of well-dressed men you see enjoying themselves at the latter, have made over the thousands of well-dressed women you saw exhibited at the former, into the hands of the priests, at least, for the day. The American people arrogate to themselves a character of superior morality and religion, but this division of their hours of leisure does not give me a favourable idea of either.

* * * * *

I can imagine nothing more perfect than the interior of the public institutions of New York. There is a practical good sense in all their arrangements that must strike foreigners very forcibly. The Asylum for the Destitute offers a hint worth taking. It is dedicated to the reformation of youthful offenders of both sexes, and it is as admirable in the details of its management, as in its object. Every part of the institution is deeply interesting; but there is a difference very remarkable between the boys and the girls. The boys are, I think, the finest set of lads I ever saw brought together; bright looking, gay, active, and full of intelligence. The girls are exactly the reverse; heavy, listless, indifferent, and melancholy. In conversing with the gentleman who is the general superintendant of the establishment, I made the remark to him, and he told me, that the reality corresponded with the appearance. All of them had been detected in some act of dishonesty; but the boys, when removed from the evil influence which had led them so to use their ingenuity, rose like a spring when a pressure is withdrawn; and feeling themselves once more safe from danger, and from shame, hope and cheerfulness animated every countenance. But the poor girls, on the contrary, can hardly look up again. They are as different as an oak and a lily after a storm. The one, when the fresh breeze blows over it, shakes the raindrops from its crest, and only looks the brighter; the other, its silken leaves once soiled, shrinks from the eye, and is levelled to the earth for ever.

179

+   +   +   +   +

We spent a delightful day in New Jersey, in visiting, with a most agreeable party, the inclined planes, which are used instead of locks on the Morris canal.

This is a very interesting work; it is one among a thousand which prove the people of America to be the most enterprising in the world. I was informed that this important canal, which connects the waters of the Hudson and the Delaware, is a hundred miles long, and in this distance overcomes a variation of level amounting to sixteen hundred feet. Of this, fourteen hundred are achieved by inclined planes. The planes average about sixty feet of perpendicular lift each, and are to support about forty tons. The time consumed in passing them is twelve minutes for one hundred feet of perpendicular rise. The expense is less than a third of what locks would be for surmounting the same rise. If we set about any more canals, this may be worth attending to.

This Morris canal is certainly an extraordinary work; it not only varies its level sixteen hundred feet, but at one point runs along the side of a mountain at thirty feet above the tops of the highest buildings in the town of Paterson, below; at another it crosses the falls of the Passaic in a stone aqueduct sixty feet above the water in the river. This noble work, in a great degree, owes its existence to the patriotic and scientific energy of Mr. Cadwallader Colden.

There is no point in the national character of the Americans which commands so much respect as the boldness and energy with which public works are undertaken and carried through. Nothing stops them if a profitable result can be fairly hoped for. It is this which has made cities spring up amidst the forests with such inconceivable rapidity; and could they once be thoroughly persuaded that any point of the ocean had a hoard of dollars beneath it, I have not the slightest doubt that in about eighteen months we should see a snug covered rail-road leading direct to the spot.

+   +   +   +   +

I was told at New York, that in many parts of the state it was usual to pay the service of the Presbyterian ministers in the following manner. Once a year a day is fixed on which some member of every family in a congregation meet at their minister's house in the afternoon. They each bring an offering (according to their means) of articles necessary for housekeeping. The poorer members leave their contributions in a large basket, placed for the purpose, close to the door of entrance. Those of more importance, and more calculated to do honour to the piety of the donors, are carried into the room where the company is assembled. Sugar, coffee, tea, cheese, barrels of flour, pieces of Irish linen, sets of china and of glass, were among the articles mentioned to me as usually making parts of these offerings. After the party is assembled, and the business of giving and receiving is dispatched, tea, coffee, and cakes are handed round; but these are not furnished at any expense either of trouble or money to the minister, for selected ladies of the congregation take the whole arrangement upon themselves. These meetings are called spinning visits.

Another New York custom, which does not seem to have so reasonable a cause, is the changing house once a year. On the 1st of May the city of New York has the appearance of sending off a population flying from the plague, or of a town which had surrendered on condition of carrying away all their goods and chattels. Rich furniture and ragged furniture, carts, waggons, and drays, ropes, canvas, and straw, packers, porters, and draymen, white, yellow, and black, occupy the streets from east to west, from north to south, on this day. Every one I spoke to on the subject complained of this custom as most annoying, but all assured me it was unavoidable, if you inhabit a rented house. More than one of my New York friends have built or bought houses solely to avoid this annual inconvenience.

There are a great number of negroes in New York, all free; their emancipation having been completed in 1827. Not even in Philadelphia, where the anti-slavery opinions have been the most active and violent, do the blacks appear to wear an air of so much consequence as they do at New York. They have several chapels, in which negro ministers officiate; and a theatre in which none but negroes perform. At this theatre a gallery is appropriated to such whites as choose to visit it; and here only are they permitted to sit; following in this, with nice etiquette, and equal justice, the arrangement of the white theatres, in all of which is a gallery appropriated solely to the use of the blacks. I have often, particularly on a Sunday, met groups of negroes, elegantly dressed; and have been sometimes amused by observing the very superior air of gallantry assumed by the men, when in attendance on their *belles*, to that of the whites in similar circumstances. On one occasion we met in Broadway a young negress in the extreme of the fashion, and accompanied by a black beau, whose toilet was equally studied; eye-glass, guard-chain, nothing was omitted; he walked beside his sable goddess uncovered, and with an air of the most tender devotion.

*   *   *   *   *

Most of the houses in New York are painted on the outside, but in a manner carefully to avoid disfiguring the material which it preserves: on the contrary, nothing can be neater. They are now using a great deal of beautiful stone called Jersey free-stone; it is of a warm rich brown, and extremely ornamental to the city wherever it has been employed. They have also a grey granite of great beauty. The trottoir paving in most of the streets is extremely good, being of large flag stones, very superior to the bricks of Philadelphia.

At night the shops, which are open till very late, are brilliantly illuminated with gas, and all the population seem as much alive as in London or Paris. This makes the solemn stillness of the evening hours in Philadelphia still more remarkable.

There are a few trees in different parts of the city, and I observed many young ones planted, and guarded with much care; were they more abundant it would be extremely agreeable, for the reflected light of their fierce summer sheds intolerable day.

Ice is in profuse abundance; I do not imagine that there is a house in the city without the luxury of a piece of ice to cool the water, and harden the butter.

The hackney coaches are the best in the world, but abominably dear, and it is necessary to be on the *qui vive* in making your bargain with the driver; if you do not, he has the power of charging immoderately. On my first experiment I neglected this, and was asked two dollars and a half for an excursion of twenty minutes. When I referred to the waiter of the hotel, he asked if I had made a bargain. "No." "Then I expect" (with the usual look of triumph) "that the Yankee has been too smart for you."

The private carriages of New York are infinitely handsomer and better appointed than any I saw elsewhere; the want of smart liveries destroys much of the gay effect, but, on the whole, a New York summer equipage, with the pretty women and beautiful children it contains, look extremely well in Broadway, and would not be much amiss any where.

The luxury of the New York aristocracy is not confined to the city; hardly an acre of Manhatten Island but shews some pretty villa or stately mansion. The most chosen of these are on the north and east rivers, to whose margins their lawns descend. Among these, perhaps, the loveliest is one situated in the beautiful village of Bloomingdale; here, within the space of sixteen acres, almost every variety of garden scenery may be found. To describe all its diversity of hill and dale, of wood and lawn, of rock and river, would be in vain; nor can I convey an idea of it by comparison, for I never saw any thing like it. How far the elegant hospitality which reigns there may influence my impressions, I know not; but, assuredly, no spot I have ever seen dwells more freshly on my memory, nor did I ever find myself in a circle more calculated to give delight in meeting, and regret a parting, than that of Woodlawn.

* * * * *

CHAPTER XXXI

(omitted)

CHAPTER XXXII

Journey to Niagara . . . Hudson . . .
West Point . . . Hyde Park . . . Albany . . .
Yankees . . . Trenton Falls . . . Rochester . . .
Genesee Falls . . . Lockport . . .

How quickly weeks glide away in such a city as New York, especially when you reckon among your friends some of the most agreeable people in either hemisphere. But we had still a long journey before us, and one of the wonders of the world was to be seen.

On the 30th of May we set off for Niagara. I had heard so much of the surpassing beauty of the North River, that I expected to be disappointed, and to find reality flat after description. But it is not in the power of man to paint with a strength exceeding that of nature, in such scenes as the Hudson presents. Every mile shews some new and startling effect of the combination of rocks, trees, and water; there is not interval of flat or insipid scenery, from the moment you enter upon the river at New York, to that of quitting it at Albany, a distance of 180 miles.

For the first twenty miles, the shore of New Jersey on the left, offers almost a continued wall of trap rock, which from its perpendicular form, and lineal fissures, is called the Palisades. This wall sometimes rises to the height of a hundred and fifty feet, and sometimes sinks down to twenty. Here and there, a watercourse breaks its uniformity; and every where the brightest foliage, in all the splendour of the climate and the season, fringed and checquered the dark barrier. On the opposite shore,

185

Manhatten Island, with its leafy coronet gemmed with villas, forms a lovely contrast to these rocky heights.

After passing Manhatten Island the eastern shore gradually assumes a wild and rocky character, but ever varying; woods, lawns, pastures, and towering cliffs all meet the eye in quick succession, as the giant steam-boat cleaves its swift passage up the stream.

*   *   *   *   *

About forty miles from New York you enter upon the Highlands, as a series of mountains which then flank the river on both sides, are called. The beauty of this scenery can only be conceived when it is seen. One might fancy that these capricious masses, with all their countless varieties of light and shade, were thrown together to shew how passing lovely rocks, and woods, and water could be. Sometimes a lofty peak shoots suddenly up into the heavens, shewing in bold relief against the sky; and then a deep ravine sinks in solemn shadow, and draws the imagination into its leafy recesses. For several miles the river appears to form a succession of lakes; you are often enclosed on all sides by rocks rising directly from the very edge of the stream, and then you turn a point, the river widens, and again woods, lawns, and villages are reflected on its bosom.

The state prison of Sing Sing is upon the edge of the water, and has no picturesque effect to atone for the painful images it suggests; the "Sleepy Hollow" of Washington Irving, just above it, restores the imagination to a better tone.

West Point, the military academy of the United States, is fifty miles from New York. The scenery around it is magnificent, and though the buildings of the establishment are constructed with the handsome and unpicturesque regularity which marks the work of governments, they are so nobly placed, and so embosomed in woods, that they look beautiful. The lengthened notes of a French horn, which I presume was attending some of their military manœuvres, sounded with deep and solemn sweetness as we passed.

About thirty miles further is Hyde Park, the magnificent seat of Dr. Hosack; here the misty summit of the distant Kaatskill begins to form the outline of the landscape; it is hardly possible to imagine any thing more beautiful than this place. We passed a day there with great enjoyment; and the following morning set forward again in one of those grand floating hotels called steam-boats. Either on this day, or the one before, we had two hundred cabin passengers on board, and they all sat down together to a table spread abundantly, and with considerable elegance. A continual succession of gentlemen's seats, many of them extremely handsome, borders the river to Albany. We arrived there late in the evening, but had no difficulty in finding excellent accommodation.

Albany is the state capital of New York, and has some very handsome public buildings; there are also some curious relics of the old Dutch inhabitants.

The first sixteen miles from Albany we travelled in a stage, to avoid a multitude of locks at the entrance of the Erie canal; but at Scenectedy we got on board one of the canal packet-boats for Utica.

With a very delightful party, of one's own choosing, fine temperate weather, and a strong breeze to chase the mosquitos, this mode of travelling might be very agreeable, but I can hardly imagine any motive of convenience powerful enough to induce me again to imprison myself in a canal boat under ordinary circumstances. The accommodations being greatly restricted, every body, from the moment of entering the boat, acts upon a system of unshrinking egotism. The library of a dozen books, the backgammon board, the tiny berths, the shady side of the cabin, are all jostled for in a manner to make one greatly envy the power of the snail; at the moment I would willingly have given up some of my human dignity for the privilege of creeping into a shell of my own. To any one who has been accustomed in travelling, to be addressed with, "Do sit here, you will find it more comfortable," the "You must go there, I made for this place first," sounds very unmusical.

There is a great quietness about the women of America, (I speak of the exterior manner of persons casually met,) but somehow or other, I should never call it gentleness. In such trying moments as that of *fixing* themselves on board a packet-boat, the men are prompt, determined, and will compromise any body's convenience, except their own. The women are doggedly stedfast in their will, and till matters are settled, look like hedgehogs, with every quill raised, and firmly set, as if to forbid the approach of any one who might wish to rub them down. In circumstances where an English woman would look proud, and a French woman *nonchalante,* an American lady looks grim; even the youngest and the prettiest can set their lips, and knit their brows, and look as hard, and unsocial as their grandmothers.

Though not in the Yankee or New England country, we were bordering upon it sufficiently to meet in the stages and boats many delightful specimens of this most peculiar race. I like them extremely well, but I would not wish to have any business transactions with them, if I could avoid it, lest, to use their own phrase, "they should be too smart for me."

It is by no means rare to meet elsewhere, in this working-day world of our's, people who push acuteness to the verge of honesty, and sometimes, perhaps, a little bit beyond; but, I believe, the Yankee is the only one who will be found to boast of doing so. It is by no means easy to give a clear and just idea of a Yankee; if you hear his character from a Virginian, you will believe him a devil; if you listen to it from himself, you might fancy him a god—though a tricky one; Mercury turned righteous and notable. . . . In acuteness, cautiousness, industry, and perseverance, he resembles the Scotch; in habits of frugal neatness, he resembles the Dutch; in love of lucre he doth greatly resemble the sons of Abraham; but in frank admission, and superlative admiration of all his own peculiarities, he is like nothing on earth but himself.

The Quakers have been celebrated for the pertinacity with which they avoid giving a direct answer, but what Quaker could ever vie with a Yankee in this sort of fencing? Nothing, in fact, can equal their skill in evading a question, excepting that with which they set about asking one. I am afraid that in repeating a conversation which I overheard on board the Erie canal boat, I shall spoil it, by forgetting some of the little delicate doublings which delighted me—yet I wrote it down immediately. Both parties were Yankees, but strangers to each other; one of them having, by gentle degrees, made himself pretty well acquainted with the point from which every one on board had started, and that for which he was bound, at last attacked his brother Reynard thus:—

Well, now, which way may you be traveling?"

"I expect this canal runs pretty nearly west."

"Are you going far with it?"

"Well, now, I don't rightly know how many miles it may be."

"I expect you'll be from New York?"

"Sure enough I have been at New York, often and often."

"I calculate, then, 'tis not there as you stop?"

"Business must be minded, in stopping and in stirring."

"You may say that. Well, I look then you'll be making for the Springs?"

"Folks say as all the world is making for the Springs, and I expect a good sight of them is."

"Do you calculate upon stopping long when you get to your journey's end?"

" 'Tis my business must settle that, I expect."

"I guess that's true, too; but you'll be for making pleasure a business for once, I calculate?"

"My business don't often lie in that line."

"Then, may be, it is not the Springs as takes you this line?"

"The Springs is a right elegant place, I reckon."

"It is your health, I calculate, as makes you break your good rules?"

"My health don't trouble me much, I guess."

"No? Why that's well. How is the markets, sir? Are bread stuffs up?"

"I a'nt just capable to say."

"A deal of money's made by just looking after the article at the fountain's head."

"You may say that."

"Do you look to be making great dealings in produce up the country?"

"Why that, I expect, is difficult to know."

"I calculate you'll find the markets changeable these times?"

"No markets ben't very often without changing."

"Why, that's right down true. What may be your biggest article of produce?"

"I calculate, generally, that's the biggest, as I makes most by."

"You may say that. But what do you chiefly call your most particular branch?"

"Why, that's what I can't justly say."

And so they went on, without advancing or giving an inch, 'till I was weary of listening; but I left them still at it, when I stepped out to resume my station on a trunk at the bow of the boat, where I scribbled in my note-book, this specimen of Yankee conversation.

+ + + + +

The Erie canal has cut through much solid rock, and we often passed between magnificent cliffs. The little falls of the Mohawk form a lovely scene; the rocks over which the river runs are most fantastic in form. The fall continues nearly a mile, and a beautiful village, called the Little Falls, overhangs it. As many locks occur at this point, we quitted the boat, that we might the better enjoy the scenery, which is of the wildest description. Several other passengers did so likewise, and I was much amused by one of our Yankees, who very civilly accompanied our party, pointing out to me the wild state of the country, and apologizing for it, by saying, that the property all round thereabouts had been owned by an Englishman; "and you'll excuse me, ma'am, but when the English gets a spot of wild ground like this here, they have no notions about it like us; but the Englishman have sold it, and if you was to see it five years hence, you would not know it again; I'll engage there will be by that, half a score elegant factories—'tis a true shame to let such a privilege of water lie idle."

We reached Utica at twelve o'clock the following day, pretty well fagged by the sun by day, and a crowded cabin by night; lemon-juice and iced-water (without sugar) kept us alive. But for this delightful recipe, feather fans, and eau de Cologne, I think we should have failed altogether; the thermometer stood at 90°.

At two, we set off in a very pleasant airy carriage for Trenton Falls, a delightful drive of fourteen miles. These falls have become within the last few years only second in fame to Niagara. The West Canada Creek, which in the map shews but as a paltry stream, has found its way through three miles of rock, which, at many points, is 150 feet high. A forest of enormous cedars is on their summit; and many of that beautiful species of white cedar which droops its branches like the weeping-willow,

190

grow in the clefts of the rock, and in some places almost dip their dark foliage in the torrent. The rock is of a dark grey limestone, and often presents a wall of unbroken surface. Near the hotel a flight of very alarming steps leads down to the bed of the stream, and on reaching it you find yourself enclosed in a deep abyss of solid rock, with no visible opening but that above your head. The torrent dashes by with inconceivable rapidity; its colour is black as night, and the dark ledge of rock on which you stand, is so treacherously level with it, that nothing warns you of danger. Within the last three years two young people, though surrounded by their friends, have stepped an inch too far, and disappeared from among them, as if by magic, never to revisit earth again. This broad flat ledge reaches but a short distance, and then the perpendicular wall appears to stop your farther progress; but there is a spirit of defiance in the mind of man; he will not be stayed either by rocks or waves. By the aid of gunpowder a sufficient quantity of the rock has been removed to afford a fearful footing round a point, which, when doubled, discloses a world of cataracts, all leaping forward together in most magnificent confusion. I suffered considerably before I reached the spot where this grand scene is visible; a chain firmly fastened to the rock serves to hang by, as you creep along the giddy verge, and this enabled me to proceed so far; but here the chain failed, and my courage with it, though the rest of the party continued for some way farther, and reported largely of still increasing sublimity. But my knees tottered, and my head swam, so while the rest crept onward, I sat down to wait their return on the floor of rock which had received us on quitting the steps.

A hundred and fifty feet of bare black rock on one side, an equal height covered with solemn cedars on the other, an unfathomed torrent roaring between them, the fresh remembrance of the ghastly legend belonging to the spot, and the idea of my children clinging to the dizzy path I had left, was altogether sombre enough; but I had not sat long before a tremendous burst of thunder shook the air; the deep chasm answered from either side, again, again, and again; I thought the rock I sat upon trembled: but the whole effect was so exceedingly grand, that I had no longer leisure to think of fear; my children immediately returned, and we enjoyed together the darkening shadows cast over the abyss, the rival clamour of the torrent and the storm, and that delightful exaltation of the spirits which sets danger at defiance. A few heavy rain drops alarmed us more than all the terrors of the spot, or rather, they recalled our senses, and we retreated by the fearful steps, reaching our hotel unwetted and unharmed. The next morning we were again early a-foot; the last night's storm had refreshed the air, and renewed our strength. We now took a different route, and instead of descending, as before, walked through the dark forest along the cliff, sufficiently near its edge to catch fearful glimpses of the scene below. After some time the path began to descend, and at length brought us to the Shantee. . . . This is by far the finest point of the falls. There is a little balcony in front of the Shantee, literally hanging over the tremendous whirlpool; though frail, it makes one fancy oneself in safety, and reminded me of the feeling with which I have stood on one side a high gate, watching a roaring bull on the other. The walls of this Shantee are literally covered with autographs, and I was inclined to join the laugh against the egotistical triffling, when one of the party discovered "Trollope, England," amidst the innumerable scrawls. The well known characters were hailed with such delight, that I think I shall never again laugh at any one for leaving their name where it is possible a friend may find it.

We returned to Utica to dinner, and found that we must either wait till the next day for the Rochester coach, or again submit to the packet-boat. Our impatience induced us to prefer the latter, not very wisely, I think, for every annoyance seemed to increase upon us. The Oneida and the Genesee country are both extremely beautiful, but had we not returned by another route we should have known little about it. From the canal nothing is seen to advantage, and very little is seen at all. My chief amusement, I think, was derived from names. One town, consisting of a whiskey store and a warehouse, is called Port Byron. At Rome, the first name I saw over a store was Remus, doing infinite honour, I thought, to the classic lore of his godfathers and godmothers; but it would be endless to record all the drolleries of this kind which we met with. We arrived at Rochester, a distance of a hundred and forty miles, on the second morning after leaving Utica, fully determined never to enter a canal boat again, at least, not in America.

Rochester is one of the most famous of the cities built on the Jack and Bean-stalk principle. There are many splendid edifices in wood; and certainly more houses, warehouses, factories, and steam-engines than ever were collected together in the same space of time; but I was told by a fellow-traveller that the stumps of the forest are still to be found firmly rooted in the cellars.

The fall of the Genesee is close to the town, and in the course of a few months will, perhaps, be in the middle of it. It is a noble sheet of water, of a hundred and sixty feet perpendicular fall; but I looked at it through the window of a factory, and as I did not like that, I was obligingly handed to the door-way of a sawing-mill; in short, "the great water privilege" has been so ingeniously taken advantage of, that no point can be found where its voice and its movement are not mixed and confounded with those of "the admirable machinery of this flourishing city."

          *   *   *   *   *

Our journey now became wilder every step, the unbroken forest often skirted the road for miles, and the sight of a loghut was an event. Yet the road was, for the greater part of the day, good, running along a natural ridge, just wide enough for it. This ridge is a very singular elevation, and, by all the enquiry I could make, the favourite theory concerning it is, that it was formerly the boundary of Lake Ontario, near which it passes. When this ridge ceased, the road ceased too, and for the rest of the way to Lockport, we were most painfully jumbled and jolted over logs and through bogs, till every joint was nearly dislocated.

Lockport is, beyond all comparison, the strangest looking place I ever beheld. As fast as half a dozen trees were cut down, a *factory* was raised up; stumps still contest the ground with pillars, and porticos are seen to struggle with rocks. It looks as if the demon of machinery, having invaded the peaceful realms of nature, had fixed on Lockport as the battleground on which they should strive for mastery. The fiend insists that the streams shall go one way, though the gentle mother had ever led their dancing steps another; nay, the very rocks must fall before him, and take what form he wills. The battle is lost and won. Nature is fairly routed and driven from the field, and the rattling, crackling, hissing, splitting demon has taken possession of Lockport for ever.

We slept there, dismally enough. I never felt more out of humour at what the Americans call improvement; it is, in truth, as it now stands, a most hideous place, and gladly did I leave it behind me.

*   *   *   *   *

CHAPTER XXXIII

Niagara . . . Arrival at Forsythes . . .
First sight of the Falls . . . Goat Island . . .
The Rapids . . . Buffalo . . . Lake Erie . . .
Canandaigua . . . State-coach adventures . . .

At length we reached Niagara. It was the brightest day that June could give; and almost any day would have seemed bright that brought me to the object which, for years, I had languished to look upon.

We did not hear the sound of the Falls till very near the hotel, which overhangs them; as you enter the door you see beyond the hall an open space, surrounded by galleries, one above another, and in an instant you feel that from thence the wonder is visible.

I trembled like a fool, and my girls clung to me, trembling too, I believe, but with faces beaming with delight. We encountered a waiter, who had a sympathy of some sort with us, for he would not let us run through the hall to the first gallery, but ushered us up stairs, and another instant placed us where, at one glance, I saw all I had wished for, hoped for, dreamed of.

It is not for me to attempt a description of Niagara; I feel I have no powers for it.

After one long, stedfast gaze, we quitted the gallery that we might approach still nearer, and in leaving the house had the good fortune to meet an English gentleman, who had been introduced to us at New York; he had preceded us by a few days, and knew exactly how and where to lead us. . . . I can only say that wonder, terror, and delight completely overwhelmed me. I wept with a strange mixture of pleasure and of pain, and certainly was, for some time, too violently affected in the *physique* to be capable of much pleasure; but when this emotion of the senses subsided, and I had recovered some degree of composure, my enjoyment was very great indeed.

*   *   *   *   *

Exactly at the Fall, it is the Fall and nothing else you have to look upon; there are not, as at Trenton, mighty rocks and towering forests, there is only the waterfall; but it is the fall of an ocean. . . .

The noise is greatly less than I expected; one can hear with perfect distinctness every thing said in an ordinary tone, when quite close to the cataract. The cause of this, I imagine to be, that it does not fall immediately among rocks, like the far noisier Potomac, but direct and unbroken, save by its own rebound. The colour of the water, before this rebound hides it in foam and mist, is of the brightest and most delicate green; the violence of the impulse sends it far over the precipice before it falls, and the effect of the ever varying light through its transparency is, I think, the loveliest thing I ever looked upon.

We descended to the edge of the gulf which receives the torrent, and thence looked at the horse-shoe fall in profile; it deems like awful daring to stand close beside it, and raise one's eyes to its immensity. I think the point the most utterly inconceivable to those who have not seen it, is the centre of the horse-shoe. The force of the torrent converges there, and as the heavy mass pours in, twisted, wreathed, and curled together, it gives an idea of irresistible power, such as no other object ever conveyed to me.

The following anecdote, which I had from good authority, may give some notion of this mighty power.

After the last American war, three of our ships, stationed on Lake Erie, were declared unfit for service, and condemned. Some of their officers obtained permission to send them over Niagara Falls. The first was torn to shivers by the rapids, and went over in fragments; the second filled with water before she reached the fall; but the third, which was in better condition, took the leap gallantly, and retained her form till it was hid in the cloud of mist below. A reward of ten dollars was offered for the largest fragment of wood that should be found from either wreck, five for the second, and so on. One morsel only was ever seen, and that about a foot in length, was mashed as by a vice, and its edges notched like the teeth of a saw. What had become of the immense quantity of wood which had been precipitated? What unknown whirlpool had engulphed it, so that, contrary to the very laws of nature, no vestige of the floating material could find its way to the surface?

Beyond the horse-shoe is Goat Island, and beyond Goat Island the American fall, bold, straight, and chafed to snowy whiteness by the rocks which meet it; but it does not approach, in sublimity or awful beauty, to the wondrous crescent on the other shore. There, the form of the mighty cauldron, into which the deluge pours, the hundred silvery torrents congregating round its verge, the smooth and solemn movement with which it rolls its massive volume over the rock, the liquid emerald of its long unbroken waters, the fantastic wreaths which spring to meet it, and then, the shadowy mist that veils the horrors of its crash below, constitute a scene almost too enormous in its features for man to look upon. "Angels might tremble as they gazed;" and I should deem the nerves obtuse, rather than strong, which did not quail at the first sight of this stupendous cataract.

Minute local particulars can be of no interest to those who have not felt their influence for pleasure or for pain. I will not tell of giddy stairs which scale the very edge of the torrent, nor of beetling slabs of table rock, broken and breaking, on which, shudder as you may, you must take your stand or lose your reputation as a tourist. All these feats were performed again and again, even on the first day of our arrival, and most earthly weary was I when the day was done, though I would not lose the remembrance of it to purchase the addition of many soft and silken ones to my existence.

By four o'clock the next morning I was again at the little shantee, close to the horse-shoe fall, which seems reared in water rather than in air, and took an early shower-bath of spray. Much is concealed at this early hour by the heavy vapour, but there was a charm in the very obscurity; and every moment, as the light increased, cloud after cloud rolled off, till the vast wonder was again before me.

It is in the afternoon that the rainbow is visible from the British side; and it is a lovely feature in the mighty landscape. The gay arch springs from fall to fall, a fairy bridge.

After breakfast we crossed to the American side, and

explored Goat Island. The passage across the Niagara, directly in face of the falls, is one of the most delightful little voyages imaginable; the boat crosses marvellously near them, and within reach of a light shower of spray. Real safety and apparent danger have each their share in the pleasure felt. The river is here two hundred feet deep. The passage up the rock brings you close upon the American cataract; it is a vast sheet, and has all the sublimity that height and width, and uproar can give; but it has none of the magic of its rival about it. Goat Island has, at all points, a fine view of the rapids; the furious velocity with which they rush onward to the abyss, is terrific; and the throwing a bridge across them was a work of noble daring.

Below the falls, the river runs between lofty rocks, crowned with unbroken forests; this scene forms a striking contrast to the level shores above the cataract. It appears as if the level of the river had been broken up by some volcanic force. The Niagara flows out of Lake Erie, a broad, deep river; but for several miles its course is tranquil, and its shores perfectly level. By degrees its bed begins to sink, and the glassy smoothness is disturbed by a slight ripple. The inverted trees, that before lay so softly still upon its bosom, become twisted and tortured till they lose their form, and seem madly to mix in the tumult that destroys them. The current becomes more rapid at every step, till rock after rock has chafed the stream to fury, making the green one white. This lasts for a mile, and then down sink the rocks at once, once hundred and fifty feet, and the enormous flood falls after them. God said, let there be a cataract, and it was so. When the river has reached its new level, the precipice on either side shews a terrific chasm of solid rock; some beautiful plants are clinging to its sides, and oak, ash, and cedar, in many places, clothe their terrors with rich foliage.

This violent transition from level shores to a deep ravine, seems to indicate some great convulsion as its cause, and when I heard of a burning spring close by, I fancied the volcanic power still at work, and that the wonders of the region might yet increase.

* * * * *

It was a sort of pang to take what we knew must be our last look at Niagara; but "we had to do it," as the Americans say, and left it on the 10th June, for Buffalo.

The drive along the river, above the Falls, is as beautiful as a clear stream of a mile in width can make it; and the road continues close to it till you reach the ferry at Black Rock.

* * * * *

At Black Rock we crossed again into the United States, and a few miles of horrible jolting brought us to Buffalo.

Of all the thousand and one towns I saw in America, I think Buffalo is the queerest looking; it is not quite so wild as Lockport, but all the buildings have the appearance of having been run up in a hurry, though every thing has an air of great pretension; there are porticos, columns, domes, and colonnades, but all in wood. Every body tells you there, as in all their other newborn towns, and every body believes, that their improvement, and their progression, are more rapid, more wonderful, than the earth ever before witnessed; while to me, the only wonder is, how so many thousands, nay millions of persons, can be found, in the nineteenth century, who can be content so to live. Surely this country may be said to spread rather than to rise.

Lake Erie has no beauty to my eyes; it is not the sea, and it is not the river, nor has it the beautiful scenery generally found round smaller lakes. The only interest its unmeaning expanse gave me, arose from remembering that its waters, there so tame and tranquil, were destined to leap the gulf of Niagara. A dreadful road, through forests only beginning to be felled, brought us to Avon; it is a straggling, ugly little place, and not any of their "Romes, Carthages, Ithacas, or Athens," ever provoked me by their names so much. This Avon flows sweetly with nothing but whisky and tobacco juice.

The next day's journey was much more interesting, for it shewed us the lake of Canandaigua. It is about eighteen miles long, but narrow enough to bring the opposite shore, clothed with rich foliage, near to the eye; the back-ground is a ridge of mountains. Perhaps the state of the atmosphere lent an unusual charm to the scene; one of those sudden thunderstorms, so rapid in approach, and so sombre in colouring, that they change the whole aspect of things in a moment, rose over the mountains, and passed across the lake while we looked upon it. Another feature in the scene gave a living, but most sad interest to it. A glaring wooden hotel, as fine as paint and porticos can make it, overhangs the lake; beside it stands a shed for cattle. To this

199

shed, and close by the white man's mushroom palace, two Indians had crept to seek a shelter from the storm. The one was an aged man, whose venerable head in attitude and expression indicated the profoundest melancholy: the other was a youth, and in his deep-set eye there was a quiet sadness more touching still. There they stood, the native rightful lords of the fair land, looking out upon the lovely lake which yet bore the name their fathers had given it, watching the threatening storm that brooded there; a more fearful one had already burst over them.

Though I have mentioned the lake first, the little town of Canandaigua precedes it, in returning from the West. It is as pretty a village as ever man contrived to build. Every house is surrounded by an ample garden, and at that flowery season, they were half buried in roses.

It is true these houses are of wood, but they are so neatly painted, in such perfect repair, and shew so well within their leafy setting, that it is impossible not to admire them.

Forty-six miles farther is Geneva, beautifully situated on Seneca Lake. This, too, is a lovely sheet of water, and I think the town may rival its European namesake in beauty.

We slept at Auburn, celebrated for its prison, where the highly-approved system of American discipline originated. In this part of the country there is not want of churches; every little village has its wooden temple, and many of them two; that the Methodists and Presbyterians may not clash.

We passed through an Indian reserve, and the untouched forests again hung close upon the road. Repeated groups of Indians passed us, and we remarked that they were much cleaner and better dressed than those we had met wandering far from their homes. The blankets which they use so gracefully as mantles, were as white as snow.

We took advantage of the loss of a horse's shoe, to leave the coach, and approach a large party of them, consisting of men, women, and children, who were regaling themselves with I know not what, but milk made a part of the repast. They could not talk to us, but they received us with smiles, and seemed to understand when we asked if they had mocassins to sell, for they shook their sable locks, and answered "no."

A beautiful grove of butternut trees was pointed out to us, as the spot where the chiefs of the six nations used to hold their senate; our informer told me that he had been present at several of their meetings, and though he knew but little of their language, the power of their eloquence was evident from the great effect it produced among themselves.

Towards the end of this day, we encountered an adventure which revived our doubts whether the invading white men, in chasing the poor Indians from their forests, have done much towards civilizing the land. For myself, I almost prefer the indigenous manner to the exotic.

The coach stopped to take in "a lady" at Vernon; she entered, and completely filled the last vacant inch of our vehicle; for "we were eight" before.

But no sooner was she seated, than *her beau* came forward with a most enormous wooden best-bonnet box. He paused for a while to meditate the possibilities—raised it, as if to place it on our laps—sunk it, as if to put it beneath our feet. Both alike appeared impossible; when, in true Yankee style he addressed one of our party with, "If you'll just step out a minute, I guess I'll find room for it."

"Perhaps so. But how shall I find room for myself afterwards?"

This was uttered in European accents, and in an instant half a dozen whisky drinkers stepped from before the whisky store, and took the part of *the beau*.

"That's because you'll be English travellers I expect, but we have travelled in better countries than Europe—we have travelled in America—and the box will go, I calculate."

We remonstrated on the evident injustice of the proceeding, and I ventured to say, that as we had none of us any luggage in the carriage, because the space was so very small, I thought a chance passenger could have no right so greatly to incommode us.

"Right!—there they go—that's just their way—that will do in Europe, may be; it sounds just like English tyranny, now—don't it? but it won't do here." And thereupon he began thrusting in the wooden box against our legs, with all his strength.

"No law, sir, can permit such conduct as this."

"Law!" exclaimed a gentleman very particularly drunk, "we makes our own laws, and governs our own selves."

"Law!" echoed another gentleman of Vernon, "this is a free country, we have no laws here, and we don't want no foreign power to tyrannize over us."

I give the words exactly. It is, however, but fair to state, that the party had evidently been drinking more than an usual portion of whiskey, but, perhaps, in whisky, as in wine, truth may come to light. At any rate the people of the Western Paradise follow the Gentiles in this, that they are a law unto themselves.

During this contest, the coachman sat upon the box without saying a word, but seemed greatly to enjoy the joke; the question of the box, however, was finally decided in our favour by the nature of the human material, which cannot be compressed beyond a certain degree.

For great part of this day we had the good fortune to have a gentleman and his daughter for our fellow-travellers, who were extremely intelligent and agreeable; but I nearly got myself into a scrape by venturing to remark upon a phrase used by the gentleman, and which had met me at every corner from the time I first entered the country. We had been talking of pictures, and I had endeavoured to adhere to the rule I had laid down for myself, of saying very little, where I could say nothing agreeable. At length he named an American artist, with whose works I was very familiar, and after having declared him equal to Lawrence, (judging by his portrait of West, now at New York), he added, "and what is more, madam, he is perfectly *self-taught*."

I prudently took a few moments before I answered; for the equalling our immortal Lawrence to a most vile dauber stuck in my throat; I could not say Amen; so for some time I said nothing; but, at last, I remarked on the frequency with which I had heard this phrase of self-taught used, not as an apology, but as positive praise.

"Well, madam, can there be a higher praise?"

"Certainly not, if spoken of the individual merits of a person, without the means of instruction, but I do not understand it when applied as praise to his works."

"Not understand it, madam? Is it not attributing genius to the author, and what is teaching compared to that?"

I do not wish to repeat all my own *bons mots* in praise of study, and on the disadvantages of profound ignorance, but I would willingly, if I could, give an idea of the mixed indignation and contempt expressed by our companion at the idea that study was necessary to the formation of taste, and to the development of genius. At last, however, he closed the discussion thus,—"There is no use in disputing a point that is already settled, madam; the best judges declare that Mr. H°°°°°g's portraits are equal to that of Lawrence."

"Who is it who has passed this judgment, sir?"

"The men of taste of America, madam."

I then asked him, if he thought it was going to rain?

+   +   +   +   +

The stages do not appear to have any regular stations at which to stop for breakfast, dinner, and supper. These necessary interludes, therefore, being generally *impromptu*, were abominably bad. We were amused by the patient manner in which our American fellow-travellers ate whatever was set before them, without uttering a word of complaint, or making any effort to improve it, but no sooner reseated in the stage, than they began their complaints—"'twas a shame"—"'twas a robbery"—"'twas poisoning folks"—and the like. I, at last, asked the reason of this, and why they did not remonstrate? "Because, madam, no American gentleman or lady that keeps an inn won't bear to be found fault with."

We reached Utica very late and very weary; but the delights of a good hotel and perfect civility sent us in good humour to bed, and we arose sufficiently refreshed to enjoy a day's journey through some of the loveliest scenery in the world.

Who is it that says America is not picturesque? I forget; but surely he never travelled from Utica to Albany. I really cannot conceive that any country can furnish a drive of ninety-six miles more beautiful, or more varied in its beauty. The road follows the Mohawk River, which flows through scenes changing from fields, waving with plenty, to rocks and woods; gentle slopes, covered with cattle, are divided from each other by precipices 500 feet high. Around the little falls there is a character of beauty as singular as it is striking. Here, as I observed of many other American rivers, the stream appears to run in a much narrower channel than it once occupied, and the space which it seems formerly to have filled is now covered with bright green herbage, save that, at intervals, large masses of rock rise abruptly from the level turf; these are crowned with all such trees as love the scanty diet which a rock affords. Dwarf oak, cedars, and the mountain ash, are grouped in a hundred different ways among them; each clump you look upon is lovelier than its neighbour; I never saw so sweetly wild a spot.

*   *   *   *   *

CHAPTER XXXIV

Return to New York . . . Conclusion . . .

The comfortable Adelphi Hotel again received us at Albany, on the 14th of June, and we decided upon passing the following day there, both to see the place, and to recruit our strength, which we began to feel we had taxed severely by a very fatiguing journey, in most oppressively hot weather. It would have been difficult to find a better station for repose; the rooms were large and airy, and ice was furnished in most profuse abundance.

           *   *   *   *   *

Some parts of the town are very handsome; the Town Hall, the Chamber of Representatives, and some other public buildings, stand well on a hill that overlooks the Hudson, with ample enclosures of grass and trees around them.

Many of the shops are large, and showily set out. I was amused by a national trait which met me at one of them. I entered it to purchase some *eau de Cologne*, but finding what was offered to me extremely bad, and very cheap, I asked if they had none at a higher price, and better.

"You are a stranger, I guess," was the answer. "The Yankees want low price, that's all; they don't stand so much for goodness as the English."

Nothing could be more beautiful than our passage down

the Hudson on the following day.... As we approached New York the burning heat of the day relaxed, and the long shadows of evening fell coolly on the beautiful villas we passed. I really can conceive nothing more exquisitely lovely than this approach to the city. The magnificent boldness of the Jersey shore on the one side, and the luxurious softness of the shady lawns on the other, with the vast silvery stream that flows between them, altogether form a picture which may well excuse a traveller for saying, once and again, that the Hudson river can be surpassed in beauty by none on the outside of Paradise.

It was nearly dark when we reached the city, and it was with great satisfaction that we found our comfortable apartments in Hudson Street unoccupied; and our pretty, kind (Irish) hostess willing to receive us again. We passed another fortnight there; and again we enjoyed the elegant hospitality of New York, though now it was offered from beneath the shade of their beautiful villas. In truth, were all America like this fair city, and all, no, only a small proportion of its population like the friends we left there, I should say, that the land was the fairest in the world.

*   *   *   *   *

I suspect that what I have written will make it evident that I do not like America. Now, as it happens that I met with individuals there whom I love and admire, far beyond the love and admiration of ordinary acquaintance, and as I declare the country to be fair to the eye, and most richly teeming with the gifts of plenty, I am led to ask myself why it is that I do not like it. I would willingly know myself, and confess to others, why it is that neither its beauty nor its abundance can suffice to neutralize, or greatly soften, the distaste which the aggregate of my recollections has left upon my mind.

I remember hearing it said, many years ago, when the advantages and disadvantages of a particular residence were being discussed, that it was the "who?" and not the "where?" that made the difference between the pleasant or unpleasant residence. The truth of the observation struck me forcibly when I heard it; and it has been recalled to my mind since, by the constantly recurring evidence of its justness. In applying this to America, I speak not of my friends, nor of my friends' friends.

The small patrician band is a race apart; they live with each other, and for each other; mix wondrously little with the high matters of state, which they seem to leave rather supinely to their tailors and tinkers, and are no more to be taken as a sample of the American people, than the head of Lord Byron as a sample of the heads of the British peerage. I speak not of these, but of the population generally, as seen in town and country, among the rich and the poor, in the slave states, and the free states. I do not like them. I do not like their principles, I do not like their manners, I do not like their opinions.

Both as a woman, and as a stranger, it might be unseemly for me to say that I do not like their government, and therefore I will not say so. That it is one which pleases themselves is most certain, and this is considerably more important than pleasing all the travelling old ladies in the world. I entered the country at New Orleans, remained for more than two years west of the Alleghanies, and passed another year among the Atlantic cities, and the country around them. I conversed during this time with citizens of all orders and degrees, and I never heard from any one a single disparaging word against their government. It is not, therefore, surprising, that when the people of that country hear strangers questioning the wisdom of their institutions, and expressing disapprobation at some of their effects, they should set it down either to an incapacity of judging, or to a malicious feeling of envy and ill-will.

"How can any one in their senses doubt the excellence of a government which we have tried for half a century, and loved the better the longer we have known it?

Such is the natural enquiry of every American when the excellence of their government is doubted; and I am included to answer, that no one in their senses, who has visited the country, and known the people, can doubt its fitness for them, such as they now are, or its utter unfitness for any other people.

Whether the government has made the people what they are, or whether the people have made the government what it is, to suit themselves, I know not; but if the latter, they have shewn a consummation of wisdom which the assembled world may look upon and admire.

It is matter of historical notoriety that the original stock of the white population now inhabiting the United States, were

207

persons who had banished themselves, or were banished from the mother country. The land they found was favourable to their increase and prosperity; the colony grew and flourished. Years rolled on, and the children, the grand-children, and the great grand-children of the first settlers, replenished the land, and found it flowing with milk and honey. That they should wish to keep this milk and honey to themselves, is not very surprising. What did the mother country do for them? She sent them out gay and gallant officers to guard their frontier; the which they thought they could guard as well themselves; and then she taxed their tea. Now, this was disagreeable; and to atone for it, the distant colony had no great share in her mother's grace and glory. It was not from among them that her high and mighty were chosen; the rays which emanated from that bright sun of honour, the British throne, reached them but feebly. They knew not, they cared not, for her kings nor her heroes; their thriftiest trader was their noblest man; the holy seats of learning were but the cradles of superstition; the splendour of the aristocracy, but a leech that drew their "golden blood." The wealth, the learning, the glory of Britain, was to them nothing; the having their own way every thing.

Can any blame their wish to obtain it? Can any lament that they succeeded?

And now the day was their own, what should they do next? Their elders drew together, and said, "Let us make a government that shall suit us all; let it be rude, and rough, and noisy; let it not affect either dignity, glory, or splendour; let it interfere with no man's will, nor meddle with any man's business; let us have neither tithes nor taxes, game laws, nor poor laws; let every man have a hand in making the laws, and no man be troubled about keeping them; let not our magistrates wear purple, nor our judges ermine; if a man grow rich, let us take care that his grandson be poor, and then we shall all keep equal; let every man take care of himself, and if England should come to bother us again, why then we will fight altogether."

Could any thing be better imagined than such a government for a people so circumstanced? Or is it strange that they are contented with it? Still less is it strange that those who have lived in the repose of order, and felt secure that their country could go on very well, and its business proceed without their bawling and squalling, scratching and scrambling to help it, should bless the gods that they are not republicans.

So far all is well. That they should prefer a constitution which suits them so admirably, to one which would not suit them at all, is surely no cause of quarrel on our part; nor should it be such on theirs, if we feel no inclination to exchange the institutions which have made us what we are, for any other on the face of the earth.

But when a native of Europe visits America, a most extraordinary species of tyranny is set in action against him; and as far as my reading and experience have enabled me to judge, it is such as no other country has ever exercised against strangers.

*   *   *   *   *

A single word indicative of doubt, that any thing, or every thing, in that country is not the very best in the world, produces an effect which must be seen and felt to be understood. If the citizens of the United States were indeed the devoted patriots they call themselves, they would surely not thus encrust themselves in the hard, dry, stubborn persuasion, that they are the first and best of the human race, that nothing is to be learnt, but what they are able to teach, and that nothing is worth having, which they do not possess.

The art of man could hardly discover a more effectual antidote to improvement, than this persuasion; and yet I never listened to any public oration, or read any work professedly addressed to the country, in which they did not labour to impress it on the minds of the people.

To hint to the generality of Americans that the silent current of events may change their beloved government, is not the way to please them; but in truth they need be tormented with no such fear. As long as by common consent they can keep down the pre-eminence which nature has assigned to great powers, as long as they can prevent human respect and human honour from resting upon high talent, gracious manners, and exalted station, so long may they be sure of going on as they are.

I have been told, however, that there are some among them, who would gladly see a change; some, who with the wisdom of philosophers, and the fair candour of gentlemen, shrink

209

from a profession of equality which they feel to be untrue, and believe to be impossible.

I can well believe that such there are, though to me no such opinions were communicated, and most truly should I rejoice to see power pass into such hands.

If this ever happens, if refinement once creeps in among them, if they once learn to cling to the graces, the honours, the chivalry of life, then we shall say farewell to American equality, and welcome to European fellowship one of the finest countries on the earth.